HEAVENS DECLARE

JESUS CHRIST PROPHESIED IN THE STARS

BY WILLIAM D. BANKS

THE HEAVENS DECLARE
ISBN 10: 0-89228-218-5
ISBN 13: 978-089228-218-0

Copyright © 1985, 2013
Impact Christian Books

IMPACT CHRISTIAN BOOKS, INC.
332 Leffingwell Ave., Suite 101
Kirkwood, MO 63122
(314) 822-3309

www.impactchristianbooks.com

ALL RIGHTS RESERVED

Illustrations:
Bob Shay Productions Artist,
Mary Uhring

Dedication

I dedicate this book to all seekers of Truth — both Christian and non-Christian alike — and to my parents who taught me to love the Truth. I present this book to all those who love a mystery, who are willing to honestly follow the search for Truth wherever and to whatever conclusion it may lead them.

I also dedicate this book with due respect and reverence to the Source of all Truth, who in His infinite wisdom chose to place His mysterious message in the ancient names of the stars.

New Edition

In this new edition of *The Heavens Declare*, there is a complete map of the constellations spanning pages 252 - 253 in the back of the book. This includes all 12 major constellations and their related stars and signs. A short explanation is included on page 251.

Acknowledgements

I want to express my gratitude to the following people whose assistance has made this book possible:

Sharon Kelch and Lillian Edwards who volunteered their typing skills,

Tom Sims, Rev. Joe Marting and others who read the manuscript and offered suggestions,

Pam Miltenberger for her proofreading, grammatical insights and corrections,

The people of the Thursday Night Fellowship for their prayers, and tolerance in sitting through the teaching of this material on two separate occasions,

Family and Christian friends such as Margaret Jenks, and Aria Bott for their supportive enthusiasm and encouragement throughout the ten years of ongoing research and compilation,

And finally, to my wife, Sue, and my two sons, Kevin and Steve who gave of their time with a husband and father.

I am a man greatly blessed, to have such friends and family. I love them, appreciate them, and trust that this book will in some small way bless them as they have blessed me.

- **William D. Banks**

QUOTATIONS

"I have never beheld the stars that I do not feel that I am looking into the face of God. I can see how it might be possible for a man to look down upon the earth and be an atheist, but I cannot conceive how he could look up into the heavens and say there is no God."

- Written by **Abraham Lincoln** at age 19

"Why did not somebody teach me the constellations and make me at home in the starry heavens, which are always overhead, and which I don't half know to this day?"

- **Thomas Carlyle**, 1795-1881

"The mysteries of the Incarnation, from the Conception on to the Ascenscion into heaven, are shown to us on the face of the sky, and are signified by the stars."

- **Albert Magnus**, 1200-1280

"This prospect vast, what is it?—Weighed aright, 'Tis Nature's system of divinity; 'Tis Elder Scripture, writ by God's own hand: Scripture authentic! uncorrupt by man."

- **Edward Young**, 1683-1765

"An undevout astronomer is mad!"

- **Edward Young**, 1683-1765

"What though no real voice or sound, Amid their radiant orbs be found? In reason's ear they all rejoice, And utter forth a glorious voice; Forever singing, as they shine, The hand that made us is divine."

- **Unknown**, pre 1900

TABLE OF CONTENTS

DEDICATION	iii
ACKNOWLEDGEMENTS	iv
QUOTATIONS	v
LIST of ILLUSTRATIONS	ix
PREFACE	xi

A Mystery Unfolds 13
How I Discovered The Key	14
Where To Look	17
Why Were The Stars (Signs) Placed in The Heavens?	19
How Can We Be Sure These Signs Are Ancient?	22
How Do We Read A Circular Story?	27
Sequence	27
Decans	28
The Sphinx Riddle	29

Part I - The Promise Fulfilled 31
VIRGO	The Virgin	32
COMA	The Desired	37
CENTAURUS	The Centaur	41
BOOTES	The Coming One	45
LIBRA	The Scales	49
CRUX	The Southern Cross	53
VICTIMA	The Victim	57
CORONA	The Crown	60
SCORPIO	The Scorpion	64
SERPENS	The Serpent	67
ORPHIUCHUS	The Serpent-Holder	67
HERCULES	The Mighty One	71
SAGITTARIUS	The Archer	77
LYRA	The Harp	82
ARA	The Altar	84
DRACO	The Dragon	87

Part II -	Resurrection Life Received	 91
CAPRICORN	The Goat-Fish	 93
SAGITTA	The Arrow	 98
AQUILA	The Eagle	 100
DELPHINUS	The Dolphin	 103
AQUARIUS	The Water-Pourer	 107
PISCIS AUSTRALIS	The Southern Fish	 114
PEGASUS	The Winged Horse	 116
CYGNUS	The Swan	 120
PISCES	The Fishes	 123
THE BAND	The Bands	 131
ANDROMEDA	The Chained Woman	 134
CEPHEUS	The Crowned King	 138
ARIES	The Lamb	 142
CASSIOPEIA	The Enthroned Woman	 146
CETUS	The Sea-Monster	 151
PERSEUS	The Breaker	 156

Part III -	Kingdom And Judgment Established	.. 161
TAURUS	The Bull	 162
ORION	The Glorious One	 171
ERIDANUS	The River	 176
AURIGA	The Shepherd	 180
GEMINI	The Twins	 186
LEPUS	The Enemy	 193
CANIS MAJOR	The Prince	 196
CANIS MINOR	The Redeemer	 200
CANCER	The Crab (Sheepfold)	 203
URSA MINOR	The Lesser Sheepfold	 209
URSA MAJOR	The Greater Sheepfold	 213
ARGO	The Ship	 216
LEO	The Lion	 221
HYDRA	The Serpent	 227
CRATER	The Cup	 230
CORVUS	The Raven	 233

THE TWELVE LABOURS 237
CONCLUSION   241
SALVATION IS OFFERED 243
WHAT IS THE REAL VALUE OF THESE TRUTHS? 246
WHAT ABOUT ASTROLOGY? 248

COMPLETE MAP OF THE HEAVENS 252
BIBLIOGRAPHY   254
INDEX OF STAR & SIGN NAMES 256

List Of Illustrations

VIRGO	The Virgin	33
COMA	The Desired	38
CENTAURUS	The Centaur	42
BOOTES	The Coming One	46
LIBRA	The Scales	50
CRUX	The Southern Cross	53
VICTIMA	The Victim.	58
CORONA	The Crown.	61
SCORPIO	The Scorpion.	65
SERPENS & ORPHIUCHUS		
	The Serpent.	68
	The Serpent-Holder.	68
HERCULES	The Mighty One	72
SAGITTARIUS	The Archer.	78
LYRA	The Harp	82
ARA	The Altar	85
DRACO	The Dragon	88
CAPRICORN	The Goat-Fish	94
SAGITTA	The Arrow	98
AQUILA	The Eagle	101
DELPHINUS	The Dolphin	103
AQUARIUS	The Water-Pourer.	108
PISCIS AUSTRALIA	The Southern Fish	115
PEGASUS	The Winged Horse	117
CYGNUS	The Swan	121

List Of Illustrations (cont)

PISCES	The Fishes	124
THE BAND	The Bands	132
ANDROMEDA	The Chained Woman	135
CEPHEUS	The Crowned King	139
ARIES	The Lamb	143
CASSIOPEIA	The Enthroned Woman	147
CETUS	The Sea-Monster	152
PERSEUS	The Breaker	157
TAURUS	The Bull	163
ORION	The Glorious One	173
ERIDANUS	The River	176
AURIGA	The Shepherd	181
GEMINI	The Twins	187
LEPUS	The Enemy	193
CANIS MAJOR	The Prince	196
CANIS MINOR	The Redeemer	201
CANCER	The Crab (Sheepfold)	204
URSA MINOR	The Lesser Sheepfold	210
URSA MAJOR	The Greater Sheepfold	214
ARGO	The Ship	217
LEO	The Lion	222
HYDRA	The Serpent	228
CRATER	The Cup	231
CORVUS	The Raven	235

Astronomers indicate the relative brightness of the stars by assigning to each a "magnitude." The brightest stars in the heavens are of the 1st magnitude, next brightest 2nd magnitude, etc.

Bayer in his celestial charts, Uranometria (1603), was the first to employ the letters of the Greek alphabet to rank the relative brightness of the stars within a constellation. This system is still in use today. However, in preparing our illustrations, we have used the letters of our alphabet, for the convenience of the reader unfamiliar with Greek.

The illustrations have been drawn primarily from those in Jamieson's Celestial Atlas. However, details have been added, and corrections made, where applicable, utilizing earlier sources, such as Aratus or the ancient Egyptian and Arabian astronomical records.

Preface

Anyone who approaches the study of the ancient names of the stars, will soon become aware of the great debt owed to an amazing lady, Frances Rolleston. It was she who devoted over fifty years of her life to the compilation of a massive series of notes which was published under the title Mazzaroth—The Constellations in 1863, when she was in her 80's.

Miss Rolleston was a scholar in every sense of the word. She was a classicist, a linguist, and one who worked and consulted with many of the most educated people in England during the 1800's. She also corresponded with many other experts from around the world.

Frances was a gifted student who became deeply committed to her studies and began diligently studying Hebrew in 1818 and continued as a student through 1835. She read daily from the original Hebrew Scriptures even after completing her formal study of the language. Among her other exceptional accomplishments were the following: she studied Latin and Greek doing her own translations of Homer, and other Greek poetry ("just to keep my hand in"); she also mastered French, Egyptian (Coptic and Hieroglyphics); the Semitic root languages of Arabic, Syriac, Aramaic, Sanskrit, and Chaldee; and became an authority on the origin and roots of language.

Miss Rolleston was also a poet of more than passing talent. She wrote a second part to the hymn "Rock of Ages" which touched many lives and was repeated by Prince Albert upon his death bed.

In addition Frances was a charitable person. When she heard of the plight of the American Slaves in 1811, she became actively involved in working for their emancipation at that very early date. She remained quite concerned and later sent aid for the "15000 [sic] left masterless and destitute by this dreadful [Civil] war." She regularly visited the elderly and needy in her own area. One of these was an old soldier acquaintance, whom she visited three days before his death. When she offered to bring him some reading material, the old gentleman replied,

"Nothing but the Bible will do for me now!"

"He was right," she said. "Better than he knew."

When Frances was only nine, she overheard part of a funeral service which made a lasting impression on her and shaped the course of her life. The passage which she heard quoted was, "I know that my Redeemer liveth." This became her theme and remained so in her final hours.

At the time of her death in her late 80's, she was excited about working on a new edition of Mazzaroth. It was to include a new find, seven zodiacs from India, "none older than Abraham, from the Ancient Chaldean astronomy in Sanscrit."

Even at the end of her life Miss Rolleston had things in proper perspective. This fact is evident in the closing statement of an 1862 letter to a colleague in the United States, "... what concerns you and me is, be ye ready, for ye know not in what hour your Lord cometh."

In memory of this dear lady, I offer this book in the hope that it will both inspire and cause the readers to find in it what she also found, "the most magnificent of all manuscripts, the heavens declaring the glory of God."

W. D. Banks

Kirkwood, MO 1985

A Mystery Unfolds

He telleth the number of the stars; He calleth them all by their names.
Ps. 147:4

Lift up your eyes on high, and behold who hath created these things, that bringeth out their host by number: He calleth them all by names by the greatness of his might, for that He is strong in power not one faileth.
Isa. 40:26

While reading these Scriptures years ago as a child, I felt a a pleasant chill of anticipation and excitement tingling up my spine. Wouldn't it be fantastic if we could learn what the names were that God had applied to the stars? I thought. What tremendous truths or secrets might be contained in those names! How we might be able to expand our knowledge of God, for the very inner-workings and heart-feelings of God Himself might be revealed there. How we might be enabled to better know and understand God, if we were but to know the names which He in His infinite wisdom had chosen to give to the stars.

From past experience I have come to see that God does nothing by chance: nothing is said or revealed by accident. He has a purpose in all that He does: everything has significance, if we can but come to understand it.

I thought to myself, "He must certainly have had a reason, and an important one at that, to have named the stars." And He certainly wouldn't have bothered to mention the fact twice in Scripture if He hadn't desired for us to know that the stars had names. And if He went that far, then He must have intended for us to be able to learn those names. What a titillating thought!

Then came a rush of cold logic, and I said to myself regretfully, "Well obviously it has been thousands of years since those names were given; no one throughout history to my knowledge has ever been allowed to know even one of those God-given names." Those names have definitely been lost if ever they were known to man. Certainly at this point in time, after all these centuries, we are not about to rediscover those names.

However, I am glad to say now, I WAS WRONG! Much to my amazement, God was just about to restore and reveal those names and their significance!

How I Discovered the Key

Everyone loves a mystery, at least I know that I do. Early in 1974 the previous musings of childhood long since forgotten, I was searching in a Strong's Concordance for the solution to another apparent mystery: why Jesus was said by Matthew to have been prophesied to be a Nazarene (Mt. 2.23), when no such prophecy is to be found in Scripture. I, too, was unable to find any such prophecy, however, I did find a similar word, *netzer*. I also read that some scholars felt that the prophecy was based upon a transliteration of this word which means branch or green shoot, and would therefore have valid prophetic application to the Messiah, as it does in Isaiah 11:1.

> And there shall come forth a rod out of the stem of Jesse, and a branch shall grow out of his roots.

This prophecy is perfectly applicable to the Righteous Branch, Jesus, the Messiah. As I continued tracing the roots of this word, and the Hebrew roots of Nazarene in the concordance, my eyes suddenly fell upon a strange word, "Mazzaroth." This certainly did not look like an English word, even though it's listed as one, and I don't recall reading it in the Bible. My amazement increased when I looked at its meaning and was astonished to see that it meant "Zodiac." I recoiled! How could such an obviously occult and ungodly word have gotten into the concordance and Bible? I knew that astrology was forbidden to God's people in passages such as:

> There shall not be found among you anyone... that useth divination, or an observer of times...
> **Deut. 18:10**

> Let now the astrologers, the stargazers, the monthly prognosticators, stand up, and save thee... they shall be as stubble.
> **Isa. 47:13–14**

I then turned to the reference cited as containing the word "Mazzaroth" to see if it truly appeared in the Bible, and read in **Job 38:31–33**

> "Canst thou bind the sweet influences of Pleiades, or loose the bands of Orion? Canst thou bring forth Mazzaroth in his season? or canst thou guide Arcturus with his sons? Knowest thou the ordinances of heaven? Canst thou set the dominion thereof in the earth?"

It was apparent to me that the God of the Bible was taking credit in his statement not only for establishing the Zodiac, but also for causing its components to maintain their proper sequence and perfection of timing. This really shouldn't have surprised me in light of His words in **Genesis 1:14–16**...

> And God said, Let there be lights in the firmament of the heaven to divide the day from the night; and let them be for signs, and for seasons, and for days, and years;
>
> And let them be for lights in the firmament of the heavens to give light upon the earth: and it was so.
>
> And God made two great lights; the greater light to rule the day, and the lesser light to rule the night: the stars also.

So I could see that the stars had been created and placed in the heavens as it pleased God to place them, and in accordance with His wisdom. Also the Zodiac was designed by God, even though Satan has managed to so pervert it in some men's minds as to convince them to superstitiously think that the stars will tell something about themselves and their future, rather than testifying of Him who created them.

There must be some underlying purpose and truth that God has for us in this Zodiac, which He created, since Satan has worked so hard to pervert it for his own purposes. That Satan has done his work well, is to be seen in the fact that most sincere Bible-believing Christians want nothing to do with the Zodiac or its figures, and often seem even to fear them.

God must also, I reasoned, have had a purpose in showing me the word "Mazzaroth." Thus began one of the most rewarding and challenging searches of my life; a search which has led me into many libraries in America and to rather extensive research in the fabulous British Museum Library in London. God had much amazing truth in store for me, which rather than threatening my faith, on the contrary, has enhanced and strengthened it, and given me additional understanding.

Having been a teacher and speaker at Christian meetings for a number of years, I was afraid that some people might misunderstand my research into the stars, and might assume I was getting into astrology or the occult, and so I decided to code all my research notes. I referred in my notes to this project as "Code 12" for the 12 Signs, and often abbreviated it as a star within a circle. I also began making marginal notes in my Bible using the same symbol. I soon found my Bible was becoming filled with these symbols just as it had previously begun "turning blue" when I had underlined in blue pencil references to healing, when I was "dying" as a terminal cancer patient in 1970.[1]

I had already determined that if at any point the Lord seemed to be closing the door, or the research proved not to be fruitful, or God-honoring, I would immediately cease from the search. There were also

---

[1] The amazing, faith-building account of the author's healing from terminal cancer in 1970 is recorded in *Alive Again!*

several questions to which I felt I had to have the answers if I was to be able to proceed. Some of them were:

1. Where Could I Find the Ancient Names of the Stars?
2. Why Were the Stars and Signs Placed in the Heavens?
3. How Could I Be Sure that the Names of the Stars and Signs Were Really Ancient, and had not Been Tampered with, Perhaps Even by Well Meaning Christians? Did the Signs Predate the Origins of Astrology?

Where To Look?

I now had a basic key — that there was truth to be found — and that it was to be found in the ancient, original names of the stars. Deep within myself I felt an assurance that this was not a futile task... that God Himself had put me on the trail of the names, and that somehow He would lead me to them.

But where to begin looking? Having quickly exhausted the list of star names given in the Scripture, I decided to try the local library to see if I might be able to find some clues to the names in the earliest origins of astronomy. I soon learned that in both history and tradition the Twelve Signs of the Zodiac were the same in sequence, in essential meaning of the signs, and basically the same in name in all the ancient civilizations of the world.[2] This was certainly strange, if indeed, as we've been led to believe, they had been developed to correspond to local planting seasons (which would of course differ in different parts of the world, and therefore couldn't be the true source) or merely to relate accounts of local folk or mythological heroes.

In the most ancient names that I was able to locate I found a pattern developing: a pattern which has now also been confirmed by 10 years of

---

2 It is a relatively simple matter to distinguish between the ancient constellations and those of more modern origin. The latter are named for men, Popes, kings, Napoleon, etc., and for modern inventions such as the telescope, or animals such as the giraffe.

searching ancient records. The mind-boggling discovery that I made was that God in naming the stars and numbering them, recorded the entire gospel of His Beloved Son, Jesus Christ! The story is all there, from His virgin birth, to His death, resurrection, and promised second coming, as well as His defeat of Satan and the winning of a multitude of offspring! Every detail perfectly coincides with Scripture; in no point is there disparity.

Another staggering discovery for me was that some if not all of these names were recorded prior to 4000 B.C., and there is strong evidence that the records may go back to at least 5000 B.C. It is also significant that virtually all the recording and preserving of these names was done by scholarly pagans, whose only interest was scientific, by non-Christians, and by some who were avowedly atheistic. All the records concur even though maintained around the world in different cultures, among peoples of different languages, different religions ... still the records harmonize perfectly when one possesses the simple keys which unlock the secret.

The Zodiac

The familiar word "Zodiac" does not come as we have long been told from the Greek word *zoe* meaning life, and does not refer to either animals nor a "zoo." Simple logic utilizing internal evidence within the Zodiac itself bears this out, since it contains inanimate objects such as an arrow, balancing scales, a lyre, a cup, a ship, a cross, an altar, and a crown. One sixth of the constellations are inanimate, and therefore, a word denoting animals or life could not adequately describe the constellations.

Instead the word "Zodiac" comes to us from the Hebrew root word *zodi* or *sodi* for "a Way." This latter word actually appears on some of the old star charts. "Zodiac" itself comes directly from the Greek word *zodiakos*, derived from this Hebrew word and therefore denotes The Way or The Path (lit. a way of steps) which the sun appears to follow through the heavens. Here we can note another interesting coincidence... the field of study to which the Lord had been directing me was really to be a study of The Way, His way. This is a name applied to The Way of Life or the Way to God offered by Jesus to His followers. Jesus identified Himself as The Way, The Truth, and The Life. His followers were referred to as the people of The Way.

Why Were the Stars (or Signs) Placed in the Heavens?

> ... for signs (*oth*), and for seasons (*moed*)...　　**Gen. 1:14**

The Hebrew word *oth* carries the meaning of "to come, a signal of something to come," while the word *moed* means an appointment at a fixed time; and may also mean a signal as appointed beforehand (as for example a prophetic sign).

When Scripture usage requires a season of the year as in Lev. 26:4, "I will give you rain in due season ..the word used is *oth* never *moed*. However, it is always *moed* that is used when referring to a set time for a miraculous occurrence, such as is the case in Gen. 17:21, "But my covenant will I establish with Isaac, which Sarah shall bear unto thee at this set (*moed*) time in the next year..." This is the first of three such usages of *moed* in Genesis which all refer to supernatural timing; the others being 18:14 where it is translated as "appointed," and 21:2 where again it is "set." Each refer to the supernatural fulfillment of the promised birth of Isaac.

We know that a sign is something intended to convey a message to those who come after. It is provided by someone who desires to direct, to warn, or to give guidance in advance. A highway sign, for instance, is set up by someone who knows more about the route (way or path) than those who will come later, and the sign conveys to them directions, lest they lose their way. The sign helps them follow the right path (way) without getting lost, or into danger. So it is with the Signs in the heavens.

Why are they there? They are there as signs for us. Provided by whom? They are provided by God Himself to give us guidance in advance, and to tell us of things to come, most especially and of eternal importance... of the One who is to come... The Messiah... The Promised On... Jesus Christ!

Isn't it strange that there is such a void of understanding or teaching concerning these signs which God obviously intended that we should have? Why haven't we heard more, received more teaching about these signs provided by God Himself? What has prevented it being taught to us?

This question takes us back to the most basic teaching of Scripture, to the first and, no doubt, most important prophetic revelation given to us in the written word of God... that of the first promise of a coming Saviour who would come as the seed of the woman, who would be at enmity with the seed of the serpent (Satan), who would Himself be wounded in the heel, but would nonetheless deliver a head (fatal) wound to the serpent.

This promise is found in **Genesis 3:15**. After Adam and Eve had eaten the fruit forbidden to them in the Garden, God confronted the pair, and addressing both them and the serpent announced

> "... I will put enmity between thee and the woman, and between thy seed and her seed; it shall bruise thy head, and thou shalt bruise his heel."

Here we find the great outline of the Bible which sets the stage for the entire drama which it records. In this brief passage, we find presented the cast of characters: Satan—the seed of the serpent who will be the enemy of the Seed of the woman, the Messiah, the promised Coming One, the Great Redeemer. We also have an indication of the great conflict which the Bible will chronicle: the battle between Satan and his forces, and those of the Captain of the Hosts of the Lord, the Redeemer, coming in fulfillment of this prophecy to ultimately deliver the fatal head wound to the serpent while Himself suffering a bruise in the area of His heel. This latter prophetic detail was fulfilled literally as well as figuratively when Jesus's flesh was pierced and His feet nailed to the Cross. Bruising literally took place because of the injury and also so seemed to take place that Satan's kingdom rejoiced momentarily, not realizing the true import of the victory which Jesus had actually won for mankind and His own kingdom by means of that same Cross.

A word of background understanding of the Bible account is in order. Many, especially those approaching from a secular background, have criticized the Bible for being incomplete or inaccurate as to history. They err, not knowing the word of God nor understanding the Bible's purpose. The Bible was not intended to be a complete history book. It recounts only the history of a particular seed, and does not profess to contain all of history. It is the history of the lineage through which the promised Seed either could or would come. It also chronicles the major attempts of Satan to frustrate God's purposes by either eliminating the lineage through which the seed might come, or to actually kill the Seed Himself. This Satan has attempted to do with great zeal, commencing in the beginning with the murder of Abel (using Cain as his instrument) and perhaps even earlier with his attempt to kill Adam and Eve by having them "surely die" for eating the forbidden fruit.

Throughout the Old Testament we have the historic account of Satan's attempts to murder the Seed or to eliminate the lineage through which He might come. In Jesus' day Satan's plan was still the same. This time he employed as his instrument, Herod, who "slew all the children in Bethlehem and the coasts thereof" in an attempt to kill the Messiah before the latter would be able to "bruise" his own head.

We can appreciate that Satan would also desire to prevent any knowledge of the Promised Redeemer from reaching the people. He has opposed the spreading of the Gospel by man; has opposed the making available of the written word of God, and would naturally, for the same reasons, wish to prevent the Gospel recorded in the ancient star names and star figures from being correctly understood and believed by those to whom the Redeemer was promised to come![3]

His method in this case was more subtle than murder. First he sought to pervert the star figures into objects of false worship; second to pervert and distort the truth about them, causing legends to spring up which made them out to be gods or heroes in their own right; and third by means of the former methods, he caused those who seek to obey the commands of the God of the Bible to view them with suspicion as being merely the product of superstition, legend, or false worship. Thus he causes even sincere believers to abhor and to avoid them completely, assuming them to be part of the forbidden astrology and star worship, and even in many cases to fear

---

3 Famed historian G. S. Faber also saw the Messiah in the human figures of the constellations. The Arabs early on removed all human reference from their Zodiacs and lost sight thereby of the Son of Man—the Messiah. These figures in the heavens long predate Moses' prohibition against "likenesses."

them (fear being one of Satan's favorite weapons). He has been enormously successful in camouflaging the true meaning, and in preventing God's people from becoming interested in the heavenly figures.

However, in our day God is restoring to His people the power, authority and dominion which was first given to and then lost by Adam. He is also empowering His people to stand against the powers and works of darkness, enabling them to wrest from the very hands of Satan and his minions the things which properly belong to the people of God!

A further question remained for me: it had to do with establishing the age of the names of the stars and the Signs.

How Can We be Certain These Signs are Ancient?

The first and most easily verifiable source of ascertaining the antiquity of the Signs of the Zodiac is the Bible. In it we find numerous references to the stars and the Signs of heaven.

In the **Book of Job**, considered by scholars to be the oldest of all the books of the Bible (written approximately 1520 B.C. more than 3500 years ago!), we find at least five of the principal constellations mentioned:

1.) ORION— called Kesil (9:9, 38:31)

2.) SCORPIO—"chambers of the south" (9:9)

3.) HYDRA—"the crooked serpent" (26:13)

4.) URSA MAJOR—"Arcturus with his sons" (38:32)

5.) TAURUS—referred to by its most prominent feature, the Pleiades, Kimah, or the seven stars. (38:31)

That these are mentioned without further explanation indicates that they were in common usage at the time. Both Job and the readers were expected to be familiar with them.

The Prophet Amos (circa 787 B.C.) also refers to two of these constellations, and attests to their Divine origin.

> Seek him that maketh the seven stars and Orion.... The Lord is his name.
>
> **Amos 5:8**

The Hebrew Prophets and men of God who wrote under the direction of the Holy Spirit have not been silent concerning the Signs. Moses also wrote of them,

> "And ... let them be for signs ... and it was so." **Gen. 1:14–15**

Clearly, the statement is made that they were not only to be for Signs, but that they were used as Signs! In other words they fulfilled the purpose for which they were created and did function as Signs.

If we can expand our understanding of the above passage to include the meaning of the formation of the constellations, then this statement from Holy Writ echoes the other statements of Scripture as to the Divine authorship of the arrangement and message of the heavens.

We can observe that Scripture is not silent with regard to the constellations and Zodiacal figures. God certainly doesn't fear, nor would He have His people fear His own creation, the works of His own design. The Scripture gives evidence to us not merely of the existence of the Signs from the beginning as part of God's creation, acknowledges His identification with them, but also testifies to their use and great antiquity.

The secular scientific world has also noted the great antiquity of the Constellations, for representations of them or their symbols have been found on Babylonian boundary markers dated at least 3000 B.C., as many books on the Babylonian period will attest.[4,5]

The earliest known Zodiac was discovered in the ceiling of an ancient Temple at Denderah Egypt, and a smaller one not quite so old in a temple at Esneh Egypt. The beautiful Temple of Denderah was constructed 116–107 B.C. However, it was its Zodiac which drew the most attention when it was discovered in the 1800's during the golden era of Egyptian exploration. So important was this treasure considered to be, that it was moved for Napoleon to the Louvre in Paris where it is still on display.[6] Internal evidence within this zodiac based upon the positions of the planetary bodies at the time it was drawn up indicates to astronomers that the zodiac was copied from one originally designed about 5000 years ago.

Similar truths to those noted in the Genesis account are found expressed in tablets of cuneiform writing 2000 years or more before the birth of Christ. Smith and Sayce[7] record the recovery and translation of a written account of the creation from the remains of the Assyrian and Chaldean civilization dating back to Noah's time. In their translation

---

4 As an example E. W. Maunder, famous British astronomer, in referring to the astronomical symbol for DRACO, stated, "We not only use these signs in astronomical works today, but the latter sign frequently occurs, figured exactly as we figure it now, on Babylonian boundary stones 3000 years old." (Astronomy of the Bible. London, 1908).

5 An ancient legend in the annals of Chinese astronomy indicates the high degree of development which astronomy attained at a very early date. The two court astronomers Hsi and Ho were executed by the ruler of China for failing to accurately predict an eclipse (which they missed by only a matter of days) about 2150 B.C. (various historical sources differ as to the exact date of this occurrence, but seem to place it between 2159 and 2136 B. C.) There is also recorded a five planet conjunction visible to the naked eye during the reign of Emperor Chuan Hsu, 2449-2446 B.C. (over 4430 years ago).

6 The removal was no small feat since the zodiac was carved into the rock roof and had to be removed in a slab approximately 8 feet square and 3 feet thick, weighing about 60 tons.

7 Smith & Sayce, archeological historians who wrote in early 1800's, The Chaldean Account of Genesis.

they state that it describes "the constellations of the stars, the signs of the Zodiac" as the creative work of God, and that this passage takes the place of the corresponding account in Genesis which speaks of them being "for signs."

This heavenly portrayal is then a God-designed system of symbols and pictures[8] by which mankind might receive a special body of truth: this system of constellations has everywhere been known as "the Signs."

That these pictures and representations are consistent throughout history and throughout the cultures of the world, indicates that the conformation and divisions are not arbitrary and that there has been a definite effort to maintain them without distortion. Something of how they were preserved may be gathered from the following facts and quotations.

Aratus, the poet quoted by Paul in Acts 17:28, wrote *Phainomena* — The Phenomenons — about 270 B.C. His writing was based upon an earlier work by Eudoxos (403–350 B.C.), which contained the latter's astronomical findings and compilations of earlier works.[9] Aratus lists and explains all the Signs as they were known to the Greeks of his day, although most of the original significance had already been lost to them. Modern astronomers feel that the internal evidence of the stars included, show that the original sightings must have been made at least as early as 1451 B.C., or

---

8 In all the Germanic languages except English, the word for constellation means "star-picture." (The Stars. Houghton Mifflin Co., 1952)
   Today children's books still employ pictures as a means of overcoming the hindrances and limitations of language, using instead the universal language of pictures and symbols.
   The Chinese about 2500 B.C. were developing their ideographic and pictographic language. (A Course in the Analysis of Chinese Characters. Shanghai, The Commercial Press, Ltd., 1926)

9 Eudoxos wrote The Mirror (Enoptron), a simple and familiar description of the heavens and the constellations for the use of the common people. Another work of his entitled Celestial Phenomena has been lost to us. It was this latter from which Aratus drew the material for his work *Phainomena*. This particular writing of Aratus' was so important and so revered by the ancients that it was translated by Cicero, Caesar Germanicus and Ovid, to name but a few.

more than 3400 years ago.

A strikingly significant fact emerges in this poetic work of Aratus' which bears testimony to the great antiquity of the sources of the information passed down to him, and furthers our argument that the true source is Divine. The constellations which he describes were not all visible from Tausus where the other sightings had been made. As an example, the SOUTHERN CROSS was included in his work, but had not been visible in that part of the world for over twenty centuries. It wasn't until the voyage of Amerigo Vespucci[10] toward the Cape of Good Hope in 1502, that the existence of the Southern Cross was confirmed as being more than mere legend. Here we may see God's hand unveiling the answer to another mystery: how could this constellation have been known to those who could never have seen it firsthand, unless its existence had been revealed in the past directly to man by God?

Albumazer who lived at the court of the Caliphs of Grenada early in the ninth century, in his description of the Signs and their accompanying constellations, concluded by stating that they had come down to his time "unaltered," that they "were known all over the world, and had been the objects of long speculation," and that "many had attributed to them a divine and even a prophetic virtue."

Josephus, the famous Jewish historian,[11] said that he felt, "God gave the antediluvians (the pre-flood people) such long life that they might perfect those things which they had invented in astronomy."[12] He also further attributes the source of astronomy to Seth's family. Other ancient, unrelated, sources in Arabian and Persian traditions basically concur, variously attributing the invention to Adam, Seth or Enoch. The original source, nonetheless, we know to have been God.

---

10 Amerigo Vespuci (1451–1512) Italian navigator for whom some credit for the name America.

11 Josephus (Joseph ben Matthias) born A.D. 37, died slightly after 1000 A.D.: famous Jewish historian; mentioned Jesus of Nazareth as an historical figure in but one paragraph.

12 Josephus—Complete Works

The astronomer Ptolemy (Claudius Ptolemaeus 150 A.D.) received his listing of the constellations from Hipparchus (130 B.C.) and describes them as "of unquestioned authority, unknown origin, and unsearchable antiquity."

That a well established and God-ordained connection exists between the major zodiacal figures and the plans and outworkings of God is also indicated by the easily documentable fact that each of the tribes of Israel bore one of them upon its standard.[13] This also confirms that the Signs were well known prior to 1400 B.C.

How Do We Read a Circular Story?

When a story consists of 48 constellations or star pictures scattered across the face of the heavens, in a circular pattern, how can we know where to commence reading it?

Sequence of the Signs

The 12 Signs have always and everywhere been seen in the same sequence as recorded by Sir Isaac Watts in his famous rhyme:

> The Ram, the Bull, the heavenly Twins
>
> And next the Crab, the Lion shines
>
> The Virgin and the Scales
>
> The Scorpion, Archer and Sea Goat
>
> The Man with the Water pot
>
> And Fish with glittering tails.

---

13 The Exodus took place circa 1490 B.C. See also the blessing of Jacob (approx. 1689 B.C.) in Genesis 49; and in Deut. 33 that of Moses (circa 1451 B.C.).

"That Egyptian astronomy has semetic roots as does Indian is shown in the fact that the signs were in use before the time of Jacob and were borne upon the standards of the tribes of Israel." (Dent, C., Letters. London, 1867.)

Decans

The original 48 constellations which we have had from antiquity enumerated and recorded by Ptolemy consist of the 12 major Signs, each of which is assigned thirty degrees of the circle of the Zodiac. The circle of the heavens was also divided into smaller arcs of ten degrees called 'decans' (from a Hebrew word meaning break, or division). Each of the major Zodiac signs was joined with three amplifying signs, located within its own three decans. Each of the accompanying constellations are sometimes referred to themselves as "decans."

Although most scholars attribute the invention of the decan to the Egyptians who also had 10 day weeks (360 days divided into 10 day segments), we shall see that the utilization of the decan existed long before the Egyptians.

In 1883 a book was published in the German language entitled *The Chaldean Star Bible*. Its author, Rev. George Karch, made several interesting observations which also confirm our observations and arrangement:

> "Not from the ruins of Ninevah, not from the Rosetta Stone, but there in the heights above us—there where the holy Magi beheld the Saviour's star—we find the primordial record and testimony of the way of God to us, and of our way back to God. It is there written on the heavens, to be seen and read of all men.

> "The old Persian sphere, as Aben Ezra found it, and as may be read according to Scalinger, in Petavius and Dupuis, has for each of the Twelve Signs three separate figures or constellations—three decans. The foundation (fundamental idea) of these three decans is given in general in the regular zodiacal sign to which they belong; but they give that general idea in different and special pictures.

> "These old forty-eight constellations all belong to one great hieroglyphical system, and all cohere as one original casting. They have an enigmatic meaning. They are sacred monuments. Rightly understood they are a kind of Holy Scriptures in symbolic form, given as a witness to all nations, to aid and enlighten reason and to testify of higher divine truth."

A Mystery Unfolds

We thus have the sequence of the Signs and the decans (chapter and sub chapter) relationships dividing our 48 constellations into 12 sets of four (1 Sign and 3 accompanying decans). But now, how do we find the beginning of the story? The answer is surprising, and it is portrayed graphically and dramatically for us in stone.

The Sphinx Riddle

Frances Rolleston was fascinated, as was most of her generation, by pictures of the mysterious Sphinx, as well as the Rosetta Stone and the other great treasures of Egypt brought to the British Museum during her childhood. What could be the significance of this massive, enigmatic, silent stone figure? This was a question pondered around the world by scientists and lay people alike. It seems always to have been steeped in mystery and to have been associated with a great secret as in the various legends of the riddle of the Sphinx.[14]

The word "sphinx" itself means to bind closely together; and here, graphically portrayed for us are two beings closely bound together, linked as eternally as the stone of which they are composed; preserved as they have been for centuries for all the world to see and to read in them some great message…

Miss Rolleston discovered that there was a representation of the Sphinx placed just below and between the figures of Leo and Virgo on the

---

14 The riddle was purported to have been posed to Oedipus by the Sphinx, then a living monster terrorizing the road to Thebes, killing all who failed to correctly give its answer. "What is it that goes on four feet in the morning, two feet at noon, and on three in the evening?"

Oedipus answered correctly, "Man, who as a child crawls on hands and knees, as an adult walks upright, and in old age walks with the aid of a staff." The Sphinx was so embarrassed and enraged by the solving of her riddle, that she threw herself off a cliff, perished and was turned to stone, as we see her today.

The riddle may have been suggested by the infant of Virgo, the man Orphiuchus, and the figure of Hercules, kneeling with the branch.

Zodiac of the Temple at Esneh Egypt. The Sphinx is a composite of two figures: the body of a lion with the head of a woman.[15] The head of the woman represents the starting point while the tail signifies the end of the story. Thus we have discovered both the place to commence reading our story and the Sign with which it shall conclude.[16]

We shall consider in order each of the twelve Signs, starting with Virgo and her three decans, on through the Sign of Leo. We shall conduct our study by taking note of the ancient original names for the Signs, the ancient names of the stars, the records from Denderah's Temple and such other sources as may be applicable.

With these clues in hand we can begin reading our circular story, the gospel in the stars… the true story of the stars… the secret in the stars… that which THE HEAVENS DECLARE.

---

[15] The sphinx most familiar to us (the androsphinx or part human sphinx) is normally taken to be the body of a lion with the head of a woman, fitting our interpretation perfectly. However, in recent years it has been felt that the head is rather that of a young prince of Egypt. Even if true, this does no real damage to our position for it would merely place the emphasis even more clearly upon the Seed which is the proper focus of the first constellation.

The Krio-sphinx or ram-headed lion, is also common in the monuments of Egypt. It would signify the recognition in one figure of the sacrifice aspect of the Lamb slain, and the coming of the same in victory as the Lion of Judah.

[16] The ancients according to tradition read the Zodiac in the same sequence we have employed, starting with Virgo and ending with Leo!

PART I

THE PROMISE FULFILLED

The promise of a divine hero, who will come down from heaven possessing a dual nature to be born as a child, is made and fulfilled. Because of his nature, character and work, he will win favor with man and God, and will also engage in a great conflict with a malignant enemy. This will require the payment of an unthinkably high price. Even though his death will result from that conflict and price, the outcome will be glorious.

VIRGO
(THE VIRGIN)

VIRGO, the Virgin, has been seen as a virgin by every civilization. She is normally pictured as a woman standing in a poised restful position, holding in her left hand either an ear of corn or a sheaf head of wheat, and in the right hand a small branch. We present her also holding a child in her arms as she is seen in the earliest Babylonian representations.

—NAMES FOR THE SIGN—

VIRGO has always been known to us by her Latin name The Virgin, but her name is naturally different in other languages: to the Hebrews she was either Bethulah, or Almah both meaning The Virgin; to the Greeks she was Parthenos, Maid of Virgin Pureness; while by the early Arabians she was called Adarah, The Pure Virgin, or Sunbul, meaning An Ear Of Corn, which correctly places the emphasis upon the Seed which she was carrying.

The ancient Chinese as early as 5000 B.C. called her The Barren Woman. In the Syriac language she was given the name Bethulto with the same meaning as the Hebrew root (The Virgin) used above. In Coptic she was Aspolia, The Place of the Desired Branch. The Latin word Virgo meaning Virgin from which we get our present name, may originally have been instead Virga which means Branch and is the exact word used in the Vulgate in Isaiah 11:1,

> "And there shall come forth a rod out of the stem of Jesse, and a branch shall grow out of his roots."

FIG. 1   VIRGO   The Virgin

The early Egyptians as well as the Babylonians saw VIRGO as holding an infant (Horus) in her arms. The meaning of Horus' name was He Who Comes Forth. The Babylonians called VIRGO The Great Mother, and according to Layard[17] her name was recorded in Assyrian as Mylitt or Mylitta—She Who Brings Forth.

One of the great wonders associated with this figure is that the *virgin* so consistently seen and recognized by all cultures is also associated with *motherhood*! One hundred years B.C. an altar dedicated to her was found in ancient Gaul with the inscription, "to the virgin who is to bring forth." Thus, we can see that this pure virgin was miraculously to have a child! That the emphasis is clearly upon her offspring rather than upon herself is borne out in the names associated with this figure and with the names of the individual stars in this constellation.

—NAMES OF THE STARS—

In her left hand lies one of the brightest stars in the entire heavens, Spica, a relatively modern Latin name meaning An Ear Of Corn, or the Seed of Corn. The original Hebrew name of this star was Zerah, The Seed.

> "Verily, verily, I say unto you, except a corn of wheat fall into the ground and die, it abideth alone: but if it die, it bringeth forth much fruit."
>
> **John 12:24**

The same word for corn (Zerah) is used in the Hebrew New Testament and is translated seed in Genesis 3:15. However, the most ancient name for this star in Hebrew still appears upon some of the oldest star charts and is the word "Tsemech," meaning The Branch. An ancient Arabic name is also often found on these most ancient star charts, and has the identical meaning.

This word "Tsemech" is especially interesting because it is used but four times in Scripture and each time it refers to the Messiah:

---

17 Layard, Sir A. H. (1817-1894) British author, Diplomat, first excavator of Nineveh's ruins (in 1845).

> "In that day shall the Branch of the Lord be beautiful and glorious."
>
> Isa. 4:2a

> "Behold the days come, saith the Lord, that I will raise up to David a righteous Branch and a King shall reign and prosper... and this is His name whereby He shall be called, The Lord Our Righteousness."
>
> Jer. 23:5-6

> "For, behold, I will bring forth my servant the Branch."
>
> Zech. 3:8

> "Behold the man whose name is the Branch and he shall grow up out of his place."
>
> Zech. 6:12

Thus, we note that this Branch is to be brought forth to be beautiful, glorious, a King, the Lord, righteous and yet, a servant.

The second brightest star in the constellation is Zavijaveh, located at the tip of the right shoulder, and means gloriously beautiful, which conforms perfectly to the passage just noted in Isaiah 4:2.

In the right arm holding the branch, we find a star named by the ancient Arabians as Al Murredin which means Who Shall Come Down, or Who Shall Have Dominion. This star is seen today on most charts as Vindemiatrix which in Chaldee means The Son, or The Branch Who Cometh. The Greeks called this star Prometheus, The Deliverer or Branch (Bough) Who Cometh.

In Isaiah's seventh chapter we read that God sent Isaiah to King Ahaz to confirm to him that his rule would be established, and He offered to prove His offer with a sign:

> "Ask thee a sign of the Lord thy God; ask it either in the depth, or in the height above."
>
> Isa. 7:11

Ahaz refused to ask fearing that he would be tempting God, and so the

Prophet said to him:

> "Therefore the Lord Himself shall give you a sign; behold a (literally 'The') virgin shall conceive, and bear a son, and shall call his name Immanuel."
>
> Isa. 7:14

As noted, the correct translation should read *the* virgin, since the article is in the Hebrew text. Thus we see once again, God stating authorship of a sign in the heavenlies and here taking a sign from the height (lit.) and giving clarification and amplification of its meaning to specifically point to the conception of the Virgin who would bear a son who would truly be "God with us!"

The ancient Arabians also gave names to several other stars in this constellation, the exact positions of which are not possible to determine, but the names listed upon their charts continue the message we've been reading: Subilah, Who Carries; Al Azal, The Branch or Shoot; Subilon, the Spike or (Ear) of Corn.

DENDERAH

In the Denderah Planisphere, VIRGO as the Sign carries one large palm branch, again signifying symbolically that she carries The Branch. The people who unknowingly but symbolically strew palm branches in the path of Jesus during His triumphal entry into Jerusalem were re-enacting something pictured centuries earlier.

Thus we see that the Sign called VIRGO presents to us, The Righteous One, The Righteous Branch, The Seed of the woman, Who is To Come, Whose coming will be glorious and beautiful. He Who Comes is that Promised Seed who will bruise the head of the serpent even though in that act He Himself sustains a wound in His heel.

We shall learn more of this miraculously born Coming child in the next decan, COMA.

COMA
(THE DESIRED SON)

The first amplifying constellation provided in our starry gospel advances the message of Virgo and bears the name COMA. COMA is seen as the Virgin seated with her son standing in her lap. It is interesting to notice that in our figure taken from a copy drawn at the original site in the temple at Denderah, Egypt before the Planisphere was moved to the Louvre in 1821, that the head of the son is slightly higher than the head of the mother, thus symbolizing that the son is to be greater than the mother. This is certainly true when we realize this to be a picture of the Virgin-born Son of God, figuratively standing in the lap of His mother.

—NAMES FOR THE SIGN—

COMA is the ancient Hebrew name of this constellation and means The Desired, The Longed-For. The exact same word is used by Haggai in describing the longed-for Messiah when he recorded, "And I will shake all nations, and the Desire of all nations shall come" (Hag. 2:7).

The ancient Egyptians called this figure Shes-nu — the Desired Son (lit. the Son or Offspring Desired). The Egyptians often pictured Isis and other of their goddesses holding a divine infant, the coming One, unaware they were prophetically testifying to Christ. That these interpretations put forth are correct is brought out in an amazing quotation from Albumazer,[18] the eighth century Arabian astronomer who was not a Christian. He said that the first decan of Virgo was everywhere a woman with an infant. Then he went on to state,

---

[18] Albumazer (Abu Masher, or Maaschor) 805-885, was a great Arabian Astronomer, physician. His most important work was "Flores Astrologiae" written in Arabic and translated into Hebrew by Aben Ezra.

FIG. 2   COMA   The Desired One

"There arises in the first decan as the two Hermes[19] and Aescalius teach a young woman, whose Persian name translated into Arabic is Adrenedefa a pure and immaculate virgin, holding in the hand two ears of corn, sitting on a throne, nourishing an infant, in the act of feeding him, who has a Hebrew name (the boy, I say) by some nations called Ihesu, with the signification of Ieza, which we in Greek call Christ"!

Satan couldn't permit a prophecy so obviously Messianic to remain, so he arranged history such that we find in the place of COMA, a wig!

---

[19] The two Hermes were, according to Egyptian authorities, Enoch and Seth. Early church fathers such as Eusebius as well as Jewish tradition agree, adding that Abraham taught Astronomy to the Egyptian priests at Heliopolis, and had in his possession at that time certain sacred writings of Adam, Seth, and Enoch.

Part I - The Promise Fulfilled - COMA

The Greeks not understanding or appreciating the significance of the Hebrew word "Coma" substituted for it their own word for hair, "Co-me," and to explain the word came up with a legend involving hair. Berenice, was the wife of Ptolemy III (Euergetes) King of Egypt in the 3rd century B.C., who vowed that if her husband returned from a dangerous expedition against the Assyrians, she would give her hair for which she was famous to Venus. Her hair was supposedly cut off and hung in the temple of Venus from whence it was stolen. In an attempt to console her, Conon, the astronomer of Alexandria, put forth the legend that Jupiter had placed the hair in the heavens as a constellation.[20] Thus today most of the modern star charts, since 1590 A.D. do not list COMA as they should, but rather put this constellation as COMA BERENICAE (*the Hair of Berenice*). This gives a graphic illustration of how the true names of the constellations have been distorted, either intentionally or unintentionally, over the centuries.

In Shakespeare's time the significance of this figure was still apparently known to some, for he wrote of shooting an arrow up "to the good boy in Virgo's lap."[21]

It was probably in this constellation that the Star of Bethlehem, seen and followed by the Wise Men, first appeared. A well known and carefully preserved prophecy in the east (traditionally attributed to the Prophet Daniel) was that a new star would appear in this sign when He whom it foretold was to be born! That star was indubitably a new star as both tradition and history would indicate. Ignatius, Bishop of Antioch, A.D. 69, said, "At the appearance of the Lord a star shone forth brighter than all the other stars." This information he no doubt received from actual eye-witnesses. We can only wonder if indeed a bright new star or even the same one might again appear in this constellation as one of those signs in the heavens to herald His second coming in glory.

---

20 "The belief that the stars are great men and divinities translated to the heavens occurs among nearly every people of the world." Hastings, James Encyclopedia of Religion & Ethics.

21 "Titus Andronicus" Act Iv. Sc. 3

—NAMES FOR THE STARS—

In the figure of COMA we have two individuals, the woman and her son. We know the woman's name to be Virgo from the adjoining constellation which COMA explains, as is also borne out in stars identified with the figure of COMA, Subilah, Who Bears (Hebrew) and Adrenosa, in Arabic The Virgin Who Carries. Thus we again see the woman to be The Virgin Who Bears or Carries The Seed or The Branch.

The son in her lap is seen as He to whom the name of the Sign points, Coma, The Desired, the Longed For (One). Another new star name appears here, Hazanethon (Arabic), The Branch. So we may correctly identify this son of the Virgin as the Branch, the Desired and Longed-For Son of God!

DENDERAH

As noted in the first paragraph, COMA was presented on the Denderah Zodiac as the infant held by the seated woman and called The Desired Son.

This Coming One was to be more than a Virgin-born, desired infant. He was also to possess a dual nature, to be both God and Man in one body as we shall see borne out in CENTAURUS.

CENTAURUS
(THE CENTAUR)

This figure has been seen from antiquity as a creature half man and half horse, a man holding a spear in the right hand and a shield in the left, a man down to the waist with the balance of the body being horse. Centaurs were considered in myth and legend to be mighty warriors but despised and hated by both men and gods and banished from heaven, perhaps because they had no form of comeliness or beauty. Yet in this figure we can clearly see a portrait of Immanuel, God identifying with us in our humanity. At the very heart of our faith is the doctrine that Jesus Christ was indeed God taking upon Himself human flesh and blood at the incarnation and living as the seed of the woman, truly God and truly Man in one and the same being.

—NAMES FOR THE SIGN—

This being with a dual nature is mentioned by Jamieson in his Celestial Atlas of 1822 as "On the authority of the most enlightened Orientalist of our own times, the Arabic and Chaldaic name of this constellation is … BEZEH." Bezeh is a Hebrew word meaning exactly the same as the Arabic title Al Beze also given for this figure meaning The Despised. This very word is used twice in the Messianic prophecy of Isaiah 53:3,

> "He is despised and rejected of men; a man of sorrows, and acquainted with grief: and we hid as it were our faces from him; he was despised, and we esteemed him not."

Another name in Hebrew for this constellation was Asmeath which means a Sin-Offering. To combine the two Hebrew names gives us The Despised Sin-Offering, which is an apt description of Jesus Christ who "came unto his own, and his own received him not" (Jn. 1:11) who yet offered Himself in our stead.

> "When thou shalt make his soul an offering for sin, he shall see his seed."
>
> **Isa. 53:10**

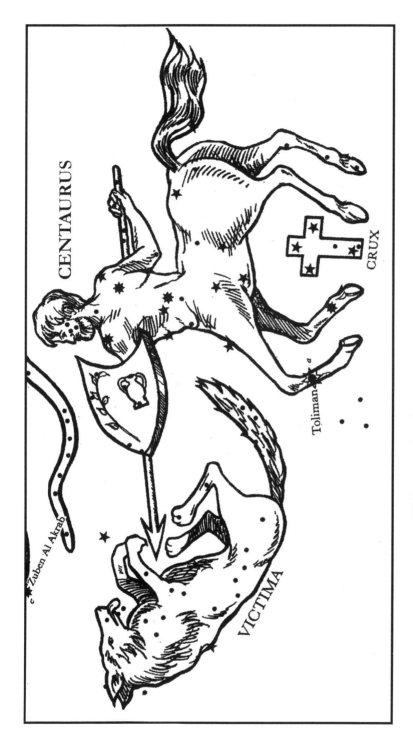

FIG. 3 CENTAURUS The Centaur

In this passage Isaiah states that when we make Jesus's sacrifice of Himself an offering for our sin, then He shall indeed have children: we by the spirit of adoption in accepting His offer enter into a son-Father relationship with God.

—NAMES OF THE STARS—

The brightest star in this constellation is Toliman (seen in the foreleg) which means The Heretofore and The Hereafter. This name recorded by Ulugh Beigh[22] in 1437, reveals that it refers to the one who "is the same yesterday, and today, and forever" (Heb. 13:8). The star Toliman was discovered to be a changeable star, meaning that its degree of brightness varies. Just so we see Jesus, who was once brightly seen, but for a brief moment His glory was diminished while He stripped Himself of the glory which was rightfully His for a season, and is now continually increasing in glory.

Another star in this figure is known by its Latin name, Proxima which means The Pierced, or Who Pierces. In the mythology of the Greeks Chiron was famed for his skill in hunting, medicine, music, athletics, and prophecy. He was also the teacher of all the great heroes of Greece. Chiron was immortal but agreed to die, and while he was battling a wild boar (an unclean animal) was wounded by a poisoned arrow intended for someone else. In dying he passed his immortality on to Prometheus[23] and was then himself installed among the constellations.

We can readily see in these fables the ignorant perversion of the original truths. Even though distorted we can vaguely see in them the underlying truth of Him who was all knowing, the perfect Teacher (Rabboni, Master) and Prophet, "who went about doing good" (Acts 10:38) even though He

---

22 Ulugh Beigh, a Tartar prince and astronomer, grandson of Tamerlane, made his observations and wrote at Gymnasium of Saracand in Persia. Utilizing ancient Arabic astronomical records, he drew up an atlas containing 1019 stars in their positions as of 1437.

23 Prometheus, (in Greek meaning to forethink or to learn beforehand), as his successor, and son of a Greek god, took pity upon mankind and stole fire from heaven and gave it to mankind for their benefit. (Webster's Dict.)

Himself was 'despised and rejected of men,' who yielded up His life that someone else might live eternally. The successor, Prometheus, also pictures the One who took pity upon mankind, left the glory which He had enjoyed from the beginning of time in the heavens, and came to earth in the form of a man that He might give "gifts unto men" (Eph. 4:8b).

The Greeks had a second unlikely name for this centaur figure. They also called him Pholas, meaning The Mediator. This, of course, can only represent him as the "one mediator between God and men, the man Christ Jesus" (Tim. 2:5).

We note that CENTAURUS is positioned directly above the SOUTHERN CROSS which speaks to us of His death upon a cross, and we see him in the act of destroying an enemy, being himself armed with a spear and shield. He also can be seen in this act to be killing or offering the life of VICTIMA (The Victim)—to be considered in the next section—thus representing him in his dual role as both sacrifice and the offerer of the sacrifice.

DENDERAH

The Egyptians at Denderah knew this figure as Knemu (from Kne— appointed, and mu — to die) meaning The Appointed Dies, Is Bruised, which perfectly restates the observation just made and we plainly see the Appointed One offering himself as a sacrifice. Also, oddly enough, in the Denderah planisphere, the form of the Centaur is reversed. That is to say, it is shown as a human body with the head of a sacrificial animal, either a ram or a calf. Thus it also clearly points us to the same truth: a human with a dual-nature who was to be sacrificed.

The Romans called this figure Rex Centaurus — The King, The Centaur. Thus we have seen outlined that the Promised Child came forth virgin-born, the Promised Seed, or Branch, grew into the strength of manhood, possessed two natures, would destroy his enemy in his death and would be a king. We have but to see his coming again in glory as BOOTES to round out our scenario.

BOOTES
(THE COMING ONE, THE HERDSMAN)

The third amplifying Sign further develops the story of this wonderful Coming One. We see BOOTES as a man coming rapidly on the run, bearing a shepherd's crook in his right hand and a sickle in his uplifted left hand.

—NAMES FOR THE SIGN—

He was called Bootes by the Greeks: a name taken from the Hebrew root word *Bo* meaning to come, thus he is seen as He Comes or The Coming One. The same word and thought appear in Scripture:

> "Rejoice before the Lord: for he cometh to judge the earth:
> He shall judge the world with righteousness and the people with his truth."
>
> Ps. 96:12–13

It is most probable that BOOTES was originally known and referred to, as he apparently is in Job 9:9 and 38:32, as Arcturus which is the name of the brightest star in the constellation, located in the left knee and which also means He Comes. This figure was called by the ancient Egyptians Smat meaning One Who Subdues, Rules and Governs. They also knew him as *Bau* which has the same meaning as the old Hebrew root *Bo*, The Coming One!

Aratus called him Arctophylax, or The Guardian of the Arctos—the Greater Flock, and intimates that this One was seen as a shepherd which is one of the most common prophetic figures applied to the Messiah.

FIG. 4   BOOTES   The Coming One

—NAMES OF THE STARS—

The same thought is to be found in the name of the star in the head of the crook held in the right hand, Al Kalurops meaning The Shepherd's Crook. This would lead me to think, as it has several astronomers, that BOOTES was probably originally a shepherd figure, even though he is often pictured with a spear in the place of the crook. The earliest star maps show him as we do in our figure, and the ancients called him, Bootes, The Herdsman.

The star Mizar or Izar located just below the waist on the right side means The Preserver or Guardian, and was apparently known still earlier as Mirac, The Coming Forth as An Arrow.

The second brightest star Nekkar located in the head of the figure means The Pierced and identifies BOOTES as the One who was pierced.

> "And they shall look upon me whom they have pierced."
>
> Zech. 12:10

Another Hebrew name for this same star carries a similar thought, Merga, Who Bruises. This identifies him as the one who was not only pierced but also bruised.

Another star located in the left calf is Murphride, Who Separates as in the sense of separating sheep from goats.

One other star in this constellation whose exact location isn't clear is Pulcherima the Latin superlative for beautiful, therefore meaning The Most Beautiful.

DENDERAH

BOOTES is portrayed at Denderah as a human figure coming, holding a ploughshare, to break or bruise the enemy. There he is named Smat, One Who Subdues, Rules, and Governs, but the name also carries the sense of "One Who Comes To, or Makes, An Ordained Place."

So we come to the close of the first section of our story recorded in the ancient star names. This ancient gospel has thus far proven to be in complete accord with the Scripture account. It has not added new truth but has itself proven to be true to the written revelation which it preshadows by thousands of years.

Thus far, in every detail it has shown us the beginning of the great gospel: the birth of the virgin-born, promised seed grown into the perfect God-man, the revealer of God to man, coming in glory and fury with love and mercy, coming as the Shepherd and Harvester of souls, coming as Shepherd for the sheep of His own flock whom He has been protecting and guarding, and coming with an upraised sickle for the harvesting of souls.

BOOTES is seen emerging, actually leaping forth from the VIRGO, COMA, CENTAURUS section as a fulfillment of the Seed full-grown, and in His dual role as Shepherd-Harvester.

"And I looked, and behold a white cloud, and upon the

cloud one sat like unto the Son of Man, having on his head a golden crown, and in his hand a sharp sickle."

"And another angel came out of the temple, crying with a loud voice to him that sat on the cloud, Thrust in thy sickle, and reap: for the time is come for thee to reap; for the harvest of the earth is ripe."

Rev. 14:14–15

SUMMARY OF VIRGO'S MESSAGE

By virtue of the inclusion of the sickle in the hand of Bootes we see intimated the prophecy of the great end-time reaping of the great harvest of souls by the Coming One, Pierced Himself, but bruising and defeating His enemy. Herein we have seen outlined the whole story, yet even though only an outline it stands as a complete message in itself. The stars and Signs truly in one accord, as one voice align themselves with the written word of God praising and declaring His glory!

LIBRA
(THE SCALES WEIGHING)

In our first series of Signs we noted that the Coming One was to sacrifice His life that others might live. In the second part of this heavenly story we shall see the means whereby that death was to be accomplished.

LIBRA, meaning The Scales in Latin, is always represented as it is in our diagram as a pair of balances with one pan in the act of being elevated and the other going downward as if a measurement has been made, even though both pans of the scales are empty.

—NAMES FOR THE SIGN—

LIBRA was known in ancient Hebrew as Mozanaim[24] — The Pair of Scales Weighing; in Arabic as Al Zubena—The Purchase, Redemption or Gain: to the Greeks it was Zugos a word meaning Yoke, Cross Bar, or Balance Beam.

—NAMES OF THE STARS—

The true meaning of LIBRA is readily apparent when we consider the ancient names of the three key stars in this constellation. The first and brightest, located in the raised pan of the balance is Zuben al Genubi, The Price Which is Deficient.

The second brightest star located in the lower pan is Zuben al Shemali, The Price Which Covers (or is sufficient). The Hebrews apparently had two names for this star, the first Graffias, meaning Swept Away and the other Kaphar, To Cover. This latter word is repeatedly used in the Old Testament where it is translated as "atonement" — the word used for the "covering up" of our sins. Under the Old Testament the best thing available

---

[24] This Hebrew word was selected as the title for the book on the Signs by Aben Ezra.

to mankind was Kaphar—the covering up of sins, so that God would not look upon them. They were not removed but only covered up so that they couldn't be seen. Under the New Covenant, offered since Calvary by Jesus Christ, something better than covering up has been made available — the complete remission and doing away with our sins, completely and forever, erased by His blood.

"The blood of Jesus Christ His Son, cleanses us from all sin."

1 Jn. 1:7

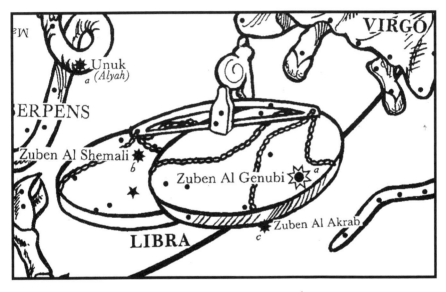

FIG. 5   LIBRA   The Scales

Here then we read the testimony of this second brightest star The Price Which Covers. Another name for this same star in Arabic is Al Gubi, meaning Heaped Up High and speaks to us of the inestimably great value of the price paid for our redemption, the very life of God in Jesus Christ.

The earliest Persian Planisphere presented this Sign as a man coming in wrath carrying in one hand a pair of scales and in the other a lamb. Thus confirming that the price to be paid, to be measured out in scales, was to be the life of the Lamb.

The names of the brightest stars put forth this situation: a transaction is to be made; a transaction of redemption; a great price is to be paid. This is due to the fact that mankind has been "weighed in the balances" like Belshazzar of old and been "found wanting."

> "None of them can by any means redeem his brother, nor give to God a ransom for him: (For the redemption of their soul is precious, and it ceaseth forever).
> Ps. 49:7–8

> "Surely men of low degree are vanity, and men of high degree are a lie: to be laid in the balance (Mozanaim), they are altogether lighter than vanity."
> Ps. 62:9

Even though man is so adjudged in Scripture and by the star names, there is yet hope for so fallen and ruined mankind: a hope that lies only in another, a substitute, to pay the ransom price. That this was indeed done, and all guilt for sin removed is confirmed by the ancient Hebrew name, Graffias meaning Swept Away. This aptly describes what has become of our sins.

Another star nearby toward the nose of Victima on the chart is the third brightest star in the constellation and indicates to us both by its position and by its name, the nature of the conflict to be involved in the paying of that redemption price, Zuben al Akrab or Zuben Akrabi, The (Redemption) Price of the Conflict. This refers to the conflict between the Seed of the woman and the seed of the serpent which will eventually be won by the Seed of the woman, but at a very great cost.

DENDERAH

The Copts, whose roots and language are traced to ancient Egypt, called Libra Lambadia, The Gracious Branch, and also designated this Sign Statio-Propitiantionis, The Place Of Propitiation. Their portrayal of the

Scales is not unlike that in the accompanying illustration.

There is another possibility as to the name and meaning of the sign of Libra which makes the story which we have been reading in it even clearer and more poignant. Dr. Budge[25] of the British Museum in his Babylonian Life and History (pg. 109) makes the statement, "The months were called after the signs of the Zodiac." This being the case the corresponding month should have been named for the scales but it was not. The Akkadian name for the seventh month was Tulku from their words *Tul*—meanings mound and *Ku*—meaning sacred. Thus their seventh month was called Sacred Mound or Holy Altar.

The present astronomical sign for Libra is (♎) which resembles an altar and tends to lend credence to this possibility. Although this name is quite different as is the shape of the figure, the thrust of the thought is very similar. If indeed the original Sign was a sacred mound or holy altar upon which the price which covers was offered for the price which was deficient, then we can see even more clearly the teaching intended in this Sign: that the great sacrifice of all time—the great redemptive price, unthinkably high, was indeed paid for mankind upon a sacred altar. The price was to entail a sacrifice, a life, a life's blood to be poured out in payment: the redeeming blood of God Himself.

"The Lamb slain from the foundation of the world."

Rev. 13:8

"They sang a new song... Thou art worthy ... for thou wast slain, and has redeemed us to God by thy blood."

Rev. 5:9

The price that was paid, by whom it was paid, and the result of its being paid, are brought out in three accompanying decans.

---

25 Budge, Sir Ernest A. W. (1857–1934) English Archeologist: became Keeper of Egyptian and Assyrian Antiquities in the British Museum; conducted excavations in Egypt and produced a long list of publications.

CRUX
(THE SOUTHERN CROSS)

This constellation was touched upon in our consideration of CENTAURUS. It is one of the most fascinating of the constellations in several respects. The figure is seen as a Cross and has always been so recognized.

It is odd that there is only one cross in the heavens as there are innumerable other possible combinations of four or more stars which could form crosses. Several of them would form a more perfectly aligned cross.

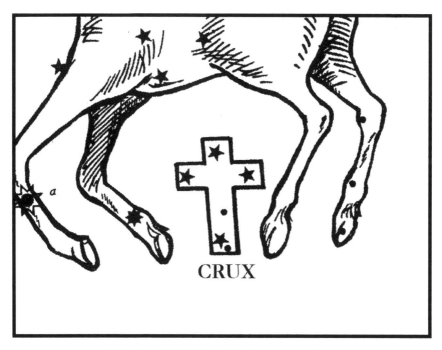

FIG. 6   CRUX   The Southern Cross

I was fascinated to learn that this constellation was visible to our earliest ancestors, and was recognized as the CROSS even then; and that it disappeared from the visible heavens in the north temperate zone at approximately the time when Jesus Christ hung upon an earthly cross, when its prophetic import had been fulfilled.[26]

Dante[27], the poet, also a great astronomer, authored The Divine Comedy and in it supposed himself to have been at Jerusalem at the beginning. He mentions what he would certainly have seen had he indeed been there: these "four stars never beheld but by the early race of man." This passage of Dante's was called to mind and quoted by Amerigo Vespucci on this third voyage toward the Cape as he viewed the starry skies of the South and boasted that he "now looked on the four stars never seen till then by any but the first human race."

An ancient Hebrew tradition passed down by Aben Ezra[28] was that this unseen Southern polar constellation was in the form of a cross, of the same shape as the pole on which the brazen serpent was lifted up:

> "And Moses made a serpent of brass, and put it upon a pole, and it came to pass, that if a serpent had bitten any man, when he beheld the serpent of brass, he lived."
>
> **Num. 21:9**

> "And as Moses lifted up the serpent in the wilderness, even so must the Son of Man be lifted up: that whosoever believeth

---

26 It was not entered on modern star charts until 1679 when Royer included it in his celestial atlas.

27 Dante, Alighiera (1265-1321) Scholar, author, poet.

28 Aben Ezra (Abraham ben Meir, Ebn Ezra) born 1092, died 1167. He established his reputation not only as a poet, but also as a Biblical commentator, a grammarian, and as an astronomer. He translated a number of works from Arabic into Hebrew and wrote treatises upon the subjects translated. His most important work was entitled Moznayim-The Scales written in 1140. In the late 1100's he made Europe acquainted with Albumazer and himself became the authority for Hebrew and Chaldee astronomy.

in him should not perish, but have everlasting life."

Jn. 3:14–15

—NAMES FOR THE SIGN—

The Hebrew name for this decan was ADOM, The Cutting Off, and this very same word is used in Scripture by the Prophet Daniel:

> "And after threescore and two weeks shall Messiah be cut off but not for himself."

Dan. 9:26

Jesus was "cut off" (had his life cut off from the land of the living) when he was condemned and crucified by the hands of wicked men.

The Cross has always been a sacred symbol. It is sacred to Christians who, like Paul, should glory in nothing "but the cross of our Lord Jesus Christ." However, it has from the earliest time been considered a symbol associated with supernatural life, after-life and some type of resurrection. The last letter of the Hebrew alphabet is the Tau (t) which was anciently in the form of a cross. It means a mark, especially a boundary mark, a limit or finish. Today this is still the letter which finishes the Hebrew alphabet. It reminds us of the cross of Jesus Christ which was also a boundary mark in history, observed by the secular world as well as the Christian. Time before Jesus' cross is referred to as B.C. and after, as A.D. The boundary mark of history was struck when Jesus completed His work upon the cross and uttered the statement, "It is *finished*."

—NAMES OF THE STARS—

Apparently none of the ancient names have been preserved for us.

DENDERAH

In the ancient Egyptian Zodiac at Denderah this first decan is seen as a lion with its head turned backward and its tongue hanging out as if in great thirst. This is none other than the "Lion of Judah" who, when hanging upon the cross, uttered one of His brief exclamations:

> "Jesus, knowing that all things were now accomplished, that the Scripture might be fulfilled saith, "I thirst."
>
> Jn. 19:28

In the same Denderah configuration a female figure is seen offering him a cup of water. So also in Scripture:

> "Now there was set a vessel full of vinegar: and they filled a sponge with vinegar... and put it to his mouth. When Jesus had received the vinegar, he said, It is finished: and he bowed his head, and gave up the ghost."
>
> Jn. 19:29–30

A third aspect of the Denderah picture bears note: there is a hieroglyphic name attached to this figure, which means running or pouring water. Hardly a descriptive term one would use to refer to a cup of water. This refers rather to what David spoke in the Spirit prophesying as if he were the Messiah,

> "I am poured out like water, and all my bones are out of joint: my heart is like wax; it is melted in the midst of my bowels. My strength is dried up like a potsherd; and my tongue cleaveth to my jaws; and that has brought me into the dust of death."
>
> Ps. 22:14–15

It is positively astounding how perfectly the ancient figures correspond with the written word of God.

The Egyptian name of the Lion, does not leave us in defeat, however, nor with a thought of death, as their name for this Lion was SERA, which means victory. This Coptic name according to Ulugh Beigh meant "victory, Triumph by a Great Conflict." Thus even though in the "valley of the shadow of death," victory is also present, as the next Signs will explain.

VICTIMA
(THE VICTIM)

In this constellation we see an animal that has been slain in the act of falling down in death. It has been slain by the spear of CENTAURUS which has apparently just pierced its heart.

—NAMES FOR THE SIGN—

It is fairly obvious that the more recent astronomical names for this figure, Latin Lupus (Wolf), Greek Therea (the Beast) and Lycos (the Wolf), and even Latin Victima (the Victim), are drawn from the figures after the fact and are not the original names.

The ancient Hebrew name Asedah as well as the Arabic Asedaton continue our developing message and fits the figures more precisely, for both mean "To Be Slain," which is exactly what we see pictured.

We observe in the Zodiac picture message that VICTIMA is being sacrificed by himself, that is, by the Centaur whom we have previously seen to be a representation of the Messiah. Even though we know "Messiah was by wicked hands crucified and slain" (Acts 2:23), still He willingly allowed Himself to face death, thus He could validly be said to have brought about His own death, or to have literally sacrificed Himself. That Jesus's death was indeed voluntary there is no question, for He makes that fact perfectly clear to us:

> "... I lay down my life, that I might take it again. No man taketh it from me, but I lay it down of myself. I have power to lay it down, and I have power to take it again."
>
> Jn. 10:17–18

> "I am the good shepherd: the good shepherd giveth his life for the sheep."
>
> Jn. 10:11

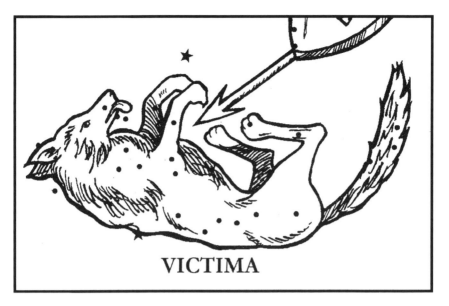

FIG. 7   VICTIMA.   The Victim

Paul also takes note of the self-sacrificing aspect of Jesus' offering up of Himself:

"...who through the eternal Spirit offered Himself without spot to God..."

Heb. 9:14

"... now once in the end of the world hath he appeared to put away sin by the sacrifice of Himself."

Heb. 9:26

—NAMES OF THE STARS—

Unfortunately none of the star names in VICTIMA have been preserved for us.

DENDERAH

Ulugh Beigh says that in the earliest Arabian figures this victim was seen as Sura, the Lamb, and as such would perfectly prefigure Jesus as "the

Lamb slain from the foundation of the world" (Rev. 13:8). This would also correspond with what we find in the ancient Denderah Zodiac and the earliest Coptic records. There, too, the victim is seen not as a wolf, but as a youth, silent and unresisting, with his finger to his lips as if signalling silence. The youth is known to the Egyptians as Horus, the Coming One, who is always associated with the bringing of life and blessing: through them known also to the Greeks and Romans by the same name signifying either justice or the victim of justice. He was also known to the Romans as the god of silence, quiet submission and uncomplaining acquiescence.

In all these clues we see the outworkings of the bruising of the heel. We see in this Him who

> "... was oppressed, and was afflicted, yet he opened not his mouth: he is brought as a lamb to the slaughter, and as a sheep before her shearers is dumb, so he opened not his mouth."
>
> Isa. 53:7

Some of the early figures of the youth show him having a horn on the side of his head marking him as a sacrificial animal. Also in some cases he has the horn in his hand: the horn being filled with fruit and flowers (the origin of the concept of the cornucopia, the horn of plenty) indicating him to be the Source or Provider of all good things.

> "And being found in fashion as a man, he humbled himself, and became obedient unto death, even the death of the cross."
>
> Phil. 2:8

Here we see the One who went willingly to His death, silently without objection or defense, obediently, that He might pour forth the greatest of blessings upon mankind.

As God never leaves us in defeat, so our story never ends a chapter on a note of defeat, but rather closes with a note of victory: so we close not with the cross but with the CROWN!

CORONA
(THE CROWN)

This constellation is one of the very few if not the only star grouping which actually resembles the figure which it presents. It consists of an arc of stars which looks almost like a crown. This figure is known to astronomers as CORONA, or Corona Borealis, The Crown or the Northern Crown.

God, the Father, rewarded the obedience of Jesus, even the obedience of His death upon the cross, with a crown.[29]

> "Wherefore God hath highly exalted Him, and given Him a name which is above every name, that at the name of Jesus every knee should bow."
>
> **Phil. 2:9**

> "But we see Jesus, who was made a little lower than the angels for the suffering of death, crowned with glory and honor."
>
> **Heb. 2:9**

The crown given to Jesus is far superior to every other crown that has ever been worn, even by those who wear them in heaven, for they will cast their crowns before the throne saying,

> "Thou art worthy, O Lord, to receive glory and honor and power, for thou hast created all things." (Rev. 4:11) and "hast redeemed us to God by thy blood out of every kindred, tongue, and people and nation" (Rev. 5:9).

29 "The stars of CORONA shone upon the night after the crucifixion ... Spica the Seed in the hand of VIRGO shone also on Eve in paradise, and on the weeping virgin mother of Christ after 4000 years, and now shines on us after two thousand more." (Dent, C., Letters. London, 1867).

Part I - The Promise Fulfilled - CORONA

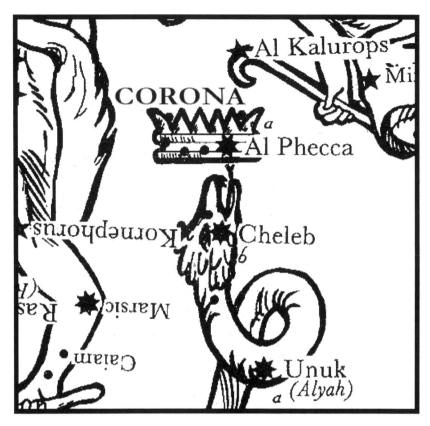

FIG. 8   CORONA   The Crown

NAMES FOR THE SIGN

The ancient Hebrew name for this constellation is Atatah, meaning a Kingly (Royal) Crown. It is a crown intended for none other than the King of Kings. Today the people in the middle east still refer to the stars in this figure as Al Iclil, An Ornament or Jewel. Isaiah employs similar symbolism to apply both to the Messiah and to His people.

> "The bridegroom decketh himself with ornaments, and as a bride adorneth herself with her jewels."
>
> **Isa. 61:10**

> "Thou also shalt be a crown of glory in the hand of the Lord, and a royal diadem in the hand of thy God."
>
> **Isa. 62:3**

—NAMES OF THE STARS—

The brightest star in the figure is Al Phecca, The Shining. The Messiah is identified in both Testaments as a shining Light—the Light which "shineth in darkness" (Jn. 1:5) and "The people that walked in darkness have seen a great light: they that dwell in the land of the shadow of death, upon them hath the light shined" (Isa. 9:2). It was probably this same star which the Romans called Gemma, The Pearl.

DENDERAH

The Denderah Zodiac represents this constellation as the figure of Sura, (the Lamb) Enthroned. They called the constellation *Api-Aaatl* which is derived from *Api*, head or chief, and *Aatl*, noble. Thus we can put them together and read the name as The Chief Noble. The same word *Aatl* in Hebrew means Strong, and would further enhance our grasp of this name, as The Chief of the Strong. We can thus see that this is not only the King of Kings, but also the Lord of Lords.

This Chief of the Strong is the same who in Scripture says of Himself,

> "But if I cast out devils by the Spirit of God, then the kingdom of God is come unto you. Or else how can one enter into a strong man's house, and spoil his goods except he first bind the strong man? And then he will spoil his house."
>
> **Mt. 12:28–29**

> "But when a stronger than he shall come upon him and overcome him, he taketh from him all his armor wherein he trusted, and divideth his spoils."
>
> **Lk. 11:22**

Clearly Jesus is here referring to Himself, in these parallel passages from Matthew and Luke as the Stronger One who has come, and will bind, overcome and strip from the former strong man (Satan) all his armor, and captives that he has attempted to hold by fear or force. Satan's defeat is again being plainly foretold, as is the glorious crowning of the Stronger Chief.

> "Then take silver and gold, and make crowns and set them upon the head of Joshua (Jesus), the son of Josedech, the high priest; and speak unto him saying, thus speaketh the Lord of Hosts: saying, Behold the man whose name is the Branch."
>
> **Zech. 6:11–12**

Now we have seen the man whose name is the Branch, the Seed of the woman, crowned with glory and honor. But our story is far from complete, for an enemy known as SCORPIO awaits us.

SCORPIO

(THE SCORPION)

The third chapter of our story written in the stars of heaven is entitled SCORPIO, The Scorpion, introduces the enemy, and will further explain the conflict introduced in the previous Sign.

The picture attached to this constellation is that of a giant scorpion attempting to sting with its poisonous tail, the foot (or heel) of a mighty man coming toward him, with one of his feet already placed upon the head of the scorpion. The mighty man is struggling with and restraining a huge serpent.

—NAMES FOR THE SIGN—

SCORPIO was identified as Akrab by the Hebrews which means Scorpion, but also means The Conflict, or War. The root of this very word is used by David in Psalm 144:1, where he blesses God for teaching his "hands to war." The Hebrew word for scorpion comes from a root meaning to cleave in conflict or battle.

The Coptic name is Isidis, meaning Attack of the Enemy. A word taken from the same Hebrew root word is used by David in Psalm 17:9 when he prays that God will protect him from "the wicked that oppress me, from my deadly enemies who compass me about."

The Arabic name is Al Akrab meaning Wounding Him Who Cometh.

Even though we know today that not all scorpions are poisonous, from earliest time they have been feared and considered a deadly enemy by man. Thus the scorpion is an apt figurative pictorial representation for Satan. The figures, names and all indications of the story agree that we have here a most deadly conflict with a wound or wounds being inflicted.

PART I - *The Promise Fulfilled* - *SCORPIO*

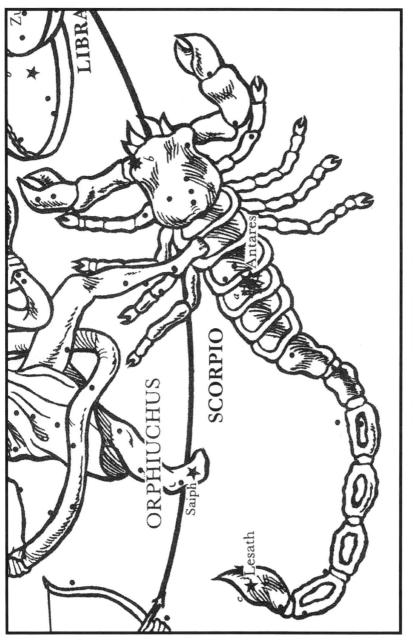

FIG. 9   SCORPIO   The Scorpion

—NAMES OF THE STARS—

The brightest star in the figure is Antares, located in the upper torso of the scorpion. This ancient Arabic name means The Wounding. In Latin the star is known as Cor Scorpii, or The Heart of The Scorpion. The star itself is recognized by its deep red light.

The star in the tail, actually in the poised and uplifted stinger is named Lesath in Hebrew (Chaldee, Lesha) and means The Perverse. Thus in this Sign we see again, restated and slightly amplified, the enmity existing between the Seed of the Woman and the perverse one, the seed of the serpent.

DENDERAH

In the ancient Egyptian Planispheres such as the one at Denderah this Sign is seen not as a scorpion, but rather as a serpent under the feet of an enthroned figure.

"In ancient zodiacs this sign is sometimes represented as a snake (Typhon)... with serpents tails for legs." So stated an early writer. The idea of serpents with legs is foreign to us, but may fit in with the curse imposed by God upon the serpent in Gen. 3:14 when He cursed the serpent and said "upon thy belly shalt thou go." The curse would obviously have been of no effect if the serpent were already crawling at that time.

The serpent of the Denderah Zodiac is entitled in hieroglyphics as Khu-or-bakh, or The Enemy Ruled, and Bowed Down; from *Khu*, Ruled; Or, Enemy; and *Bakh*, Bowed Down. The latter word comes from a Hebrew root meaning Caused to Fail, as used in the Hebrew Bible in Jer. 19:7,

> "And I will make void the counsel of Judah and Jerusalem in this place; and I will cause them to fall by the Sword before their enemies, and by the hands of them that seek their lives..."

Again we may observe that the Author and Designer of this heavenly collage did not wish any to err and assume that the Seed was to be defeated, thus especially in this Sign He has the figures closely interacting and even intertwined. The serpent will not be victorious and the scorpion will be crushed! That is the thrust of the message of the next group of stars. The following two figures we will consider together as it is almost impossible to disassociate them.

SERPENS
(THE SERPENT)

ORPHIUCHUS
(THE SERPENT HOLDER)

We see in this pair of constellations the picture of a serpent attempting to get away from the grasp of the Mighty Man with whom it is struggling in an attempt to reach the crown directly above its head. The crown we noted earlier rightfully belongs to Jesus the victor for His obedience unto death upon the cross. The battle here is definitely one for a crown. It is a battle for dominion ... the dominion lost by the first Adam through his act of high treason in the garden of Eden ... and the title to that dominion which was rightfully regained by the second Adam, Jesus Christ, through His obedience.

Satan the usurper has throughout history attempted to achieve the crown by force, violence, theft and murder, just as he stole it from Adam by deception and subtlety.

Our figures amplify the portion of the story that we noted in considering SCORPIO, wherein the enemy was attempting to sting the heel (kill) the Coming One, but here we see added the fact that the enemy also desires to steal from him the crown which is rightfully His. We note with joy that he struggles in vain, for this is the Stronger One who is not only defeating him in his grasping for power, but is in the very act of vanquishing him, dealing him a death blow upon the head (or the heart), as he tramples him underfoot.

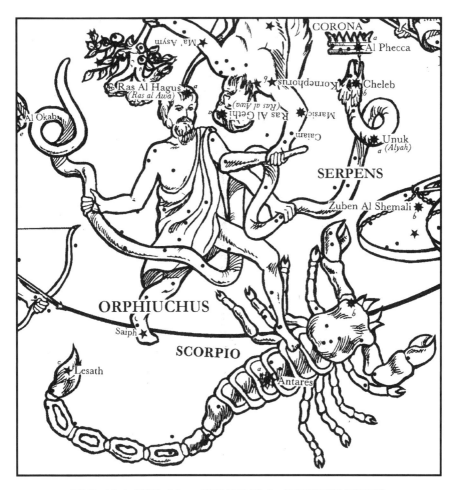

FIG. 10 & FIG. 11   SERPENS & ORPHIUCHUS
The Serpent & The Serpent Holder

—NAMES FOR THE SIGN—

The Latin name for the figure of a human holding the serpent and treading upon the serpent is Serpentarius, The Holder of the Serpent. The Greek name by which this figure is most commonly known, Orphiuchus, comes from the Hebrew and Arabic name Afeichus which translates as The

Serpent Held.[30]

—NAMES OF THE STARS—
(SERPENS)

The stars in the figure continue our story. The brightest star in SERPENS, located in its neck is Unuk meaning Encompassing. Its Hebrew name is Alyah—meaning The Accursed: confirming for us that this is indeed none other than the Accursed Enemy, first cursed by God in the Garden in the form of the serpent.

The next brightest star in SERPENS is located in the jaw and named Cheleb or Chelbalrai in Arabic meaning The Serpent Enfolding.

—NAMES OF THE STARS—
(ORPHIUCHUS)

The brightest star in ORPHIUCHUS is located in his head and bears the Arabic name Ras-Al-Hagus, The Head of Him Who Holds. This star we see bears another Arabic name which is Ras-Al-Awa, The Head of the Desired One, the same name as that of the star in the head of HERCULES.

Located in the foot which is uplifted as if injured is another important but not so bright star named Saiph (Hebrew), meaning Bruised, the same word used in Gen 3:15. Another significant star is not identifiable as to location but bears the Hebrew name Triophas, meaning Treading Underfoot. Two other unidentifiable stars in this constellation bear Hebrew names, Carnebus, the Wounding, and Megeros, Contending.

As we have noted, Orphiuchus was the Greek name meaning the Serpent-holder but came originally from two Arabic words meaning the same thing Cheleb Afei or Aesculapius (Ae-skaa-lape-us). The latter name figures prominently in mythology. He was considered to be one of the most

---

30 There is a legend that the Serpent-Holder, Orphiuchus, was really Imhotep, Egyptian ruler circa 2900 B.C. This legend, if true, would again confirm the antiquity of the astronomical records, would indicate their importance, and the desire of the monarch to be immortalized in them.

honored of all the gods. Even Socrates in the last hours of his life sacrificed to him. Although it isn't fully understood as to why, he was considered to be both a god and a man. He was thought to be the son of the Sun, and was reported to have seven children which were in actuality aspects of his own power, character, and nature. Their names are especially enlightening in our context: The Healer, the Physician, the Desired One, the Health-Giver, the Beautifier with Good Health, the One who Brings Universal Cure, and the Universal Remedy. He was also reported to bring the dead back to life by applying blood from the side of the goddess of justice and from the Gorgon which he slew, (indicating a recognition of the truth that life is in the blood). He was Himself ultimately slain by a bolt from heaven as a sin-offering but was raised to glory in heaven by the action of his father, Apollo. In all the pictures or representations of him, he is seen pictured with a serpent or its symbol.[31]

We can readily identify the truth behind the myths and legends and note their source as telling of the Seed of the Woman, the Desired One, the Desire of Nations, the One victorious over the serpent, who both gives and restores life and health, and who is the Great Physician, the Perfect Healer, the "Sun of Righteousness who arose with healing in his wings" (Mai. 4:2).

An ancient hymn reportedly composed and sung at the birth of Aesculapius is phenomenal in that it could just as well have been the hymn sung by the angels over the manger in Bethlehem:

"Hail, great Physician of the world! All hail! Hail, mighty Infant, who, in years to come, Shall heal the nations and defraud the tomb! Swift be thy growth! Thy triumphs unconfined! Make kingdoms thicker and increase mankind: Thy daring art shall animate the dead, And draw the thunder on Thy guilty head; For thou shalt die, but from the dark abode rise up victorious, and be twice a god."

Thus we can see beyond any reasonable doubt the prophetic similarity between Orphiuchus, Aesculapius of old, and the true figure to whom the

---

31 The cadeusus is an insignia composed of a staff (or pole) with two entwining serpents and at the top, wings symbolizing divinity. It is still in use today as a symbol for physicians.

prophecies actually addressed themselves. ... . The Babe of Bethlehem, the Man Jesus Christ.

DENDERAH

In the Denderah Zodiac we find ORPHIUCHUS figured as a throned figure with a hawk's head, the hawk being the natural enemy of the serpent. This figure's name is given in hieroglyphics as Api-Bau, the Chief or Head Who Cometh. Hence we can read that the enthroned figure, the Victor of the struggle is the Serpent's natural enemy (an enemy by nature). But apparently we haven't yet seen enough of this Victor who has been enthroned, as the next portrait gives us more details about him.

HERCULES
(THE BRANCH KNEELING)

Here we see the figure of a mighty man, down upon one knee with his right heel raised up as if wounded, holding a huge club in his uplifted right hand. At the same time his left foot is placed directly upon the head of DRACO, the Serpent. Our figure wears about him the skin of a lion which he has slain, and in his left hand he holds both a triple-headed snake-like monster and a branch from an apple tree which in some representations has apples on it.

Our figure corresponds to Hercules of legend and mythology in most all points. The mythological character had to perform twelve herculean tasks (origin of the phrase) among them the slaying of the Nemean lion, the offspring of Typhon the serpent; the killing of the hundred-headed Hydra; and defeating and capturing the triple-headed dragon-dog to retrieve the apples of the Hesperides, and storm the gates of Hell, which it guarded. In the battle with Gorgon this hero received a venomous bite from which he later died.

The correlation with our heavenly figure makes it evident, as does the obvious parallel with the Messianic prophecies and their fulfillment in Christ that the figure here presented and the legends associated with him spring from a far richer and more noble source than the mythology created by the minds of heathens. Jesus was the One who battled the roaring lion, Satan, and soundly defeated him; Who was Himself brought down into the dust of death by contact with the venom of the snake-like dragon-dog monster; Who won back the right of access to the tree of life, which the golden apples symbolize; and the One who wrested the keys of Hell from those attempting to guard Hell's gates.

FIG. 12   HERCULES   The Mighty One

—NAMES FOR THE SIGN—

This man is called Herakles by the Greeks and Hercules by the Romans. The Egyptians saw him and named him as they did on the Denderah Zodiac, Bau, the One Who Cometh; they, too, pictured him holding an uplifted club. Thus they also saw him as one coming to bruise and crush the head of the serpent.

The Phoenicians during five centuries before the time of the Greeks worshipped this man and honored him as representing a saviour. The Chaldeans made note of him and his legends over 4,000 years ago. The Arabians called him Al Giscale, The Strong One.

> "Who is this King of glory? The Lord strong and mighty, the Lord mighty in battle."
>
> Ps. 24:8

The Hebrew name for him is Marsic which means The Wounding.

—NAMES OF THE STARS—

The brightest star in this figure, located in the forehead of HERCULES is named in Arabic Ras-Al-Gethi, The Head of Him Who Bruises and has a second Arabic name Ras-Al-Awa, The Head of The Desired. Just as we find these two names for the star in the forehead of Hercules we saw previously two names for the star in the forehead of ORPHIUCHUS: Ras-Al- Hagus and Ras-Al-Awa, the Head of Him Who Holds and The Head of The Desired. The second name being identical confirms for us clearly that although the figures are different, they both represent one and the same Desired Coming-Conqueror and Deliverer-Saviour.

The second brightest star in HERCULES is Kornephorus, The Branch Kneeling, located in the right armpit.

The star in the right elbow area bears a Hebrew name, Marsic, meaning as noted previously The Wounding. The star in the upper left arm is Ma'asym, The Sin-Offering. The identical word is used in Isa. 53:10:

"when thou shalt make his soul an offering for sin, he shall see his seed..."

In the right arm is also located a star called in Hebrew Guiam, or Caiam meaning Punishing. The same latter word means in Arabic, Treading Underfoot.

Aratus the poet quoted by Paul as we have mentioned, speaks of HERCULES or Herakles as being "an image none knows certainly to name, Nor what he labors for" and also speaks of him as "the inexplicable image."

> "Near this, and like a toiling man, revolves a form. Of it no one can clearly speak, nor what he labors at. They call him simply 'The Man upon his knees': in desperate struggle like one who sinks, he seems. From both his shoulders His arms are high-uplifted and outstretched as far as he can reach; and his right foot is planted on the coiled Dragon's head."

As a result of Aratus' description of HERCULES, he was known for centuries simply as The Kneeler.[32]

There was much of mystery in the mythology of old, even to the Greeks who thought they were inventing this legend; yet, this figure long predates their culture. Though they didn't know who the figure really was, they had not lost much of the significant prophecy which had obviously been associated with this figure from earliest times.

These passages give some indication of the confusion and mystery which shroud so many of the mythological figures. The reason for the confusion I believe is that they are premised upon an invalid assumption—that nothing could have been known of Jesus before His birth, or before

---

32 The Encyclopedia Britannica, states under Hercules in "Astronomy," p 482... "this constellation was first known as 'the man on his knees'... and under "Hercules" .. "His name ... shows that he cannot be originally a god, since no Greek god ever has a name compounded of another diety. Probably a real man..."

the writing of the Hebrew Scriptures. On the contrary, it is our contention and one that is daily being underscored and confirmed, that God from the very beginning of His dealings with man, has made known to him knowledge of the promised Seed, the coming Saviour, to wit, the messages which we are reading here, written by the wisdom of God centuries before man's most developed mind could have fabricated them.

Many Greeks recognized that there was something greater underlying their legends and myths. In Metaphysics 10:8 Aristotle said in regard to the myths, that religion and philosophy had been lost, and that much had been, "added after the mythical style" although much was also "preserved to our times as the remains of ancient wisdom." Another ancient writer stated mythology to be "the fragments of tradition, which transmitted the knowledge of divine things possessed in the earliest times."

These accounts all predate the Greeks and even include an account of Hercules spending "three days and three nights" in the belly of a sea monster; an obvious distortion of the story of Jonah or the prediction concerning the Messiah's spending three days and nights in the belly of the earth after crucifixion. So many and such perfect coincidences would be extremely difficult for a rational man to explain by any other method than that which we are here putting forth.

This constellation has been seen and recognized in essentially its present form, from the beginning of recorded history. Astronomy books indicate its history as dating back over 5,000 years. Astronomers have also noted six bright stars in HERCULES which they feel resemble a butterfly flying to the west in the upper portion of this figure and they call this figure within a figure the Keystone. Keystone or capstone is also a name applied to Jesus who is "a chief corner stone, elect, precious .. . the stone which the builders disallowed, the same is made the head of the corner" (1 Peter 2:6–7).

The perfection of God's clues for us are even to be seen in this word for cornerstone (rendered Keystone, Capstone, head of the corner etc.) for the Greek word for corner Gonia, comes from a root *gonu* which means "knee." Everywhere we turn these truths seem to be underscored.

DENDERAH

HERCULES is seen on Denderah's Zodiac as He Who Bruises, a human figure carrying a club. An air of mystery surrounds him even there, for he is named simply, Him Who Cometh.

Hercules is thus one of the most beautiful or complete embodiments of the Messianic hero figure, perfectly picturing the Coming One crushing and trampling upon the head of the enemy in all his symbolic forms, serpent, dragon, snake, etc.

> "Thou shalt tread upon the lion and adder: the young lion and the dragon shalt thou trample underfeet."
>
> **Ps. 91:13**

Still another symbolic figure awaits us with more truth in SAGITTARIUS.

SAGITTARIUS

(THE ARCHER)

In this fourth chapter of the story written in the heavens, we come to SAGITTARIUS, the Archer, and continue the record of the Mighty One whom we saw in the last Sign, coming as Conqueror. Here once again we see the figure of a centaur, this time the human portion of the figure is drawing a bow and aiming an arrow at Antares, the very heart of the Scorpion.

He also has a quiver of arrows slung over his shoulder. The right foreleg is raised as if it might have been injured.

—NAMES FOR THE SIGN—

This Sign was called by the Hebrews Kesith, meaning the Bending of a Bow for Shooting, hence, the Bowman, or the Archer. This exact word is used in Gen 21:20, "God was with the lad, and he grew ... and became an archer." The Syriac name was identical. The Arabic name was Al Kaus, The Arrow. To the Greeks this figure was Toxotes, The Archer, and he was seen by the Romans as Sagittarius, the Archer Who Sends Forth the Arrow.

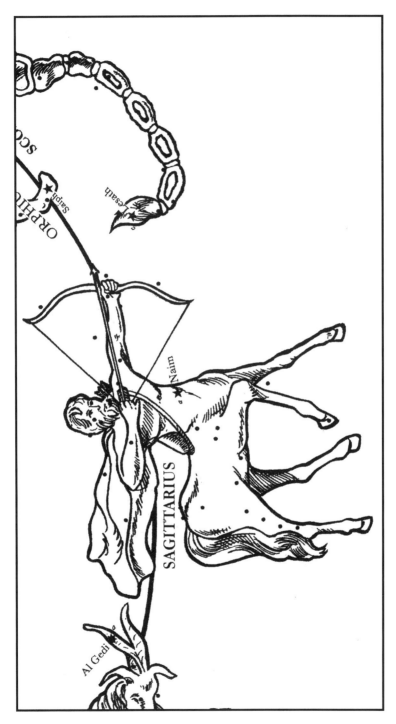

FIG. 13   SAGITTARIUS   The Archer

Part I - The Promise Fulfilled - SAGITTARIUS

We find almost a complete picture language version of the 45th Psalm of David recorded in this Sign and its accompanying decans.

> "Gird thy sword upon thy thigh, O most mighty, with thy glory and thy majesty. And in thy majesty ride prosperously because of truth and meekness and righteousness; and thy right hand shall teach thee terrible things. Thine arrows are sharp in the heart of the kings enemies, whereby the people fall under thee."
>
> Ps. 45:3–5

The Coptics called the figure Pi-Maere, The Gracious Going Forth or the Beauty of the Coming Forth. We also call to mind Gen. 9:13,

> "I do set my bow in the cloud, and it shall be for a token of a covenant[33] between me and the earth."

Aratus the poet writes of our figure

> "Midst golden stars he stands refulgent now, and thrusts the scorpion with his bended bow."

John writes of his own revelation of a figure similar to the one we are considering here:

> "And I saw, and behold a white horse; and a crown was given unto him, and he went forth conquering, and to conquer."
>
> Rev. 6:2

—NAMES OF THE STARS—

The brightest stars have names which are indeed relevant once again. The brightest star is Naim which in Hebrew is The Gracious, or The Delighted In. This is exactly what we find recorded by David earlier in the 45th Psalm in the 2nd verse:

---

[33] For further information upon the subject of covenants, we recommend an excellent book, *The Blood Covenant,* H. Clay Trumbull.

"Thou art fairer than the children of men; grace is poured into thy lips; therefore God hath blessed thee forever."

Jesus is the One "fairer than ten thousand," whom God hath blessed forever, and whose kingdom is for ever and ever.

Another Hebrew-named star in this Sign is Nushata, meaning The Going or Sending Forth. A third Hebrew-named star amplifies this thought, Terebellum, Sent Forth Swiftly.

The Arabian names for the stars in this constellation are similar in meaning: Al Naim, The Gracious One; Al Shaula, The Dart; Al Warida, The One Who Comes Forth; Ruchba er Rami, The Riding of the Bowman; Urkab er Rami, the Bowman, or the Rider and finally Al Naim, Al Sadiara, The Gracious One Who Strives.

The arrows named and seen in the quiver of SAGITTARIUS may symbolize either the present pricking of hearts with the convicting power of the truth of God, or may yet to be fulfilled in the destruction of His enemies at the end of the age.

We can see that the message thus far is that of a Mighty One who comes swiftly riding upon a great horse, who is armed with a bow and has his arrow aimed at the heart of the enemy. He is coming swiftly and with mighty vengeful power even though he is also seen to be both gracious and blessed of God.

A final star name to be noted in this Sign is that of Croton, the Greek word meaning The Purchaser! Jesus is the One who is the Purchaser, the Redeemer of His people, His lost and straying sheep. He has bought them back at an extremely high price, as we noted in considering LIBRA. Here we are again reminded of the great sacrifice and price associated with the Coming One, who has the right to come in judgment and righteousness, to pour forth His righteous fury upon the enemies of the King.

The ancient Akkadians named this figure Nun-Ki, The Prince of the Earth.

DENDERAH

In the ancient Denderah Zodiac we find a hawk or eagle-headed torso of a human figure located centaur-like upon the body of a horse. The figure is aiming an arrow at SCORPIO. Beneath the hind foot of the figure are the hieroglyphic characters for the Egyptian word Knem, He Conquers.

In mythology this figure of Sagittarius is known to the Greeks as Cheiron, the Executer, the chief of the centaurs who was also known as "the righteous-dealing Centaur." He was recorded as possessing a nature of greatest kindness, grace, intelligence, wisdom, dignity, and power. He, like Aesculapius, was considered to be the great teacher of mankind and revealer of heavenly wisdom, music, medicine and all the noble arts. All the Greek heroes and most honored men were thought to have been educated at his feet. Cheiron is sometimes seen in art to possess Apollo's throne, and this one coming to judge, wage war and rule, is similarly to occupy a righteous throne ... as is the One to whom it was said,

> "Thy throne, O God, is forever and ever; the sceptre of thy kingdom is a right sceptre."
>
> **Ps. 45:6**

Sagittarius is thus a perfectly clear reflection of the dual-natured, God-man, Jesus Christ: who possesses two natures in one body; possesses all wisdom, all goodness and all righteousness; who is going to come swiftly, armed as a warrior to defeat His enemy, Satan, and to undo or destroy all the works of the Devil (1 Jn. 3:8). He will not rest until all His enemies are under His feet, and all dominions, principalities, and powers have acknowledged their submission unto His glorious kingdom. This we will see amplified in the accompanying decans.

LYRA
(THE HARP)

"Thine hand shall find out all thine enemies: thy right hand shall find out those that hate thee. For they intended evil against thee: they imagined a mischievous device, which they are not able to perform. Therefore shalt thou make them turn their back, when thou shalt make ready thine arrows upon thine strings against the face of them. Be thou exalted, Lord in thine own strength: so will we sing and praise thy power."

Ps. 21:8,11–13

The harp or the lyre is one of the oldest musical instruments, mentioned as being in use during the lifetime of Adam (Gen. 4:21). In our figure LYRA is shown as a harp combined with an eagle or an eagle rising with a harp.

FIG. 14   LYRA   The Harp

The thought thus presented is that of a triumphant eagle, which like the hawk is a natural enemy of the serpent, rising heavenward, with the lyre the symbol for praise, singing, and rejoicing. In the national emblem of Mexico we see such an eagle with a dead or defeated snake in its beak.

The harp, the first decan of SAGITTARIUS, indicates that there is joy, singing, and rejoicing to be associated with this Sign, and that there is to be praise offered to the Archer-Bowman for what he is about to accomplish. The Archer-Bowman is seen in the act of regaining his dominion, by putting an arrow into the heart of his great enemy. His reign is about to commence thus the occasion for praise.

This is similar to the message of the song which Moses sang,

> "I will sing unto the Lord for he hath triumphed gloriously."
>
> Ex. 15:1

This is also what John spoke of when he wrote,

> "The kingdoms of this world are become the kingdoms of our Lord, and of his Christ; and he shall reign for ever and ever. And the four and twenty elders, which sat before God on their seats, fell upon their faces, and worshipped God. Saying, We give thee thanks, O Lord God Almighty, which art, and wast, and art to come, because thou hast taken to thee thy great power, and hast reigned."
>
> Rev. 11:15b–18

—NAMES FOR THE SIGN—

LYRA was apparently known to the early Hebrews as The Fishing Eagle from the name of its second brightest star. No other early names are available to us.

—NAMES OF THE STARS—

The brightest star in this constellation is Vega, a pure white star, one of the brightest in the heavens, and means He Shall Be Exalted. The same root word from which Vega comes is used in the song of Moses quoted above and from it also comes our word "victory." The second brightest star in the figure is called in Hebrew Shelyuk, which means The Fishing Eagle. Another name for the same is Sulaphat, meaning Springing Up. Thus the Hebrew names are telling us that the Fishing Eagle is Springing Up. As we observe birds fishing today, they dive for their prey and then having made the kill, spring upward again. The Arabians called this second brightest star Al Nesr, The Eagle.

DENDERAH

The ancient Egyptians at Denderah saw this decan as the figure of a triumphant hawk or eagle ruling over the serpent and called it Fent-kar meaning The Serpent Ruled.

Again the reason for this praise and worship offered to our God who reigns may be summed up in the words of John in Rev. 19:1-2,

> "Alleluia; Salvation, and glory, and honor, and power, unto the Lord our God: For true and righteous are his judgments."

What the judgments are beyond the arrow for the great enemy we shall see in the next decan, ARA.

ARA
(THE ALTAR)

ARA, The Altar, is figured in our illustration and in the heavens as an altar topped with burning fire, upside down, with the obvious message of fiery judgment to be poured out upon the earth.

—NAMES FOR THE SIGN—

This figure is named in the Arabian tongue, Al Mugamra meaning the Completing or the Finishing with the thought of Perfecting. The same roots are used in the Hebrew word utilized by David when He states, "The

Lord will perfect that which concerneth me" (Ps. 138:8).

The Greeks had apparently two words or names which they applied to this figure, Ara and Thusiasterion which meant respectively, the Altar or the Imprecation (a curse). In the Latin language the word Ara meant an elevated platform of stone, wood, or earth used as an altar, but also used for a funeral pyre. Thus in all the names for the constellation we see a harmony and a clear sense of a holy, completion or fulfilling of the appointed time that the fires or means of judgment might be poured out. This is exactly the message of the 9th verse of Psalm 21 omitted earlier as we considered the Psalm in connection with the Sign LYRA.

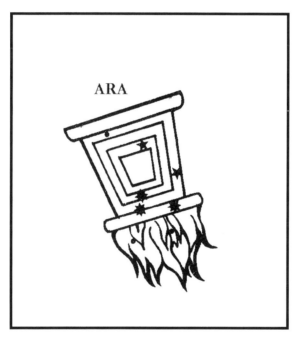

FIG. 15   ARA   The Altar

"Thou shalt make them as a fiery oven in the time of thine anger: the Lord shall swallow them up in his wrath, and the fire shall devour them."

The Greek word Ara was personified in the name of the Greek goddess of destruction and revenge. The Hebrews used two terms rooted in the same word Ara: Aram and Mara to mean utter destruction and a curse. Thus the thought is clearly presented of the curse brought upon the people by their rejection of God, being fulfilled in the judgment of utter destruction being poured out by God.

—NAMES OF THE STARS—

There are no bright stars in ARA, and no names have come down to us.

DENDERAH

The ancient Denderah Zodiac pictures this constellation somewhat differently for us, yet the messages are parallel. In Denderah's illustration we find an enthroned human figure holding a flail, the instrument for bruising. The Egyptian name for him is Bau, He Who Cometh, as we saw earlier in SCORPIO.

Scripture presents us with a picture, or really a series of pictures, line upon line, precept upon precept, whereby we learn progressively of the coming defeat, humiliation, and ultimate destruction of Satan. Jesus Himself spoke prophetically to those whom he referred to as "goats,"

> "Depart from me, ye cursed, into everlasting fire, prepared for the devil and his angels."
>
> Mt. 25:41

John in Revelation also spoke of the "devil that deceived them (being)... cast into the lake of fire and brimstone, where the beast and the false prophet are, and shall be tormented day and night for ever and ever..." (Rev. 20:10).

This is the curse placed upon the enemy of man. And God has promised to us the humiliating defeat of Satan, both in the Scripture and in the pictures recorded in the heavens, when He so named the constellations and recorded, in advance, Satan's demise. This explains why Satan has worked so hard to camouflage the astronomical signs with astrological confusion and foolishness.

Who is this figure who is coming to flail the enemy and to dispense judgment upon the serpent Satan, the old dragon and his followers? We will see in the third decan associated with the heavenly Bowman-Archer, DRACO, The Dragon.

> "And he laid hold on the dragon, that old serpent, which is the Devil, and Satan and bound him a thousand years."
>
> Rev. 20:2

DRACO
(THE DRAGON)

This brings us to the third and final decan associated with the great Archer, DRACO, the Dragon. It is seen as a huge winding serpent, fierce, but as we noted earlier, firmly under the crushing foot of HERCULES.

—NAMES FOR THE SIGN—

Its name in Greek, Drakon, the Dragon also means Trodden Down. This is none other than the dragon, that old serpent to which the last quoted Scripture refers.

We are faced with an obvious question, what is a dragon? No one has ever seen one, no such creature has ever been proven to exist. Yet every culture, in every age, in every part of the world has references to such creatures in their art, and folklore or mythology. The dragon has always represented the personification of evil that is militant: armed with sharp, fierce teeth, scales, spikes and sharp spear-like tails and sometimes breathing fire. It personifies the destructive, warlike aspect of the malignant corollary to the serpent which portrays the slippery, subtle, deceptive, sneaky, insinuating, secretive, poisonous, venomous creature which usually operates undercover in stealth, striking the unwary from behind, in darkness or from hiding.

How could such creatures which have never been seen and never existed have become so universally the symbol of evil? Probably no explanation other than that we are offering here: that God placed this figure in the heavens and explained the story which accompanies it. This would account for such worldwide acceptance and parallel association with the nature and character of these non-existent creatures.

Our figure is none other than the dragon "cast down" (Rev. 12:10), and humiliated under the foot of HERCULES who stands as a figure for the Victorious Christ.

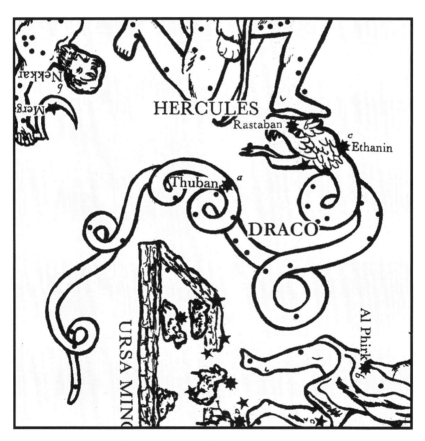

FIG. 16   DRACO   The Dragon

Part I - *The Promise Fulfilled - DRACO*

—NAMES OF THE STARS—

The brightest star in the figure is called in Hebrew Thuban, located in the second coil from the tip of the tail. Thuban means the Subtle. This was the pole star more than 4,700 years ago[34], and indicates the position of Satan as "the prince of this world" as Jesus identified him (Jn. 14:30). However it is no longer the Pole Star[35] as we shall see in connection with Ursa Minor.

The Arabs called Thuban, Al Dib, The Reptile. Another Arabian name for it is Al Waid, meaning Him Who is About to be Destroyed.

> "For God is my King of old, working salvation in the midst of the earth. Thou didst divide the sea by thy strength: thou breakest the heads of the dragons in the waters."
>
> **Ps. 74:12–13**

> "In that day the Lord with his sore and great and strong sword shall punish leviathan ... and he shall slay the dragon that is in the sea."
>
> **Isa. 27:1**

> "He divideth the sea with his power, and by his understanding he smiteth through the proud. By his spirit he hath garnished

---

[34] "And DRACO was the polar constellation when Chaldea became the cradle of astronomy. The Greeks therefore did not invent this constellation."
"... 4620 years ago alpha in DRACO was the polar star." (Jamieson, Alexander A Celestial Atlas. London, 1822.)

[35] In 1874 S. G. Bayne, author of The Pith of Astronomy visited an astronomical observatory in China said to be 4000 years old, which had two bronze eyeholes on a slanting granite wall which had been designed for the purpose of sighting Thuban. By the time of his visit they focused upon empty space, because the stars had moved over the centuries.
The long tunnel in the Pyramid of Cheops was so designed and focused as to permit, even in daylight, observation of Thuban, original Pole Star in DRACO.

the heavens; his hand hath formed the crooked serpent."

Job 26:12–13

The word "garnished" used in the preceeding passage has the meaning of "to make to glisten" which even more aptly describes what God did in placing this figure in the heavens. He indeed made the heavens to glisten when He placed this and the other constellations in them.

The second brightest star is Rastaban (Hebrew), The Head of the Subtle, or The Head of the Serpent. The third brightest star also bears a Hebrew name, Ethanin or Etanino, The Long Serpent or Dragon. Other Hebrew names for stars not identifiable as to position in this constellation are Grumian, The Subtle and Giansar, The Punished Enemy. Similar names occur in Arabic El Athik, The Fraudful and El Asieh, The Bowed Down.

DENDERAH

In the Denderah Zodiac, we find the same message, yet shown differently. They present the Serpent (*fent*) being trampled under the forefoot of Sagittarius. Their name for the figure is Her-fent, The Serpent Accursed.

Thus we find all the Signs bearing symphonic accord as they record the same theme. All concur perfectly with what we find in Scripture, in presenting the Seed of the woman coming to bruise the head of the serpent; coming as the Mighty Hero momentarily afflicted, yet coming forth in ultimate total and glorious victory, while dealing to the enemy a head wound of utter defeat, including final judgment and destruction.

As we come to the end of the first one third of the heavenly story we can but gasp in wonder at the perfection of the prophetic truths recorded so perfectly in the star signs and star names, and the beauty of the way they dovetail with each other and with Scripture. However, this really shouldn't surprise us if our premise is true, and both accounts were written by the same Divine Hand.

In the next Sign we shall meet another strange being, CAPRICORN.

PART II

RESURRECTION LIFE RECEIVED

As a result of the extreme price paid, the pouring out of the life of this hero for his people, they will be spared and receive the gift of life. He will be supernaturally raised from death, for death cannot hold so great a heaven-sent hero. By virtue of his obedience, he will win the right to pour out a flood of blessings from heaven upon the people of his choosing. His people who are also obedient and receptive, will receive all he has for them; to be rescued, loosed from bondage and promised an opportunity to reign with him in his kingdom when he himself is enthroned, after defeating his great opponent.

CAPRICORN

(THE GOAT-FISH)

CAPRICORN we find to be portrayed as the head and forepart of a goat sinking down in death with the right foreleg tucked under its body as if it had been injured. The body of CAPRICORN terminates in a healthy looking fish-like tail. We have a dual-natured figure, half goat and half fish.

Once again in this Sign we find two creatures incorporated into one body, symbolizing, as we have previously seen, the dual nature of the God-man Jesus Christ. But there is more that is new in this Sign; the goat as a sacrificial animal speaks to us of the atonement, and the sacrifice by which that atonement was accomplished:

> "And unto the children of Israel thou shalt speak, saying take ye a kid of the goats for a sin offering: And he brought the people's offering, and took the goat, which was the sin offering for the people, and slew it, and offered it for sin."
>
> Lev. 9:3,15

Here then is the foreshadowing of the sacrificial death of Jesus for the sins of the people. This figure speaks of His having gone to the cross for us in our place; His having offered up His own life that others might be given life, that those who believe upon Him might have life eternally with Him in heaven.

Another thought is also incorporated in this figure and brought out in the fish symbolism. As we have previously noted, Jesus identified Himself as the Seed, the promised Seed of the woman, which must fall into the ground and die in order that it might produce much fruit. As the poet Wordsworth so beautifully put it, "My death will be their birth." So here we see that death-to-birth process illustrated, by virtue of the goat's death, life is apparently being given to the fish.

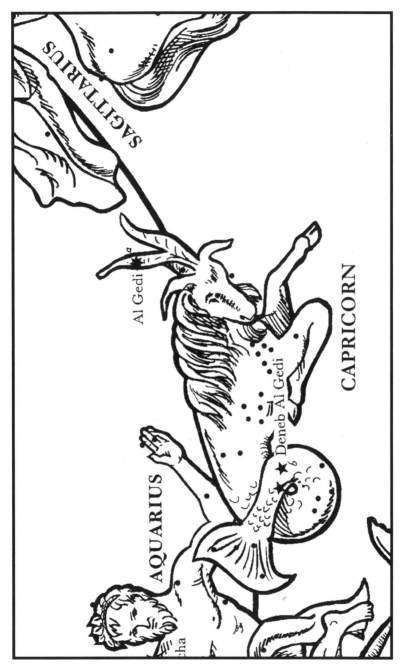

FIG. 17 CAPRICORN The Goat-Fish

Jesus upon several occasions used symbolism in speaking of those who would believe upon Him as being "fish." He said he would make those who follow Him to be "fishers of men" (Mt. 4:19). Jesus also spoke of His saved ones as being "born of water" (Jn. 3:5). Even as fish are born in the water, so these creatures whose environment is "living water." In much the same way God in the Old Testament promised Israel that He would restore them to their land and He said,

> "I will send for many fishers saith the Lord, and they shall fish them."
>
> **Jer. 16:16**

In other words God would retrieve His people from wherever they had been driven, woo them back to himself (luring them as a fisherman lures fish), and would restore them to their rightful land.

We can note here beautifully portrayed for us the sacrificial atoning death of Jesus Christ which gave birth to His mystical earthly Body, the Church, which is represented as a fish. Jesus' name was often associated with fish: one of the most popular Christian symbols still in use today is that of the fish. This symbol was chosen for several reasons: the early Christians referred to themselves both as people of The Way and as His fish and would identify themselves to one another by inconspicuously drawing the sign of the fish. The Icythus, Greek word for fish is usually pictured as the outline of a fish, sometimes containing the Greek letters "ICYTHUS" which create an acrostic of the first letters of the Greek words for Jesus - Christ - God's - Son - Saviour. So it is tremendously significant to find the same symbolic application of the fish emblazoned in the heavens and recorded as being there thousand of years before it was first used by the Christians.

Let's see if the names of the Sign correspond with the observations which we have made.

—NAMES FOR THE SIGN—

The Hebrew name for this sign is Gedi, meaning the Kid; or cut off and carries the additional thought of hewn down or a sacrifice slain.

> "He was taken from prison and from judgment; and who shall declare his generation? For he was cut off out of the land of the living."
>
> **Isa. 53:8**

The modern name Capricorn comes from the Latin name Capricornus and both merely mean the name of the Sign, The Goat. The Arabic and Syriac names are the same as the Hebrew. The Coptic, however, introduces an additional thought. It is Hupenius, The Station of Bearing (or the Place of Birth). This is hardly what one would read into the Sign as we see it. Perhaps the stars will help us to understand.

—NAMES OF THE STARS—

The ancient names of the stars involved are also in harmony with our interpretation. The brightest star in the constellation is located in the left horn area and is named Al Gedi (Arabic) which means The Kid or Goat. The next most prominent star, for which we have a name, is located in the tail and known to the Arabians as Deneb Al Gedi, The Lord, Judge, or Sacrifice Cometh. The other stars for which we have names are not identifiable as to position but their names are significant: Al Dabih (Arab.) The Sacrifice Slain; Al Dshabeh, The Slaying of the Sacrifice; MaAsad, The Slaying, The Destroying; Sa'ad al Naschira, The Record of the Cutting Off.

Here then we see the unanimous agreement of the names with the message of the Sign: that the Messiah, the sacrificial scapegoat, sin offering, was to be cut off and to sink down into death for us that He might bring forth many brethren and obtain a people for the Father and Himself, as it is written:

> "He was cut off out of the land of the living: for the transgression of my people was he stricken."
>
> **Isa. 53:8b**

> "He was wounded for our transgressions, he was bruised for our iniquities; the chastisement of our peace was upon him, and with his stripes we are healed."
>
> Isa. 53:5

Jesus was truly the Good Shepherd who laid down His life for the sheep. We see Him here figured as dying and yet "bringing forth much fruit." The life of the one dying is being reproduced in the body into which it is metamorphosing. This is the mystical union between Jesus and His Body which He attempts to convey by using many examples to help us understand: the Bride, the Vine and the Branches interrelated, one body yet composed of many members; Christ in us the hope of Glory!

DENDERAH

The ancient record of Denderah's Temple concurs with what we've seen: it also shows a goat-fish and is called The Place Of The Sacrifice, Hupenius.

Of course there is no such goat-fish creature to be found in nature, and it is obvious that it was created and placed in the heavens to graphically express a new thought. It pictures for us the act by which the Redeemer created or brought forth the redeemed ("the much fruit").

We shall find the three accompanying decans confirming this message.

SAGITTA
(THE ARROW)

SAGITTA, is the awesome arrow of God, the instrument of divine justice sent forth from His almighty bow to inflict the penalty due for sin upon the meek and submissive Lamb of God. It is the arrow of death speeding out toward Him who said, "Lo, I come to do thy will, O God" (Heb. 10:7). The effect of this arrow is seen in the sinking down of the goat, the sacrifice, into death. Its effect is also to be seen according to ancient legend upon the nearby falling Eagle which we will next consider.

FIG. 18   SAGITTA   The Arrow

"O Lord, rebuke me not in thy wrath: neither chasten me in thy hot displeasure. For thine arrows stick fast in me, and thy hand presseth me sore. There is no soundness in my flesh because of thine anger."

Psalm 38:1-3a

> "He hath bent his bow, and set me as a mark for the arrow. He hath caused the arrows of his quiver to enter into my reins (or heart)."
>
> **Lam. 3:12–13**

Jesus said of Himself by the Spirit in Zechariah:

> "... they shall look upon me whom they have pierced, and they shall mourn for him, as one mourneth for his only son."
>
> **Zech. 12:10**

That a message is intended to be conveyed by this Sign is clearly indicated by the inclusion of the piece of paper or parchment being carried by the Arrow. If a specific message was intended we cannot discern, but there is a message of obedience contained in the symbolism of an arrow. An arrow has no will of its own, it speeds directly toward the target chosen for it by the Archer: it fulfills the will of the Sender. In a certain sense, Jesus Himself is the Arrow of God. He, too, came to do the will of Him who sent Him. He said of Himself, "I can of mine own self do nothing... I seek not mine own will, but the will of the Father which hath sent me."

—NAMES FOR THE SIGN—

The Hebrew name for this constellation is Scham (or Sham) meaning Destroying, bearing out the thought that the arrow is sent indeed to destroy. Its work is seen, as we noted, in the death and dying of the goat as well as the falling of the Eagle.

—NAMES OF THE STARS—

The only name for a star in this figure to have been preserved for us is that of the second brightest, Kaus or Al Kaus, meaning as it did in SAGITTARIUS, The Arrow.

DENDERAH

The ancient Egyptians of Denderah saw this constellation, as a tailed figure with a hawk's head, standing over the junction of the head of the Kid with the Body of the Fish, and called it Fent- Kar (*Fent* being Serpent, and *Kar* being Enemy). So they also associated this Sign with The Serpent, the enemy, being defeated or destroyed.

Our message and perhaps also the target of the Arrow will be seen next in AQUILA.

AQUILA
(THE EAGLE FALLING)

This decan adds even greater impact to the message presented thus far as we consider AQUILA, the pierced, wounded and falling eagle. The head is downward toward the ecliptic, away from the center of the heavens. As we mentioned previously ancient legends tell us the arrow, SAGITTA, is said to have pierced AQUILA. In fact certain very early Greek Planispheres show the tip of the arrow touching the eagle.

AQUILA is another picture of the seed of wheat falling down in death that it might cause the bringing forth of much fruit.

—NAMES FOR THE SIGN—

The ancient Hebrew name for this figure Tarared is taken from the name of the third brightest star which is located at the base of the left wing and means The Wounded.

—NAMES OF THE STARS—

The same name is reflected in the Arabian name for the brightest star located in the neck, Al Tair, The Wounding. The second brightest star is located also in the neck, just behind the mouth, and carries another Arabic name Al Shain, meaning The Bright or The Scarlet-Colored. The root of this very word is used in the following passage:

> "Behold when we come into the land, thou shalt bind this line of scarlet thread in the window which thou didst let us down by."
>
> **Josh. 2:18**

The scarlet thread and the word used as the star's name point us once again to the sacrificial death of Jesus and to the power released in that death and made available to us in His blood.

Also to be found in this figure are two additional stars named in Arabic with symbolic names, the fourth brightest, Al Cair, located in the edge of the lower wing means the Piercing and the fifth brightest, Al Okab, in the tail means Wounded in the Heel.

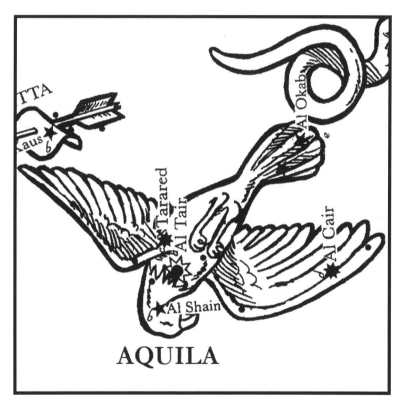

FIG. 19   AQUILA   The Eagle

Another star, whose exact position cannot be pinpointed is Deneb, Hebrew for The Lord or Judge Cometh. This same name appeared in CAPRICORN and indicates once again that these refer to the same individual.

DENDERAH

This constellation is represented at Denderah as Su-at, the Bird of the Nile Coming. The name is derived from *Su* meaning He and *At* meaning Cometh, and is translated He Cometh.

Scripture contains many references to the Eagle as a type of God or the action or provision of His Spirit in behalf of His people, for example,

> "As an eagle stirreth up her nest, fluttereth over her young, spreadeth abroad her wings, taketh them, beareth them on her wings, so the Lord alone did lead him, and there was no strange god with him."
>
> **Deut. 32:11–12**

> "Ye have seen what I did to the Egyptians, and how I bare you on eagles' wings, and brought you unto myself."
>
> **Ex. 19:4**

The eagle gives us a beautiful expression of the love of God for us. It is reported that if an eagle has no other food for its young, it will tear its own flesh to feed and nourish its young with its own blood. God, in Jesus, did just that, taking upon Himself humanity and allowing His own flesh to be torn, the blood to pour forth to nourish us and make us whole! He even said, "Whoso eateth my flesh, and drinketh my blood, hath eternal life; and I will raise him up at the last day" (Jn. 6:54). The Eagle is the ruler of the skies just as the Lion, another symbol for Jesus, is the animal king of the earth.

The next Sign will change our emphasis from the point of death and return us once again to a message of victory and glory as we consider the DOLPHIN.

DELPHINUS
(THE DOLPHIN)

In the final decan associated with CAPRICORN, we find the figure of DELPHINUS, the Dolphin, a healthy fish, no longer coupled with a dying goat, but alone and free. Considering the Dolphin in our heavenly picture to be the released, fully born fish-portion first seen in the later half of the dying goat, we get the thought of life springing up out of death. The dolphin has been known in legend, myth and history from the beginnings of recorded history. It was taken as an early symbol of Christianity and was commonly used in the 4th century in commemoration of Christ's crucifixion and resurrection.

FIG. 20   DELPHINUS   The Dolphin

Jesus not only died for our sins, but He told those whom He would have to leave behind, "I go to prepare a place for you. And if I go and prepare a place for you, I will come again and receive you unto myself; that where I am, there ye may be also" (Jn. 14:2b–4). Thus He clearly speaks of going down into the depths of the grave and death:

> "For Christ also hath once suffered for sins, the just for the unjust, that He might bring us to God, being put to death in the flesh, but quickened by the Spirit."
>
> 1 Pet. 3:18

> "But now is Christ risen from the dead, and become the first fruits of them that slept"
>
> 1 Cor. 15:20

And,

> "Know ye not, that so many of us as were baptized unto Jesus Christ were baptized unto His death? Therefore we are buried with Him by baptism unto death: that like as Christ was raised up from the dead by the glory of the Father, even so we also should walk in newness of life."
>
> Rom. 6:3–4

We see prefigured both in the DOLPHIN and in the quotations from Scripture the truth that Jesus willingly dove briefly into death and hell for us. But, He also sprang up again, rising in a new and even more powerful life. The corn of wheat which had to fall into the ground did so, and the results are glorious: a whole new Body of Christians, or "little Christs" springing forth from the seed of His death and resurrection. This was the message implied in our principal Sign, CAPRICORN, the combined Goat-Fish, but it could not convey to us what the DOLPHIN alone tells us of the new fish which have sprung forth. This truth is underscored as we note that the tail of the DOLPHIN is exactly like the tail of CAPRICORN.

We note with interest that the head of the Dolphin is always pictured upward, as it springs up into life, contrasting with the head of the adjacent

EAGLE which is always falling downward in death. The two pictures together show Jesus going down into death, when He could with the Psalmist say, "All thy waves and thy billows are gone over me" (Ps. 42:7). Yet that is not the end, but really the beginning, for the Dolphin symbolizes Him also springing back up into a vigorous, healthy life. Jesus said to His followers, those who desired to have a part in this new Body which is here portrayed as a fish, "Ye must be born again" (Jn. 3:7) and then went even further, "Except a man be born of water and of the Spirit, he cannot enter the kingdom of God" (Jn. 3:5). So there must be a "birthing in water," a new in-Living-Water-birth; a being "born again" which precedes entry into His mystical body, illustrated here for us by the DOLPHIN.

—NAMES FOR THE SIGN—

Although this Sign has always been seen as the DOLPHIN, no other really ancient names have come down to us, it having been known as it was to the Romans, as DELPHINUS. However, we'll find its most ancient form and name at Denderah.

—NAMES OF THE STARS—

The ancient star names advance the same theme, although none of them can be pinpointed as to location. The first name is Hebrew, Dalaph, meaning Pouring Out of Water.

> "For I will pour out water on him that is thirsty, and floods upon the dry ground: I will pour my Spirit upon thy seed, and my blessing upon thine offspring."
>
> **Isa. 44:3**

Four other stars have similar meanings: an Arabian name identical to the Hebrew name above Dalaph, meaning Coming Quickly, Scalooin (also Arabian) meaning Swift (as the flowing of water); and finally both the Syrian name and the Chaldean names Rotaneb and Rotaneu mean Swiftly Running (as water in a trough). The thought being brought forth is that of waters being swiftly poured out in which the birthing of new fish creatures may take place, which thought will be more fully developed when we consider another pair of fish in the Sign, PISCES.

DENDERAH

The most ancient Zodiac at our disposal, that of the Denderah Temple, shows a fish which is named in hieroglyphics Khau which means The Longed For, a Multitude, Fish, or Hoped For.

Thus we still find the message of a hoped for multitude of fish creatures resulting from the action of the dying of the Goat-Fish in order to release its fish portion. This death-to-life concept and process is often mentioned in Scripture, Jesus Himself said,

> "Thus it is written, and thus it behoved Christ to suffer, and to rise from the dead the third day: And that repentance and remission of sins should be preached in his name among all nations, beginning at Jerusalem. And ye are witnesses of these things."
>
> **Lk. 24:46–48**

One of these witnesses was Paul who declared the gospel unto the Corinthians saying,

> "For I delivered unto you first of all that which I also received, how that Christ died for our sins according to the Scriptures; and that he was buried, and that he arose again the third day according to the scriptures."
>
> **1 Cor. 15:3–4**

Jesus thus introduces the law of life as Paul also states it,

> "For the law of the Spirit of life in Christ Jesus hath made me free from the law of sin and death."
>
> **Rom. 8:2**

> "And if Christ be in you, the body is dead because of sin; but the spirit is life because of righteousness."
>
> **Rom. 8:10**

Another exciting water figure, AQUARIUS, awaits us...

AQUARIUS

(THE WATER POURER)

We see the sixth major Zodiacal figure, AQUARIUS, The Water Pourer, presented as a man kneeling with his left arm uplifted, and perhaps pointing in the direction of the three decans which we last considered (SAGITTA, AQUILA, and DELPHINUS). Thus indicating that his action is in some way related to, or a result of the message represented by those constellations. With his right arm he is supporting an urn and is pouring out its contents. From the urn we see a stream of water pouring forth and running rapidly as a mightily rushing torrent, as a river running at flood. The stream poured forth is being received and apparently completely consumed by a huge fish.

The hero figure in this Sign is unnamed, but is clearly associated with the pouring out of water. Those familiar with the Scripture would naturally expect to find reference to water somewhere in this heavenly gospel, since Scripture is resplendent with references to water and its life giving powers, as well as the overall blessedness of its presence and the corresponding spiritual applications.

> "For I will pour water upon him that is thirsty, and floods upon the dry ground; I will pour my spirit upon thy seed, and my blessing upon thy offspring, and they shall spring up as among the grass, as willows by the water courses."
>
> **Isa. 44:3–4**

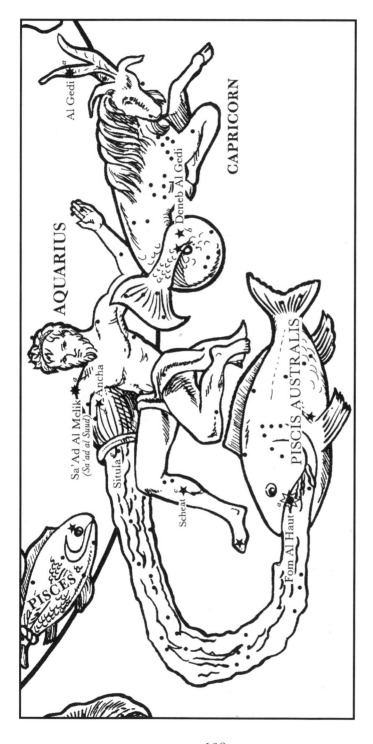

FIG. 21   AQUARIUS   The Water-Pourer

Balaam also used references to water in describing Israel in his prophecy:

> "As the valleys are they spread forth, as gardens by the river's side, as the trees of lign aloes which the Lord hath planted, and as cedars beside the waters. He shall pour the water out of his buckets, and his seed shall be in many waters, and his king shall be higher than Agag and his kingdom shall be exalted.
>
> God brought him forth out of Egypt; he hath as it were the strength of an unicorn; he shall eat up the nations his enemies, and shall break their bones, and pierce them through with his arrows."
>
> Num. 24:6–8

That "His seed shall be in many waters" tells us that His offspring — His progeny — shall be water-related creatures, and that their birthing shall somehow result from this pouring out.

Hosea likewise uses watery references:

> "Come let us return unto the Lord: for He hath torn, and he will heal us; he hath smitten, and he will bind us up. After two days will he revive us: in the third day He will raise us up, and we shall live in his sight. Then shall we know, if we follow on to know the Lord: his going forth is prepared as the morning; and he shall come unto us as the rain, as the latter and former rain unto the earth."
>
> Hos. 6:1–3

Joel also in a very familiar passage speaks of the Lord as the One who pours forth blessings:

> "And it shall come to pass afterward, that I will pour out my Spirit upon all flesh; and your sons and your daughters shall prophesy, your old men shall dream dreams, and your young men shall see visions:

> And also upon the servants and upon the handmaidens in those days will I pour out my spirit.
>
> And I will shew wonders in the heavens and in the earth: blood, and fire, and pillars of smoke.
>
> The sun shall be turned into darkness, and the moon into blood, before the great and the terrible day of the Lord come.
>
> And it shall come to pass, that whosoever shall call on the name of the Lord shall be delivered: for in Mount Zion and in Jerusalem shall be deliverance, as the Lord hath said, and in the remnant whom the Lord shall call."
>
> Joel 2:20–32

I have quoted this rather lengthy passage in full so as not to miss any of its significant points. Each time I have taught the truths contained in this book someone has come up to me with a confirming word using this passage and stating that the Lord had impressed them that the "wonders in the heavens" could be the very wonderful truths which are being presented here just as they were initially to Adam and his offspring. Also this passage has been a keystone of the renewal movement which started in the early 1900's in the Azuza Street revival that precipitated the Pentecostal movement in this country and around the world. The Pentecostal movement itself was actually a restoring of truths which had been allowed to be lost or lie fallow since being poured forth at Pentecost.

The basic truth is that God desires to pour out His Spirit upon His people and to cause them thereby to enter into a closer relationship with Himself, closer than any human being had ever dared dream might be possible.[36] He also desires to empower His people beyond their wildest hopes.

To this outpouring bear witness many of the Bible's characters. Luke in Acts 1:4 noted that Jesus commanded His followers not to leave Jerusalem,

---

36 The author learned this truth first hand and has seen it bless thousands of hungry souls. It is recorded in his book *Alive Again!*

but to await the baptism of the Holy Spirit which He said was " the promise of the Father." Luke then noted that Jesus also promised,

> "Ye shall receive power, (*Dunamis* power, not *Exousia* power)[37] after that the Holy Ghost is come upon you: and ye shall be witnesses unto me both in Jerusalem, and in all Judea, and in Samaria, and unto the uttermost part of the earth."
>
> **Acts 1:8**

Peter, subsequent to Pentecost in Acts 2:16, equated what had just transpired with the very words of Joel which we are considering. So we can clearly see the Holy Spirit inspiring Peter to associate Joel's prophecy with the fulfillment of it in the occurrence at Pentecost recorded in Acts the second chapter. This was the beginning of the end of the age, and of the era of the Holy Spirit which has and will continue to become more powerful until the age closes. Also, as the last verse of Joel's prophecy indicates, this period will be characterized by deliverance!

We should also note, that the beginning of the church occurred at Pentecost. When the Spirit was poured out, this empowering took place transforming the group of fear-filled disciples into a small but mighty army of inspired witnesses who immediately commenced evangelizing the world.

Who is the hero figure pouring out his water? It is, I submit to you, none other than He to whom all our Signs have ultimately pointed and who Himself said,

> "If any man thirst, let him come unto me, and drink. He that believeth on me, as the scripture hath said, out of his belly shall flow rivers of living water. (But this spake He of the Spirit, which they that believe on him should receive: for the

---

37 These two Greek words are both translated as power, but their actual meanings differ significantly. *Dunamis* is the root from which we get our words, expressive of great energetic power, dynamo and dynamite, and is defined as miraculous power. *Exousia*, on the other hand, connotes authority, or legal right to act.

Holy Ghost was not yet given; because that Jesus was not yet glorified)."

Jn. 7:37–39

Jesus is referred to in Scripture as the Rock which was struck by Moses and from which water sprang, that the Israelites might have the life-giving water they needed (Ex. 17:6). Jesus is that spiritual Rock from which all did drink and "that Rock is Christ" (1 Cor. 10:4). It is interesting to note that the tail (fish portion) of CAPRICORN slightly overlaps AQUARIUS. This again shows us the connection between the death and resurrection symbolism of the Goat-Fish and the winning of the right to pour forth this water of Life.

We also note that the followers of Jesus, elsewhere mentioned as being His fish, need a life-giving water environment in which to exist, and to one of them He said that He,

> "... would have given thee living water... Whosoever drinketh of this water shall thirst again: But whosoever drinketh of the water that I shall give him shall never thirst; but the water that I shall give him shall be in him a well of water springing up into everlasting life."
>
> **Jn. 4:10b,13–14**

In the Book of Revelation Jesus repeats this offer of living water:

> "I will give unto him that is athirst of the fountain of the water of life freely."
>
> **Rev. 21:6**

> "And he shewed me a pure river of water of life, clear as crystal, proceeding out of the throne of God and of the Lamb."

> "And the Spirit and the bride say, Come. And let him that heareth say, Come. And let him that is athirst come. And whosoever will, let him take of the water of life freely."
>
> **Rev. 22:1,17**

So I think we can safely say that our figure is beautifully compatible with the picture which we find painted of Jesus in His owns words and in the words of Scripture.

Do the ancient names of the Sign and its stars correspond equally as well?

—NAMES FOR THE SIGN—

The ancient Hebrew name for this Sign is Deli, the Water Urn and a form of this very word is used by Balaam in the passage from Numbers when he spoke of "buckets." The Arabic and Syriac names are both Delu, with the identical meaning as the Hebrew. The Coptic name is Hupei Tirion, The Station of the Pouring Out, or the Place of His Coming Down, As Rain. The Greeks called this Sign Hydrokoeus, the Pourer Forth of Water. The Latin name with which we are most familiar Aquarius means either the Rising Up Of or The Pouring Forth of Water.

Jesus as we have seen is the One who rose up and who both began pouring and continues to pour forth the water of life, freely.

—NAMES OF THE STARS—

The ancient names of the stars are also in harmony once again with the constellation's theme. AQUARIUS does not have very bright stars; the brightest are of the third magnitude yet four of these bear significant names for us. The brightest is Sa'ad al Melik (Arabic), The Record of The Pouring Out, located in the shoulder above the urn. Another Arabian name apparently applied to the same star is Saad al Suud which means He Who Goeth and Returneth, The Pourer Out of the Stream. The third brightest star is to be found in the right shin and carries the Hebrew name by which it is yet known today, Scheat (as in CAPRICORN and in PEGASUS), Who Goeth and Returneth. The fourth star is located in the Urn and is named for it, as Ancha, the Vessel of Pouring Out, The Urn. Another small star is located just inside the mouth of the urn, identified as Situla, Latin, meaning A Small Urn for Drawing Water.

DENDERAH

At Denderah AQUARIUS is pictured as a man pouring forth streams from two urns! One is held in each hand, and the fish (corresponding to the SOUTHERN FISH) appears also to have been poured out from the urn. The Egyptian name given for AQUARIUS is Aru, The River.

Thus we can clearly observe that both the Sign and the names of its component stars have been recorded to denote the fact or promise of the pouring out of a great blessing likened unto the pouring forth of a flood, by One who went away but came again in order to pour out a flood of blessings like a stream of liquid.

If our interpretations are correct, we should find them confirmed and substantiated in the accompanying decans.

PISCIS AUSTRALIS
(THE SOUTHERN FISH)

The SOUTHERN FISH is seen as a huge fish at the termination of the stream pouring forth from the Urn of Aquarius. It is apparently drinking in all of the flow as the stream pours right into the mouth of the fish and goes no further.

The SOUTHERN FISH is a perfect representation of the fulfillment of Jesus' invitation to "come unto me and drink," for here we find the huge fish receiving, and drinking in all that is being poured forth. The fish as we have seen is a mystical representation of the followers of Jesus Christ, and the word "fish" being either singular or plural can therefore uniquely stand as a symbol for an individual believer or for the church as a whole, the body of believers. In fact in one of the most ancient Persian Planispheres, the Persians pictured the fish as having the head of a woman. Both in Revelation and elsewhere in Scripture, the woman has been a symbol for the church. The body is spoken of as being female, the Bride of Christ. Our symbolism is even more clear: the stream (of living water) is literally being received by the woman, the head of the fish; the woman represents the church—the body—the espoused Bride of Christ.

Herein also we have a very positive message: that the blessings bought, provided, and poured out at so great a cost by our redeemer are all being received; there is none wasted! Just as was the case with the "feeding of the five thousand," even the leftovers were not wasted, all will be put to use. We also note that the fish looks only to the stream, it isn't doubled-minded (James 1:6-8). It looks only to the True Source, wholeheartedly, single-mindedly.

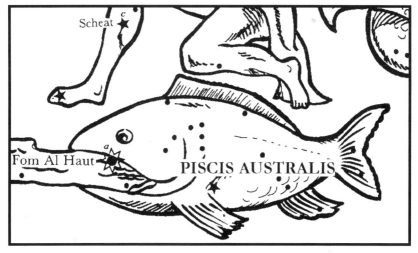

FIG. 22   PISCIS AUSTRALIS   The Southern Fish

—NAMES FOR THE SIGN—

The only ancient name of this Sign to have come down to us, is the name of its brightest star which from great antiquity has been known by the Arabic name still in use today, Fom al Haut (Fomalhaut), The Mouth of the Fish.

—NAMES OF THE STARS—

Fomalhaut's name (the only one preserved for us) again confirms the thought that the emphasis of the Sign is upon the mouth of the fish. The mouth is the instrument whereby the mystic fish representing the body of believers receives, drinks in, and partakes of the blessings being poured forth by the True Aquarius.

DENDERAH

The ancient records of Denderah's Temple have a similar message for us. There the figure of the first decan seems to include both the fish and the stream of water. Its name given in hieroglyphics is Aar, a Stream. This same root word is used in Gen. 41:1 when it is said that Pharoah dreamed that he stood by a river. Thus we can again observe the theme of blessings coming like a river or flood upon the blessed recipients, the mystic fish-people.

We'll learn more as we examine the familiar, but improbable figure of a half-horse in PEGASUS.

PEGASUS
(THE WINGED HORSE)

Once again we are confronted with the picture of an animal which has never existed in nature; never has there been a winged half-horse. There must then be a symbolic message contained in the figure other than the picture itself. This could be a representation of one half of the dual-natured Centaur: of one portion of that dual nature being set free from the hindrance of the other half—The God portion breaking free from the Man portion.

—NAMES FOR THE SIGN—

The Greek and the Latin names are the same, and they provide the only name we have, Pegasus, meaning Coming Quickly, Joyfully.

PART II - *Resurrection Life Received - PEGASUS*

—NAMES OF THE STARS—

Let's start our consideration of this figure by turning to the ancient names of the stars as we seek help in unraveling the mystery of the significance of this non-existent creature.

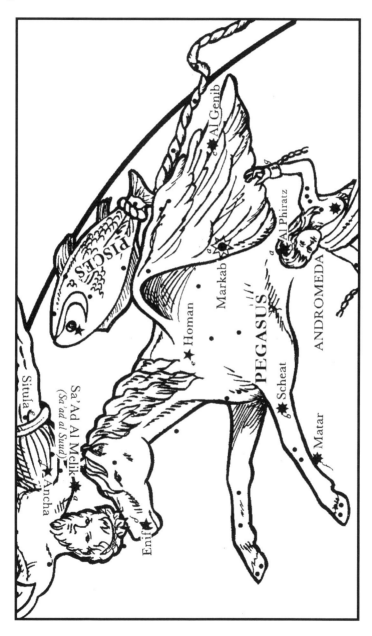

FIG. 23   PEGASUS   The Winged

The brightest star is located in the lower fore-edge of the visible wing. Its name is Hebrew is Markab, meaning Returning From Afar. The second brightest star is seen near the shoulder of the left foreleg and also bears a Hebrew name Scheat, with which we are already familiar as the same name appeared in AQUARIUS, He Who Goeth and Returneth. The third brightest star, located at the edge of the wing near the rear tip, bears an Arabic name Al Genib, Who Carries. The next brightest star is located at the nostril and named in Hebrew Enif meaning The Branch. The next brightest star is Homan located below the eye and meaning The Water. (This star is listed in modern astronomy books as having the meaning in Arabic of The Great King). The next star is located in the near leg and carries the Arabic name of Matar, which means To Cause to Overflow. This star is today considered the "rain star" by the Arabians who call it the "Lucky Star of the Rain." Another star carries a less ancient Arabic name Biham which means a Flock of Kids or Lambs.

It is difficult not to get really excited when one reads these ancient names and finds them so closely aligned with Scripture and its truths.

Here we clearly read an account of One called the Branch, a Great King, who has gone away, but who has also returned from Afar and Carries Water and will cause the blessings of the recipients of that water to overflow; He is Coming Quickly and His coming is accompanied with Joy, and His coming will in some way include a flock of Kids or Lambs. Perhaps critics will accuse us of mixing our metaphors here, but even if mixed, the metaphors are all consistent with the varied Scriptural symbolic usage.

So the stars, so the Scripture: Jesus said that He would have to leave His followers for a time but,

> "I go to prepare a place for you. And if I go and prepare a place for you, I will come again, and receive you unto myself; that where I am, there ye may be also."
>
> Jn. 14:2b–3

"Ye have heard how I said unto you, I go away, and come again unto you. If you loved me, ye would rejoice, because I said, I go unto the Father: for my Father is greater than I. And now I have told you before it come to pass, that, when it is come to pass, ye might believe."

Jn. 14:28–29

"And ye now therefore have sorrow: but I will see you again, and your heart shall rejoice, and your joy no man take from you."

Jn. 16:22

"I came forth from the Father, and am come into the world: again, I leave the world, and go to the Father."

Jn. 16:28

"Nevertheless I tell you the truth; It is expedient for you that I go away: for if I go not away, the Comforter will not come unto you; but if I depart, I will send him unto you."

Jn. 16:7

DENDERAH

The ancient Denderah figure does not have a listed hieroglyphic name in the case of PEGASUS, but beneath the figure taken to be PEGASUS, represented as a human figure wearing a crown and leading with his hand the head of a horse, are to be seen two characters *Pe* and *Ka*. Pega or Peka in Hebrew means Chief (as used in the word Pasha) and Sus means the Horse seen coming swiftly. Thus the most ancient source of the name of this constellation seems to be Denderah, with roots of the current name apparently in use even there.

It is also worthy of note that on the Denderah Zodiac there is located directly beneath PISCES a headless form which some have associated with PEGASUS. It marks the ascending node of which PEGASUS is an emblem marking the point at which the winter solstice had been in B.C. 4,000. This is another internal indication of the extreme antiquity of this Egyptian source.

In the Signs thus far we see Jesus' promise to go and yet to come again, and that the coming again was to be advantageous for His followers; that the believers would be blessed thereby.

We have yet one decan to consider. Will CYGNUS also confirm this understanding?

CYGNUS
(THE SWAN)

Our final decan is pictured as a Swan flying. The graceful swan oddly enough is a beautifully apt figure for Jesus, full of grace and truth, the One who has gone away and yet is coming back again. The Swan is not falling in death as was the pierced Eagle. It has its wings spread, healthfully flying, and is a creature equally suited to two environments, the earth or the air. Just as Jesus the God-Man could be said to be equally at home on earth or in heaven, so this bird portrays for us that which is also true of the Returning One: the One whose return will be glorious!

The swan in all ages has been considered something of a king of birds, certainly of water birds, because of its grace and elegance. For the same reasons it has been associated with music, poetry, beauty and purity throughout history. Mythology, legends and the arts have associated something of sweetness, grace and mystery with its death (the "swan song"). The stars of this constellation by their arrangement form one of the most beautiful and conspicuous of the crosses in the heavens, reminding us of the Cross of Jesus and the means by which His death was brought to pass.

—NAMES FOR THE SIGN—

The Greek name Cygnos, The Swan Circling is similar in meaning to the Latin name Cygnus, Who Comes and Goes or Circles. Thus inherent in each of our names is a reminder of the fulfillment of the promised return of the One who said, "I go," and yet, "I will come again" (Jn. 14:3).

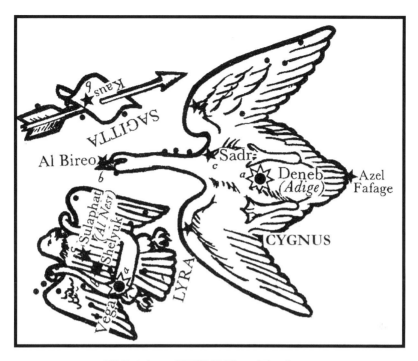

FIG. 24   CYGNUS   The Swan

—NAMES OF THE STARS—

The ancient names associated with the stars of this decan are also enlightening. The brightest star among them is named in Hebrew Deneb, as in CAPRICORN, located toward the back of the body, and means The Lord or Judge Cometh. This same star is also called in Hebrew Adige or Flying Swiftly. The second brightest is located in the beak and named in Arabic Al Bireo, Flying Quickly. The third brightest star is located in the lower shoulder and named in Hebrew Sadr, Who Returns, as in a Circle. Two additional stars are located in the tail and carry Hebrew names Azel, Who Goes and Returns Quickly, and Fafage, The Glorious Shining Forth. Another Hebrew named star is Arided, He Shall Come Down.

The star names of CYGNUS are all in agreement, The Lord or Judge is Coming Again Quickly. His journey has been similar to a circle, in that it brings Him back again from whence He departed. He Shall Come Down, and His Coming Down Again shall be a Glorious Shining Forth of His resplendent majesty.

DENDERAH

The ancient Denderah account concurs with our story. It presents the Swan also, and names it in Hieroglyphics as Tes-Ark meaning This (One) From Afar.

This is the same Jesus who came back again to us from the dead, appearing to the disciples and many witnesses at His first resurrection, and who has promised that He will yet come to us again from heaven the second time when He comes in glory and judgment.

> "And when He had spoken these things, while they beheld, he was taken up; and a cloud received him out of their sight. And while they looked steadfastly toward heaven as he went up, behold, two men stood by them in white apparel; Which also said, Ye men of Galilee, why stand ye gazing up into heaven? This same Jesus, which is taken up from you into heaven, shall so come in like manner as ye have seen him go into heaven."
>
> **Acts 1:9–11**

> "I will not leave you comfortless: I will come to you."
>
> **Jn. 14:18**

Our story will continue in a watery vein in the next Sign, PISCES, and will tell us more about the recipients of His blessings.

PISCES

(THE FISHES)

We find as the seventh major Sign, PISCES, The Fishes, figured for us as two fish with a band uniting them; the band in the form of a ribbon or rope tied securely around the tail portion of the body of each fish. The two fish are not swimming in the same direction: the one is swimming in the path of the ecliptic (the Sun's path), while the other is swimming perpendicular to it, heading upward toward the Pole-star. Additionally we note that the band securing the fish to one another is attached to the back of the head of CETUS, the Sea-Monster, and that ARIES, the Ram, has his foreleg placed upon the band also.

What does our figure symbolize? We have already established that the fish is a mystic symbol for the body of Christ. We can also observe that the two fish composing PISCES are each about one half the size of the SOUTHERN FISH; thus an obvious possibility is that perhaps they, together represent two composite portions of that mystic body. Let's see if this fits Scripture.

Jesus taught His disciples both by His words and by His deeds, or actions. In other words He often put them in learning situations, wherein the circumstances would illustrate truths for them, truths even greater than the actual situations; His parables had greater import, and parabolic truths contained within them. As an example, on two occasions in Scripture, Jesus directed His disciples who had fished throughout the night without any success at all, to again cast forth their nets, and the results were staggering in both instances.

> "Let down your nets for a draught... we have toiled all the night and have taken nothing, nevertheless, at thy word I will let down the net. And when they had this done, they inclosed a great multitude of fishes: and their net brake ... and filled both the ships, so that they began to sink."
>
> **Lk. 5:4–7**

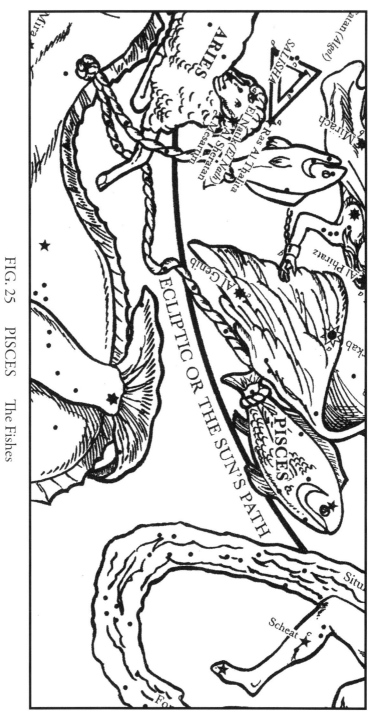

FIG. 25   PISCES   The Fishes

Part II - Resurrection Life Received - PISCES

On the next occasion Jesus was not in the boat with the disciples but was directing them from the shore while they were in their ships on the sea. Again the situation was the same, a long night of fishing without a single fish:

> "And he said unto them, Cast the net on the right side of the ship, and ye shall find. They cast therefore, and now they were not able to draw it in for the multitude of fishes."
>
> "Simon Peter went up, and drew the net to land full of great fishes, a hundred and fifty and three: and for all there were so many, yet was not the net broken." **Jn. 21:6,11**

In these accounts we have a parable in actions; along with the disciples we are being taught an illustrative truth about being "fishers of men." Just as they found great success attending their obedience to the spoken words of Jesus in catching actual fish in the natural realm, so will obedience to the words of Jesus bear fruit in the realm of "spiritual (human) fishes." In going forth and using His words and the gospel as "bait," multitudes of spiritual fishes may be "caught" for His kingdom. "Even so, must the Son of Man be lifted up ... And I, if I be lifted up" (used as bait)... "I will draw all men unto me" (Jn. 3:14, 12:32).

In the former Scripture, the net broke, no doubt allowing some fish to escape, but in the latter Scripture quoted from John, there is apparently another miracle implied, in that the net did not break in spite of the amazing quantity of great fishes. It is important to note that the ones amazed here were not just a group of men in training for the ministry, these were experienced fishermen, some professional fishermen by trade, and had spent most of their lives fishing... for them to be amazed by the miracles of the catching of fish adds additional weight to the truly miraculous nature of these catches.

Why the distinction regarding the nets breaking in one case and not the other? This gives another clue to this mystery of the fishes. There are many fish in the sea; even the miraculous catches did not encompass them all. Similarly, there are many men in the world; some will respond to the

125

bait of the gospel and the bait of the message of Jesus, and some will not. Some are apparently valid candidates for the kingdom of God and some apparently are not. Some fish are of proper size and ready to be caught, while others are too small and need to be allowed more time to develop. Jesus gave additional teaching on this theme when He declared that:

> "The kingdom of heaven is like unto a net, that was cast into the sea, and gathered of every kind; which when it was full, they drew to shore, and sat down, and gathered the good into vessels, but cast the bad away."
>
> Mt. 13:47–48

We can see therefore that there are good and bad, or those who will receive the message of the gospel and those whose hearts will apparently never be softened. So we see a contrast being drawn between those who are fish in name only and those who are truly fish, or true fish fit for the kingdom of God. This same contrast may be applied to those who claim to be Christian. The Word of God and experience tell us that there are true Christians and that there are those who are Christian in name only. These have been described as the "professing church" and the "true church": all who call themselves Christians are not necessarily Christians, as in the cults. Also there are the so-called "Christian" political parties in the middle-east which are waging war and murdering soldiers and civilians alike. Obviously, by their fruit, they are neither Christian, nor Christ-like.

We many also observe from our heavenly fish pictures that one of the fish is swimming along the path of the Sun toward the very Urn of AQUARIUS, from which the SOUTHERN FISH is drinking—perhaps speaking to us of the fact that there has always been a segment of the body of Christ which has desired "more" of what God has to offer, and which has actively sought more of His Spirit, more aggressively sought the gifts of the Spirit and a deeper walk with God. Other segments of the body more closely parallel the church in bondage as portrayed by ANDROMEDA, which we shall shortly consider. The uppermost fish, in fact, extends into the constellation of ANDROMEDA.

The fact that there are two fishes suggests an additional thought. In

Scripture the symbol of "two" has always spoken of multiplicity, as in Adam's two sons, born in connection with God's command to be fruitful and to multiply. It also speaks of contrasts: as in the case of Adam's two sons (or any of the parables of men with two sons) wherein we find a contrast between the two sons born apparently as twins yet with extremely different courses to their lives, natures and relationship with God (another clear argument against astrological influence upon lives. Twins should have identical fates, if astrology were valid, having been born under the same natal sign).

Is there a possible contrast expressed by the two fish? I believe we can see valid contrasts within the body of true believers which will ultimately be united at the marriage supper of the Lamb. For instance there are the saints who received the gospel as Abraham did by faith, before Jesus was manifested in the flesh, but who nonetheless believed in the promise of God that a Redeemer, a Messiah, was to come, and therefore were counted among the righteous. There would be a corresponding second segment of the Body of true believers composed of those of us who have had the privilege of coming to know and accept Jesus Christ as Saviour and confessing Him as Lord. The one segment are those who were accounted worthy by faith prior to Calvary, and the other, are those whose righteousness came by faith after Calvary. This may indeed be what is portrayed in the two fishes: one swimming toward the stream of 'living water' being poured out by the 'True Aquarius' at Calvary, and the other seen swimming directly heavenward, upward toward the Pole, perhaps presenting that portion of the Body striving Godward before the Living Water was poured out at the Cross.

The dual symbolism of the two fishes is so rich we dare not be dogmatic as to the significance, but rather would offer five additional possible interpretations, any or all of which could be correct. First, in the beautiful symbolism of the two fishes of PISCES we are reminded of any of the contrasts existing in the Church: as the two bodies of believers before and after Calvary, as mentioned; the body of believers here on earth and those who have already gone on to be with the Lord; the church weak and afflicted presently, contrasted with the Church strong and gloriously victorious as it will be at the end.

Second, the two fish differ in size as has been noted. Jesus made a statement concerning the fact that He had sheep who were not "of this flock," "other sheep" (i.e. of the other flock), and He addressed His followers on at least one occasion as "little flock." We see the larger and smaller fish corresponding perhaps to the "little" and the larger flocks which Jesus possesses, and which we will consider in detail when we come to the Big and Little Dippers.

A third possibility is that the two fish can stand for the contrast between those believers who shall bypass death and be raptured directly to heaven. Elijah and Enoch stand as Scriptural types and foreshadowings of that group. Other believers shall go the longer route, indicated in the heavenly portrayal by the longer band attached to the lower fish and following the path of the Sun, which is a type of Jesus who went through the doorway of death, or the way of days through a longer time.

The fact that the smaller fish overlaps ANDROMEDA may also have a bearing upon the truth contained in the Sign and offers our fourth possibility. The smaller and perhaps weaker of the fish is identified with the woman in chains, thus indicating the case of those believers who must undergo imprisonment, persecution and perhaps even martyrdom for the cause of the kingdom.

The fifth possibility is that this may also be a picture of the Jewish[38] and the Gentile believers united in one body. They are united and held together by the agencies of Jesus; united in one body by Him "who hath made both one, and broken down the middle wall of partition between us... for to make in Himself of twain one new man, so making peace" (Eph. 2:14b–15).

There is a final observation which must also be made, that is that both fishes although vigorous, healthy and swimming are definitely not free ... they are in bondage. They are being restrained by the tying of their bodies to the back of the head of CETUS. CETUS we will see shortly is

---

[38] The Jews have always associated themselves with this Sign. Their early Rabbis claim it as "peculiarly theirs" and both astronomers and historians in the past have noted its connection with their fate.

a representation of Satan, from whose bondage Jesus came to set us free.

> "The creature itself also shall be delivered from the bondage of corruption into the glorious liberty of the children of God."
>
> Rom. 8:21

> "Even so we, when we were children were in bondage under the elements of the world: but when the fullness of time was come, god sent forth his Son, made of a woman, made under the law, To redeem them that were under the law, that we might receive the adoption of sons."
>
> Gal. 4:3–5

> "Stand fast therefore in the liberty wherewith Christ hath made us free, and be not entangled again with the yoke of bondage.
>
> Gal. 5:1

What of the ancient names of the Sign and of the stars therein, do they concur with our assumptions?

—NAMES FOR THE SIGN—

The ancient Hebrew name for this Sign is Dagim, The Fishes (containing the thought of Multitudes). The Arabic name is Al Haut, meaning The Fish, reminiscent of the name of the SOUTHERN FISH's brightest star. The Syriac name Nuno means the Fish Lengthened Out (as in Posterity). The Coptic name is Pi-Cot-Orion, or The Fish, Congregation, or Company of Him That Cometh. The Greek name Icythus have already mentioned as an acrostic representation of Jesus' name and title, and it is their word for Fish. The Latin name Pisces with which we are most familiar does mean Fish but also carries the connotation of Multiplying.

Thus we see a commonality in the names: a message of fish belonging to Him that is to come, and the fish to be multiplied as in posterity. This is certainly compatible with our thought of fish as representing Jesus' body, or offspring, which will multiply and be fruitful as His posterity. The Sign reiterates the thought found in the SOUTHERN FISH of the blessed recipients of the Redeemer's completed work.

—NAMES OF THE STARS—

There are two stars named from antiquity in this constellation, but they are not identified for us as to position; the first bears the Hebrew name Okda, meaning The United; the second called in Arabic Al Samaca, The Upheld. These names apply beautifully to the body of Christ which is indeed united in and through Him, and which is also upheld, sustained, and supported by Him.

> "But thou, Israel, art my servant Jacob whom I have chosen, the seed of Abraham, my friend. Fear thou not; for I am with thee: be not dismayed; for I am thy God: I will strengthen thee; yea, I will help thee; yea, I will uphold thee with the right hand of my righteousness.
>
> **Isa. 41:8,10**

This Scripture speaks of a chosen seed, united in God, belonging to God, strengthened by God's help, and upheld by God according to His own word. This truth is echoed by the stars. This same thought of unity is expressed in Jesus' prayer:

> "That they all may be one; as thou, Father, art in me, and I in thee, that they also may be one in us: that the world may believe that thou hast sent me."
>
> **Jn. 17:21**

DENDERAH

The most ancient record of Denderah Egypt adds the name Piscis Hori which means The Fish of Him Who Comes. The Sign is presented as a human figure with a tail and an animal's head walking. The figure holds in his right hand the midpoint of THE BANDS, each half of which goes out in a straight line to the two fish which are restrained or upheld thereby. The presence of the animal's head points to the sacrificial aspect of this

One whose coming quickly is indicated by the tail, while both his name given above and the holding of their reins indicates his right of ownership to the Fishes.

PISCES' decans will provide more information about these Fish.

THE BAND
(THE BANDS)

The first decan of PISCES is THE BAND, which has always been taken to be a separate constellation from the Sign itself. Antarah, an Arabian poet of the sixth century, made reference in his poetry to THE BAND as a separate constellation, distinguishing it plainly from PISCES with which it is so obviously connected. THE BAND as we noted connects the two fish, but also makes two interesting intersections. The first intersection is made with the back of the head of CETUS, the Sea-Monster, a type of Satan, and the other important juncture is with the foreleg of ARIES in the next sign. However, we must not miss the great truth that by means of THE BAND, the two fish are inseparably bound to one another!

The desire and fulfillment of all which we are seeking or longing for as Christians is inseparably bound up with what is to be done by Jesus. Although He has already done for us more than eye can see or hearts can understand, there still remains a great deal that has been promised and prophesied yet to be accomplished.

The two fish bodies may stand for the people of the two great covenants of Scripture: for those under the law, and us who are under grace. They are the chosen and blessed by God with membership as His people through obedience to the law. We, on the other hand, are adopted into His family by our acceptance of the offer of salvation and by our relationship with the Offerer, Jesus Christ.

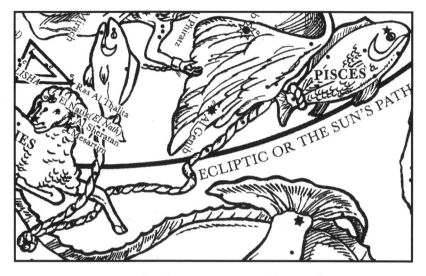

FIG. 26   THE BAND   The Bands

"For ye have not received the spirit of bondage again to fear; but ye have received the spirit of adoption, whereby we cry, Abba, Father." (Abba in Hebrew is a loving term of familiar endearment for a father, like "Daddy" in English). "The Spirit itself beareth witness with our spirit, that we are the children of God."
Rom. 8:15–16

Concerning these covenants it has been truly said, "The New is in the Old concealed, and the Old is in the New revealed."[39] The two covenants and the people of each are inexorably linked to one another, and cannot be separated without a loss to each. The Old relies upon the promise of fulfillment in the Messiah, to be complete; and the New confirms, completes, and consummates the Old.

"Think not that I am come to destroy the law, or the prophets: I am come not to destroy, but to fulfill."
Mt. 5:17

---

39 I attribute this quotation to Henrietta Mears, authoress of *What The Bible Is All About*, however, it may not have originated with her.

As the two fishes and the two covenants both find their point of agreement and unity in Jesus, not too surprisingly we find that point illustrated in the heavens. The foreleg (or hand) of ARIES placed upon THE BAND, affirms His ownership or control and states thereby His right of possession to those whose "reins" He holds.

This illustrates that formerly we were our own, going our own wayward way, ("wherein in time past ye walked according to the course of this world, according to the prince of the power of the air ... but God hath quickened us together with Christ... it is the gift of God..." Eph. 2:2,5,8). But now we are restrained from pursuing our old careers in sin and are changed by the inward force of a new nature. We have had our passions checked, (thus far and no further) and our natures bridled, harnessed, reined-in by our conversion and relationship with Jesus Christ: by the One who has promised to, and does gently lead, guide and direct our paths.

—NAMES FOR THE SIGN—

Do the names associated with this decan affirm our interpretation? The ancient Arabian name for THE BAND is Al Risha, the Band or Bridle. The same Hebrew root word is used is Psalm 32:9 "Be ye not as the horse, or as the mule, which have no understanding, whose mouth must be held in with bit and bridle, lest they come near unto thee."

Just as Peter's physical net held the literal fishes in the earlier Scripture, here we see these two fishes being held, supported, sustained and upheld by the bands ("reins" of Jesus) as we noted in the passage from Isa. 41. These BANDS also figure for the mystic bonds which exist between all believers at all times and in all places, which unite us in the faith and with our Center, Jesus.

—NAMES OF THE STARS—

Unfortunately, none of the stars in this constellation have names that have been preserved.

DENDERAH

The ancient Egyptian Zodiac presented THE BAND as a human figure with a tail, walking. The tail indicates in hieroglyphics He Comes. The Ancient name recorded for this figure in their list of names, reads U-or with the meaning of He who Cometh (its literal meaning is He To Come, He To Come).

One point not to be overlooked is that the fish are bound, and they are connected in that bondage with CETUS, or with Satan whom he represents. He "Who Is To Come" is to establish His right of ownership to the two fish bodies by taking up the reins. Even though the picture indicates that two parties are contending for possession, Jesus will ultimately win.

> "I drew them with cords of a man, with bands of love: and I was to them as they that take off the yoke on their jaws."
>
> **Hos. 11:4**

If we are correct in the application of the church as the fulfillment of these Signs, then the remainder of the amplifying decans should also picture more truths concerning the earthly Body of Christ.

In ANDROMEDA a confirmation awaits us...

ANDROMEDA
(THE CHAINED WOMAN)

ANDROMEDA is the figure of a healthy, beautiful woman in what appears to be a seated position, bound with chains upon her hands and feet. Her head is usually pictured bowed down as if despairing of help. She apparently has been ravaged, or been taken advantage of, as her dress is ripped exposing her left breast.

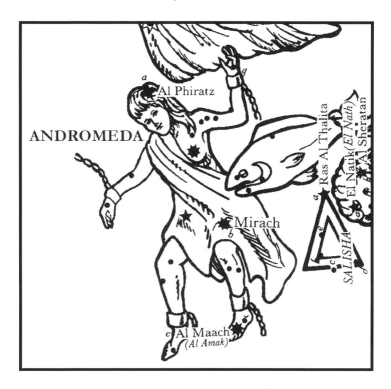

FIG. 27   ANDROMEDA   The Chained Woman

This woman is familiar to us through Greek mythology which presents her as the daughter of Cepheus and Cassiopeia who was desired as a bride by her own uncle, Phineas. When she was not enamoured toward him, other gods sent the sea monster, Cetus, to ravage the countryside because of the jealousy of the beautiful nymphs of the country who were her competitors. Finally Jupiter Ammon insisted that Andromeda be chained to a rock near Joppa in Palestine to be devoured by the sea-monster. However, she was rescued by Perseus who then married her. Her name in Greek, (Andromedo), means Man-Ruler.

Here is a beautiful representation of the church, the mystic body often symbolized in Scripture as a beautiful woman, destined to be the Bride of the Son of God. She is destined also to rule with Him as King and Priest, and to execute judgment over men as well as angels. However, that is not yet her experience; rather she is weak and afflicted, and subjected to the bondages and ravages of this world system to which she finds herself chained. The Scriptures describe her thus:

> "For the Lord hath called thee as a woman forsaken and grieved in spirit, and a wife of youth when thou was refused, saith thy God. O thou afflicted, tossed with tempest, and not comforted, behold, I will lay thy stones with fair colors, and lay thy foundations with sapphires.
>
> Isa. 54:6,11a

> "For a small moment have I forsaken thee, but with great mercies will I gather thee"
>
> Isa. 54:7

> "The Spirit of the Lord God is upon me, because the Lord hath anointed me to preach good tidings unto the meek; he hath sent me to bind up the broken-hearted, to proclaim liberty to the captives, and the opening to the prison to them that are bound."
>
> Isa. 61:1

> "Shake thyself from the dust, arise, and sit down, O Jerusalem; loose thyself from the bands of the neck, O captive daughter of Zion. For thus saith the Lord, Ye have sold yourselves for naught, and ye shall be delivered without money."
>
> Isa. 52:2–3

Thus, clearly the picture which we see in the heavens corresponds with the one in Scripture of the afflicted, chain-bound daughter of Zion in the Old Testament and equally applies to Paul and Silas as representatives of the same figure in the New Testament where we find them in the chains of the Macedonian jailer (Acts 16:19ff).

But what of the ancient stars and Sign names?

—NAMES FOR THE SIGN—

The most ancient Hebrew name for this Sign is Sirra meaning The Chained, while another Hebrew name is Persea, The Stretched Out. The Greeks knew the Sign as Andromeda, as mentioned, which also carries the meaning Set Free From Death. Aratus, the poet, refers to her as Desma, The Bound.

—NAMES OF THE STARS—

The same thoughts are echoed in the names of the stars. The brightest star located in the head is called in Arabic Al Phiratz, The Broken Down. The second brightest star Mirach (Hebrew) is located in the left hip area and bears the meaning of The Weak. The third brightest star is in the left ankle, and named in Arabic Al Maach and Al Amak both carrying the meaning The Struck Down.

Additional stars with Hebrew names are associated with this Sign but not identifiable as to position: Adhil, The Afflicted, and Mizar, The Bound. Stars with Arabic names continue the story for us. Al Mara, These include the Afflicted, Misam al Thuraiya (applied to the nebula), The Assembled, The Abundance, and a name that would be totally unbelievable were it not of such obvious antiquity, Al Mosealah, Delivered From The Grave, Sheol, Hades, or Hell.

> "For thou wilt not leave my soul in hell: neither wilt thou suffer thine Holy One to see corruption."
>
> Ps. 16:10

Moses told Pharoah, "Thus saith the Lord God of Israel, 'Let My People Go!'"

Ex. 5:1

Scripture in these two passages uses the same identical Hebrew words or root words in the Hebrew Bible to express the thought that neither Pharoah, not Satan for whom he stands in a figure, can withstand God. "Let My People Go!" Even hell cannot hold the people whom God hath called.

DENDERAH

The ancient Denderah Zodiac gives her the hieroglyphic name of Set meaning Set Up As A King or Queen. It also has characters placed below her figure for Sirra the first Hebrew name meaning The Chained. She is seen in that portrayal as a female, touching the BANDS of PISCES and is assumed to be a regal personage.

The thought which might summarize ANDROMEDA is that throughout the Sign we find a beautiful, regal personage afflicted and in chains temporarily, but she has a lover, CEPHEUS, who is coming to her aid as we shall see next.

CEPHEUS
(THE KING)

The figure of CEPHEUS is presented as a bearded kingly personage who wears a crown upon his head, has a royal robe drawn about him, and is in a seated position as if upon a throne. In his uplifted left hand he holds a scepter and with his right he holds a portion of his robe. His right foot is firmly upon the pole star, so that the heavens revolve around, and are under his feet!

This figure correlates so closely with the Scriptural descriptions of Jesus enthroned that we hardly need go into further detail. In earlier figures we noted references to the kingly crown that the Redeemer would win and wear; here for the first time we see it actually upon his head.

—NAMES FOR THE SIGN—

The ancient names bear out our assumption once again. The most ancient Hebrew name for this figure is Cepheus, The Branch. The best introduction of this man might be the name given to him on the ancient Denderah Zodiac. There he is identified as Per-Ku-Hor, This One Cometh To Rule!

PART II - Resurrection Life Received - CEPHEUS

FIG. 28　　CEPHEUS　　The Crowned King

The constellation was also called by the Ethiopians, Hyk, The King. The Greeks who took their name Cepheus from the Hebrew word also give it the meaning of The Branch, but it is rendered by others of the Greeks, such as Euripides, as The King.

—NAMES OF THE STARS—

The stars contain the same message. The brightest star located in the right shoulder is Al Deramin (Arabic) meaning Coming Quickly As In A Circle. The second brightest star in the midriff also has an Arabian name, Al Phirk, The Redeemer. Another star named in Arabic is Al Rai, or Errai, located in the left knee, meaning He Who Bruises or Breaks. This latter name has been taken by the Arabians to commonly mean The Shepherd. Another Arabian-named star echoes an earlier name Al Derab or Al Deraf and means Coming in a Circle. Two additional Hebrew-named stars which are not identifiable as to position bear the name Cheicus, or Caucus meaning To Come as in a Circle, and Regulus which means Treading Underfoot.

In Greek mythology Cepheus was presented as the father of Andromeda, and Perseus was her returning husband. Andromeda as the church undergoing persecution in the world fits this mythological scenario, the heavenly picture story, and the Scriptural account equally well. She stands in sore need of the return of her Beloved from afar.

The story thus far tells us of CEPHEUS, that he is the "Branch, enthroned as a King, the One who is going to return, quickly coming as in a circle." As was seen earlier in CYGNUS, He is the great Redeemer and the One who is to bruise and break His enemies while coming as The Shepherd for His own; and once He returns will tread His enemies underfoot.

CEPHEUS is also seen to be extending his scepter towards CASSIOPEIA whom is understood to be another representation of ANDROMEDA, pictured as enthroned and in glory.

DENDERAH

The ancient Denderah Zodiac, in addition to giving the aforementioned name Per-Ku-Hor, This One Cometh to Rule, also pictures CEPHEUS as the large foreleg of an animal and connects it with a small figure of a lamb in the same pose as ARIES in the next Sign. Thus, the ancient Egyptians also identify the thought of the Lamb with His foreleg stating possession over the BAND of the FISHES: this makes it clear for us that our Glorious King, enthroned, is the same Lamb who is the owner of, and upholder of the FISHES.

CEPHEUS[40] as we noted has one hand uplifted and a scepter

---

[40] There is a legend that the Egyptian Pharaoh Cheops, or Khufu, (circa 2700 B.C.) remembered for the pyramid which bears his name, was CEPHEUS.

outstretched in the other to CASSIOPEIA. This can be none other than the One also seen in Scripture:

> "The Lord brought us forth out of Egypt with a mighty hand and with an outstretched arm and with great terribleness, and with signs, and with wonders."
> **Deut. 26:8**

He could also be the One whom Isaiah described as

> "I saw also the Lord sitting upon a throne, high and lifted up and his train filled the temple."
> **Isa. 6:1**

Could there be any connection between such a regal figure and a ram or a lamb?

ARIES

(THE LAMB, or THE RAM)

The eighth constellation figure is a horned lamb or a ram lying in quiet repose, not sinking down in death as was CAPRICORN, but rather resting peacefully with his head turned back over his body, and his one foreleg placed over the Band of Pisces.

We observe that this figure along with CAPRICORN, forms a pair of either sheep, or Lamb-type bookends to the second section or major division of the story told in the heavens. (The chapters of this heavenly account might well be divided into three sets of four chapters each, as we have done, and has been done in the past by others). They face in opposite directions, away from each other. CAPRICORN is facing back reflectively towards the struggle, conflict and battle which led to the final "sacrifice to end all sacrifices." ARIES is looking forward from the water and fish dominated segment of the story which dealt with the "multitudes of the redeemed" and the Redeemer, toward the next phase of the story—that of the blessed hope, the completion of the age, the Second Coming in glory and judgment, and the establishing of the New Jerusalem, the new heavens and the new earth.

The body of CAPRICORN links him with, and identifies his work as being for the Fish-People; the positioning of the paw or foreleg of ARIES also indicates his identification with the Fish-People of The Way.

Both ARIES and CAPRICORN bear horns indicating the obvious fact that these are male animals, which points to the first-born, male, Son of God, Jesus Christ.

Part II - Resurrection Life Received - ARIES

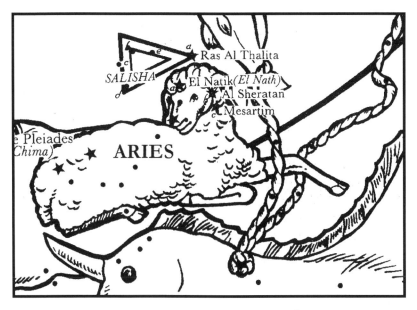

FIG. 29   ARIES   The Lamb

ARIES in his restful pose, possesses the reins of his people, and by means of the same BAND binds or holds back CETUS, the Sea Monster (or Satan). This scene looks forward to the translation of the church, when Jesus, with all His work completed, will gather His people to Himself:

> "For the Lord himself shall descend from heaven with a shout, with the voice of the archangel, and with the trump of God: and the dead in Christ shall rise first."
>
> **1 Thess. 4:16**

> "And I beheld, and, lo, in the midst of the throne and of the four beasts, and in the midst of the elders, stood a Lamb as it had been slain, having seven horns and seven eyes, which are the seven spirits of God sent forth into all the earth."
>
> **Rev. 5:6**

It is to the glory of the Lamb pictured in Scripture and also in the heavenly figure of ARIES, that the stars and the elders of Revelation numbering "ten thousand times ten thousand, and thousands of thousands" will all join in a chorus to sing with a loud voice:

> "Worthy is the Lamb that was slain to receive power and riches, and wisdom, and strength, and honour, and glory, and blessing. And every creature which is in heaven, and on the earth, and under the earth, and such as are in the sea, and all that are in them, heard I saying, Blessing and honour, and glory, and power, be unto him that sitteth upon the throne, and unto the Lamb, for ever and ever.
> **Rev. 5:12–13**

And again in verse 9:

> "And they sung a new song, saying Thou art worthy to take the book and to open the seals thereof: for thou wast slain, and hast redeemed us to God by thy blood out of every kindred, and tongue, and people, and nation; And hast made us unto our God kings and priests: and we shall reign on the earth."
> **Rev. 5:9**

ARIES the Ram is a perfect figure to represent the ram provided for Abraham which took the place of his son Isaac upon the altar, to die in order that Isaac might live (Gen. 22:12–13).

Is this interpretation correct? Is this indeed a figure in the heavens for the Lamb of God so figured and described in Scripture? Thus saith the ancient star witnesses.

—NAMES FOR THE SIGN—

The ancient name of ARIES is Taleh, meaning the Lamb Sent Forth. The Arabian name is Al Hamal, The Sheep Gentle, and Merciful. The Syriac is Amroo, meaning The Lamb. The Greek name Krios also means The Lamb as does the Latin Aries, although the latter adds the thought of Coming Forth. According to Ulugh Beigh the Coptic name is Tametouris Ammon or Regnum Ammonis normally taken to be the Reign of Ammon, but carries the clearer meaning of The Dominion or Government Established.

The ancient Akkadians called this figure Baraziggar. (Bar means Altar, or Sacrifice; while Ziggar means Making Right. The full name could be read as The Altar, or The Sacrifice of (Righteousness) Making Right.

Thus the Sign names in all languages and cultures bear an amazing unanimity in stating that this Sign represents the Lamb Sent Forth, who is to Come Forth, and to Establish His Dominion or Government, and he is characterized as being Gentle and Merciful. Perhaps most amazing of all, he is identified as The Sacrifice of Making Right (Righteousness) even though the Ram is pictured as whole and healthy. Now, how say the stars?

—NAMES OF THE STARS—

The brightest star located in the horn, El Natik or El Nath (Arabic) means The Wounded or The Slain. The second brightest star's name is also Arabic, Al Sheratan[41] meaning The Bruised or The Wounded. A third star located in the same horn bears the Hebrew name Mesartim, the Bound or The Binding.

Another interesting point in connection with ARIES is that Aratus, the poet, and others place a triangle over the head of ARIES. Many of the earliest star pictures include the triangle. The triangle is identified in Hebrew as Salisha which means The Exalted or The Chief. The Arabs called it Ras Al Thalita, The Head of the Triangle. The Greeks named it Deltoton, The Triangle, or High. This same word to the Arabs meant Lifted Up.

> "Behold, my servant shall deal prudently, he shall be exalted and extolled, and be very high"
>
> **Isa. 52:13**

> "I saw also the Lord sitting upon a throne, high and lifted up."
>
> **Isa. 6:1**

Thus the stars are consistent in bearing a message of One who is to be

---

[41] Al Sheratan, The Bruised was at the Equinox during the supernatural darkness and would have shown down upon the Crucifixion.

the Head or Chief, who is to be exalted, or lifted up high, but who is also to be bound, wounded, bruised and finally slain as a sacrifice of making-right. This perfectly applies to our Saviour and His work leading up to, and culminating in the Cross. Jesus, of course, is also a member of the Trinity, which has long been represented symbolically by the triangle.

DENDERAH

In the ancient Denderah Zodiac, ARIES[42] is pictured as the Ram, but apparently has three horns rather than two: two are those of a bull, and one of a Ram; indicating that the figure possesses in addition to the nature of the Ram, that of the Bull which we shall examine later in TAURUS. Their figure carries, as noted, the name recorded by Ulugh Beigh meaning The Dominion or Government Established.

How say the accompanying decans?

CASSIOPEIA
(THE ENTHRONED WOMAN)

The first of the accompanying decans, CASSIOPEIA, pictures a beautiful woman regally seated upon a throne with her hands above her head. Her right arm is raised holding the straps of her gown or garment as if dressing, while in the other hand she holds aloft a branch. In some early planispheres she is presented as holding her own hair in one hand and is brushing it with the branch held in her other hand.

---

42 The sun was in the Sign of the other sacrificial animal, ARIES, at the very hour of the crucifixion. This truth was reconfirmed by two astronomers in 1984.

The sun arose "... in the Ram of the Egyptian Planisphere of Denderah, the oldest Planisphere in the world, apparently referring to a time when the winter solstice ... (occurred in) ... 4000 B.C." Broome, J. H., The Astral Origin of the Emblems. London, 1881.

PART II - Resurrection Life Received - CASSIOPEIA

She is a picture of the True Church of Jesus Christ and stands in opposition to the picture we saw of her as ANDROMEDA, in chains and defeat. Here she holds aloft the victory branch symbolic of her becoming the Victorious Church that Jesus prophesied she would ultimately be. With her other hand she is preparing herself, perhaps fixing her hair, making the final preparations for her wedding, the Marriage Supper of the Lamb, and the consummation of her purpose: becoming a Bride fit for Jesus Christ. She is preparing herself to be seated with Him permanently, in heavenly places upon her throne and to rule with Him throughout eternity.

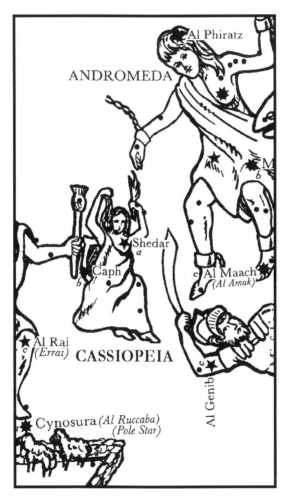

FIG. 30   CASSIOPEIA   The Enthroned Woman

This beautiful woman was said by Albumazer (9th century poet and astronomer) to have been anciently called "the daughter of splendor" and therefore was also "the glorified woman." This perfectly ascribed to her the attributes which Scripture also applies to the "glorified church."

> "For the marriage supper of the Lamb is now come, and his wife hath made herself ready. And to her was granted that she should be arrayed in fine linen, clean, and white: for the fine linen is the righteousness of saints."
>
> Rev. 19:7–8

> "And I John saw the holy city, New Jerusalem coming down from God out of heaven, prepared as a bride adorned for her husband."
>
> Rev. 21:2

> "Christ also loved the church and gave himself for it; that he might sanctify and cleanse it with the washing of water by the word, that he might present it to himself a glorious church, not having spot, or wrinkle, or any such thing, but that it should be holy without blemish."
>
> Eph. 5:25b–27

Those who are a part of this glorified body "shall be priests of God and of Christ, and shall reign with him a thousand years" (Rev. 20:6). Psalm 45 contains a prophecy applicable to the Messiah's beautiful bride-to-be.

> "Thy throne, O God, is for ever and ever: the sceptre of thy kingdom is a right sceptre. Thou lovest righteousness, and hated wickedness: therefore God, thy God, hath anointed thee with the oil of gladness above thy fellows. Upon thy right hand did stand the queen in gold of Ophir. So shall the king greatly desire thy beauty: for he is thy Lord and worship thou him."
>
> Psalm 45:6–7,9,11

PART II - Resurrection Life Received - CASSIOPEIA

Do these Scriptures correlate with the heavenly picture? Definitely. Queenly Cassiopeia is seated upon a throne to the right of King CEPHEUS who is extending his royal scepter unto her, even as a similar scepter was mercifully extended to Queen Esther, sparing her life when she found grace and favor in the sight of Ahasuerus (Es. 5:2).

So the Scripture fits. But what of the constellation's names and those of its scars?

—NAMES FOR THE SIGN—

The decan of Cassiopeia was known to the Hebrews as The Enthroned, The Beautiful, and, in fact, the same root word, *yofee*, is used in the 11th verse just quoted from Psalm 45 when David speaks of the queen's beauty. The Chaldean and Arabic names are the same Dat Al Cursa, The Set (Queen) Enthroned. Another Arabic name applied to this figure was Ruchba, also meaning The Enthroned or The Seated. Pluche gives her name as The Boundary of Typhon's (The Sea Monster) Power: The Delivered From All Evil.

—NAMES OF THE STARS—

The ancient names of the stars again join in a joyful chorus of truth. The brightest star is located in the area of the right breast and bears the Hebrew name, Shedar, The Freed. Another star named in Hebrew is found in this constellation in the back of the throne chair, Caph, meaning The Branch. Thus both the throne and her position upon it are determined by, or related to, the Branch.

This is a good place to make several astronomical observations. First the four principal stars of the third magnitude which form the throne upon which Cassiopeia is seated, never set! They are always visible, underscoring that this throne is indeed forever! Another interesting fact was introduced in the year 1572 when Tycho Brahe[43] discovered an extremely bright star which shone brilliantly for about a year and a half after it appeared on November 10th, and then mysteriously disappeared from view completely in 1574. This could foreshadow the mysterious catching away of the church from view, since it appeared in a constellation associated with the glorification of the Church, the Bride of Christ. It may also speak of another form of hiding away from view which is also mentioned in Revelation:

> "And to the woman were given two wings of a great eagle, that she might fly into the wilderness, into her place, where she is nourished for a time, and times, and half a time, from the face of the serpent."
>
> **Rev. 12:14**

The time frame of the star's appearance in the late 1500's would coincide approximately with the beginning of the Reformation and would have been just prior to the exodus from Europe to America of the Christian Pilgrims, who sought a place for freedom to worship God as they desired, and who might be said to have "flown into the wilderness."

DENDERAH

The ancient Egyptians pictured CASSIOPEIA upon their Planispheres as a woman, named her Set (Queen), and placed under her feet hieroglyphics denoting a female, and an oval and a half circle indicating that she was also a daughter. Al-bumazer, the Arabian astronomer-poet, as

---

43 Tycho Brahe, celebrated Danish astronomer was born in 1546. Frederick II of Denmark, noting his exceptional talent, built an observatory for him on the island of Huen. His observations in the hands of later greats such as Newton and Kepler helped solve the major problems of astronomy. However, there is a very interesting fact about this genius which was overlooked as mere eccentricity: he never made an observation without first putting on his best court apparel, stating that if "men dressed in honor of the king and the court, they should not be less observant of such duties in the presence of their Maker!"

mentioned earlier, called her "The Daughter of Splendor."

A striking contrast from the beauty of CASSIOPEIA awaits us in the beast, CETUS.

CETUS
(THE SEA-MONSTER)

The second decan is one of the most revealing and enlightening figures for Satan in the heavenly gospel account. CETUS is presented as a fierce-looking Sea-Monster, the natural enemy of the fish or Fish-People, and as the largest constellation in the heavens.

This figure is one of the most graphic pictures of Satan, one who would devour the fish if he could catch them. However, fear not, 'little flock,' he is restrained! As we saw previously, THE BANDS of PISCES which are the reins under the foreleg of ARIES are also attached to the back of the head of CETUS. Scripture's picture agrees.

> "And I saw an angel come down from heaven, having the key of the bottomless pit and a great chain in his hand. And he laid hold on the dragon, that old serpent, which is the Devil, and Satan, and bound him a thousand years. And cast him into the bottomless pit and shut him up, and set a seal upon him, that he should deceive the nations no more, till the thousand years should be fulfilled; and after that he must be loosed a little season."
>
> Rev. 20:1–3

Peter describes the situation as it is in our day:

> "Be sober, be vigilant; because your adversary the devil, as a roaring lion, walketh about seeking whom he may devour: whom resist steadfast in the faith."
>
> 1 Peter 5:8–9

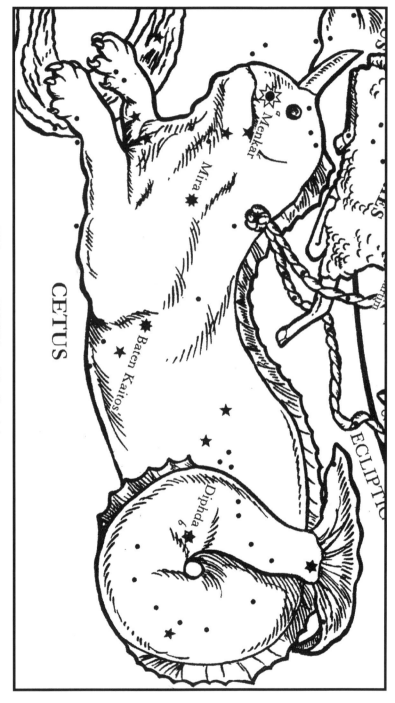

FIG. 31   CETUS   The Sea-Monster

God uses a similar figure in describing Satan to Job:

> "Canst thou put a hook in his nose? Or bore his jaw through with a thorn? Will he make supplication unto thee?
>
> Will he speak soft words unto thee? Behold the hope of him is in vain: shall not one be cast down even at the sight of him? Who can discover the face of his garments? Or who can come to him with his double bridle? Who can open the doors of his face? His teeth are terrible round about. His scales are his pride, shut up together as with a close seal. He beholdeth all high things: he is a king over all the children of pride."
>
> Job 41:2–3,9,13–15,34

This is a very accurate picture of our enemy, the king of pride, who instills fear as a weapon and seeks "whom he may devour." This is he who in mythology was the great sea-monster sent to devour Andromeda and is thus, clearly the enemy and persecutor of the church for whom she stands. From the beginning he has sought both to destroy and to deter the people of God from serving Him faithfully. But here he is bound, as if to state emphatically, thus far and no further shalt thou go. The picture story culminates in his imprisonment.

This is also he of whom God speaks in Job 41:11, "Who hath prevented me, that I should repay him? Whatsoever is under the whole heaven is mine." Thus Satan's doom is certain and predicted in John's words in Rev. 20:1-3 with which we began.

—NAMES FOR THE SIGN—

No truly ancient names for this Sign have come down to us other than CETUS. However, this Sign has been known as the Whale or the Sea-Monster for over 500 years.

That CETUS is the enemy of the Coming One, as well as of His Fish People, is also indicated by the fact that in the earliest planispheres, he has as he does in our illustration, a sharp horn protruding from his head which pricks the left foreleg of TAURUS.

—NAMES OF THE STARS—

The star names seem to sing with gusto, echoing the account which we read in Scripture.

The brightest star, located in the nose, bears a Hebrew name, Menkar, which means The Bound or Chained Enemy. The second brightest star, found in the tail, bears a Hebrew name also, Diphda meaning The Overthrown; also known by a more modern name Deneb Kaitos, taken to mean The Tail of the Whale. However, in light of the ancient meaning of Deneb, this should be read as The Lord or Judge of Cetus.

Another interesting star is Baten Kaitos, the name appears in the figure upon the belly of CETUS. It is Arabic for From the Belly of the Whale. This is another amazing name, found recorded thousands of years before Johan lived. It is also a surprisingly accurate description of the means by which Jesus defeated CETUS the symbol of Satan. Jesus said,

> "An evil and adulterous generation seeketh after a sign; and there shall no sign be given to it, but the sign of the prophet Jonas; for as Jonas was three days and three nights in the whale's belly so shall the Son of Man be three days and three nights in the heart of the earth."
>
> Mt. 12:39b–40

Later Jesus, himself went into the belly of the grave for three days and three nights, and into the belly of the earth (hell), from whence He led captivity captive and broke the bands of the fear of death by which man had been held in bondage (Heb. 2:15).

A particularly interesting star appears in the neck of CETUS, bearing the Hebrew name Mira, The Rebel (rebellion is one of the chief characteristics of Satan and his kingdom). This star is unusual and of particular interest to astronomers because it was discovered in 1596 to be a variable star. It is one of the most variable and unsteady of all the visible stars in the heavens, ranging from a star of the second magnitude (Satan has always been only second-rate) to becoming completely invisible about every three hundred and thirty days. It fluctuates from its brightest for about 15 days and then goes through stages of decreasing and increasing brilliance until it becomes completely invisible for a period at least six times every seven years.

This is an extremely revealing representation of Satan, who is the perennial enemy of the Church and of the people of God, yet who prefers to work in obscurity when it serves his purposes. Not wishing to be exposed, he normally prefers to work in secret, often being invisible—as when he crouched at the door of Cain; his presence exposed only by God's revelation. The certainty of his doom is also described by Isaiah:

> "For, behold the Lord cometh out of his place to punish the inhabitants of the earth for their iniquity: the earth also shall disclose her blood, and shall no more cover her slain.
>
> In that day the Lord with his sore and great and strong sword shall punish Leviathan, the piercing serpent, even Leviathan that crooked serpent; and he shall slay the dragon that is in the sea."
>
> Isa. 26:21; 27:1

Clearly this Scripture and the star figure relate to the same one Revelation identifies as "the great Dragon was cast out, that old serpent, called the Devil, and Satan, which deceived the whole world." The "crooked serpent" in DRACO, typified in the constellation figures of SERPENS, the triple headed HYDRA in the hand of Hercules, and now as CETUS are all the same "roaring lion" who is ultimately defeated, completely and utterly by each of the heavenly hero-figures which all point to the One, totally victorious, King of Kings.

DENDERAH

CETUS is pictured quite differently, but the message is identically the same at Denderah. There the figure is named Knem—The Subdued, The Bruised, and near it a hieroglyphic name Kan-nu meaning Victory. Victory over the subdued or bruised enemy is recorded again. Knem is presented as a monster's head being trodden underfoot by a swine, the natural enemy of the snake. The swine is joined with a wolf (the wolf is the forerunner of the dog which befriends and loves man). The wolf bears a hieroglyphic name signifying He Comes. Also above the figures is a hawk, another natural enemy of the serpent. This hawk is crowned with a mortar, the emblem for crushing and bruising. The mortar seems to correspond to the head of Medusa carried by PERSEUS in the next decan.

So we might read in this picto-language the following message: "There is one who is coming, who will be victorious over the great sea-monster which will be subdued and bruised."

In the next decan, PERSEUS expands the theme of bruising.

PERSEUS
(THE BREAKER)

The third decan contains the helmeted figure of a man coming on the run with one foot uplifted as if it had been injured, and his strong right arm raised, brandishing a great sword, while in his left hand he carries at his side the head of a vanquished enemy, apparently severed with the sword. The wings seen on his heels show that he, like other mythological figures, comes with supernatural speed.

By now you might expect this hero figure to be a type of Christ, and so it is. In the second chapter of Micah we read:

> "I will surely assemble, O Jacob, all of thee; I will surely gather the remnant of Israel; I will put them together as the sheep of Bozrah, as the flock in the midst of their fold: they shall make great noise by reason of the multitude of men. The breaker is come up before them: they have broken up, and have passed through the gate, and are gone out by it: and their king shall pass before them, and the Lord on the head of them."
>
> Micah 2:12–13

Part II - Resurrection Life Received - PERSEUS

FIG. 32   PERSEUS   The Breaker

The Scripture identifies The Breaker as Jesus, Christ coming in victory and glory, breaking down every barrier set in opposition to His kingdom, reign, and people. He is destroying the very gates by which they have been imprisoned and is eliminating all the opposing forces. The Breaker is also The Looser of Isa. 61:3 who is setting the captives at liberty and opening prison doors for them who were bound, and is the Looser or Breaker of the seals in Revelation:

> "Behold, the Lion of the tribe of Judah, the Root of David, hath prevailed to open the book, and to loose the seven seals thereof."
>
> **Rev. 5:5**

This same Breaker shall come forth with wrath for his enemies, as the

Psalmist tells us after identifying Him:

> "I will declare the decree: the Lord hath said unto me, Thou art my Son; this day have I begotten Thee. Thou shalt break them with a rod of iron; thou shalt dash them in pieces like a potter's vessel"
>
> **Psalm 2:7,9**

Once again the Psalmist writes of this aspect of His work:

> "He shall judge my people with righteousness, and the poor with judgment. He shall judge the poor of the people, he shall save the children of the needy, and shall break in pieces the oppressor."
>
> **Ps. 72:2,4**

—NAMES FOR THE SIGN—

The heavenly picture is consistent with the Scripture's presentation of the Lord as The Breaker. This mighty warrior, coming swiftly as indicated by the wings on his heels, coming with his mighty sword uplifted, already having vanquished the enemy and severed his head, is known in Hebrew by the name Perets rendered Breaker in the passage quoted from Micah. The same name adapted into Greek became Perseus and meant the same thing. The Persians called him Bershaush with the identical meaning.

—NAMES OF THE STARS—

The names of the stars involved bear out and amplify the same truth. The brightest star is Mirfak (Hebrew), located in the waist, meaning He Who Helps. The star located in the left foot also bears a Hebrew name Athik, He Who Breaks. The third brightest star is located in the uplifted right arm and carries an Arabian name Al Genib, He Who Carries Away.

Thus we indeed see that this is The Breaker who is coming to carry away His possession—His people, and is the One who helps, as elsewhere he promises to send another helper (Jn. 16:7), thereby also identifying Himself as a Helper.

But what of the enemy whom He is to defeat? Is it indeed the head of Cetus which we see in his hand? The stars will also answer this question.

The Greeks identified the head as that of Medusa, not knowing that the Hebrew word meant The Trodden Underfoot. The head or its brightest star was called by the Hebrews *Rosh Satan*, The Head of The Adversary, or *The Head of Satan*! Astounding! But it is there and it has been recorded for thousands of years.

The Arabians had two similarly enlightening names for the head, calling it Al Oneh, The Subdued or Weakened, and Al Ghoul, The Evil Spirit! The bright star in this head is the second brightest star in the entire constellation and bears a contraction of the preceding Arabic name, Algol, meaning Coming and Going, Rolling Around (i.e. the head). This star, like Mira, in CETUS is a variable star and changes from a star of the fourth magnitude to one of the second magnitude very rapidly, in about three and one half hours, just as Satan changes rapidly to suit his own wiles.

These rapid changes in the chief star of Medusa's head are reminiscent of the wiles of him who "is transformed into an angel of light" one moment and the next making himself "like a roaring lion" going about "seeking whom he may devour." At other times he appears as the beguiling serpent which enticed Eve. This one who seems to deceive, destroy, or devour the Church—the earthly body of Jesus Christ—is himself here seen to be defeated and beheaded, delivered the great head wound promised to him in Gen. 3:15. "...And her seed; it shall bruise they head"!

> "He that is our God is the God of salvation; and unto God the Lord belong the issues from death. But God shall wound the head of his enemies....."
>
> Ps. 68:20–21b

What has been anticipated is graphically portrayed for us in these stars, named thousands of years before the written accounts were recorded in the Word. Here is our soon coming Lord, and Saviour, the King of Kings and Lord of Lords pictured with a foretaste of His glory!

DENDERAH

The ancient Egyptians named Perseus Kar Knem: *Kar*, Who Fights; *Knem*, we saw previously to be the name for CETUS, The Bruised or Trodden Upon. Thus the name describes Perseus as the One Who Fights' and Subdues Cetus.

The representation of him upon the Zodiac is that of a human figure with a tail attached, signifying This One Comes. The figure also wears a royal diadem or crown upon his head, further indicating that the defeater, or breaker of CETUS is a king, a royal personage whom we recognize as the King of Kings.

The unlikely figure of a bull provides our next clue in the unravelling of our mystery…

PART III

KINGDOM AND JUDGMENT ESTABLISHED

He will come forth as a judge and governor to punish the enemy and all those who resist the establishment of his kingdom and authority. He will pour forth a river of righteous judgment upon his enemies, while coming as a compassionate, loving shepherd for his own. This shepherd has great love for his sheep whom he will guard, protect, and care for in safe sheepfolds until he takes them on a journey home with him. The shepherd will then come in great wrath as a lion rending the great enemy who will be completely destroyed.

TAURUS

(THE BULL)

The ninth figure in the heavenly ring of constellations is that of TAURUS The Bull. We see TAURUS presented as the forepart of a great raging bull rushing forth with his head lowered, charging, as if about to gore something with his mighty horns. The upper horn's tip is, in fact, piercing the heel of AURIGA The Shepherd. The space where Taurus's lower body should be, from the foreshoulder rearward, is overlaid by the body of ARIES. TAURUS doesn't look like any bull with which we are familiar.

What kind of bull is this? TAURUS is the bull of a species of animal referred to in Scripture and other ancient literature as a Rheem, an auroch, or unicorn. The Rheem as we see him pictured in our figure is not, however, a one-horned animal as the unicorn is generally pictured in mythology and literature, but is rather a member of the ox family, wild, untameable, and extremely fierce.

Julius Caesar describes such an animal as hunted in his time. According to most reliable sources it was much like an ox of today as to color and appearance, except much larger, often compared to the elephant in size, with speed and strength that were appalling. The Rheem apparently feared nothing, would charge man or any other beast with impunity. It was untameable, never having been domesticated by man, even when taken very young. Job gives a similar description of this animal:

> "Will the unicorn (Rheem) be willing to serve thee, or abide by thy crib? Canst thou bind the unicorn with his band in the furrow? Or will he harrow the valley after thee? Wilt thou trust him, because his strength is great? Or will thou leave thy labor to him? Wilt thou believe him, that he will bring home thy seed, and gather it into thy barn?"
>
> **Job 39:9–11**

PART III - Kingdom and Judgment Established - TAURUS

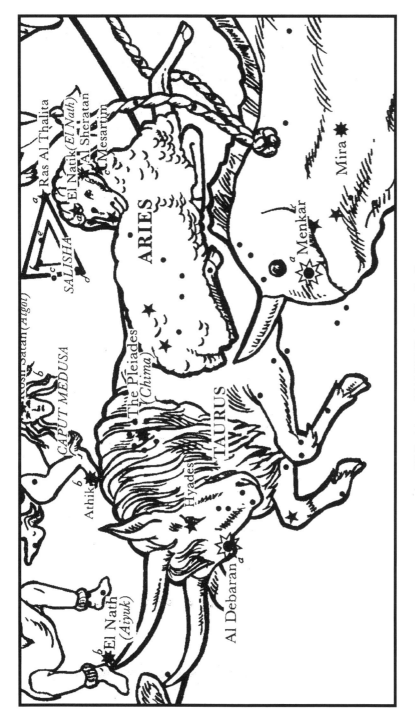

FIG. 33   TAURUS   The Bull

David also speaks of this animal:

> "But my horn shalt thou exalt like the horn of the unicorn: I shall be annointed with fresh oil."
>
> **Ps. 92:10**

Isaiah mentions the unicorn in connection with God's impending judgment:

> "And the unicorns shall come down with them, and the bullocks with the bulls; and their land shall be soaked with blood..."
>
> **Isa. 34:7**

These Scriptural references note the very great strength of these animals, their untameable fierceness and even note their being used by God to bring judgment on a land by the great slaughter which they could wreck. David, when he speaks of the exaltation of his horn (symbol of a king's power) as that of a unicorn, is using a rich term, for there is nothing else so fierce or powerful to which he could have compared his power.

There are artistic representations of these animals at least as far back as the Babylonians. I have a copy of a picture of the Rheem, or white unicorn, done in relief in enamelled bricks, that decorated the Gate of Ishtar, through which the Procession of Marduk led. Also decorating the gates and walls of this street leading to the palace of Nebuchadnezzar are the famous Lion of Babylon, which is identical to the figure of LEO in all the earliest zodiacs, and the Dragon of Babylon.[44] Both figures come as no surprise in the light of what we are learning concerning the origin of these figures, and the message behind them.

Caesar wrote of the hunters of his day proving their prowess by publicly exhibiting the horns of the great Rheem, when fortunate enough to bag one, usually taken only by luring it into a pit-type trap.

---

44 Dilitzsch, F., Babel & The Bible. London, 1903. A work that contains photographs of each.

PART III - Kingdom and Judgment Established - TAURUS

In Scripture Joseph's glory is likened to the firstling of the bullock, and his horns being like the horns of the unicorns:

> "His glory is like the firstling of his bullock, and his horns are like the horns of unicorns: With them he shall push the people together to the ends of the earth: and they are the ten thousands of Ephraim, and they are the thousands of Manasseh."
>
> **Deut. 33:17**

Since the Rheem is a symbol of greatest strength, power and fierceness, it is not surprising that Scripture should apply this symbol to Jesus in reference to His impending judgment and wrath being poured out upon his enemies.

> "For the indignation of the Lord is upon all nations, and his fury upon all their armies: he hath utterly destroyed them, he hath delivered them to the slaughter."
>
> "For my sword shall be bathed in heaven: behold, it shall come down upon Idumea, and upon the people of my curse, to judgment. The sword of the Lord is filled with blood, it is made fat with fatness, and with the blood of lambs and goats, with the fat of the kidneys of rams: for the Lord hath made a sacrifice in Bozrah, and a great slaughter in the land of Idumea."
>
> "And the unicorns shall come down with them, and the bullocks with the bulls: and their land shall be soaked with blood and their dust made fat with fatness."
>
> "For it is the day of the Lord's vengeance, and the year of recompenses for the controversy of Zion."
>
> **Isa. 34:2, 5–8**

In the preceding passage the very word translated unicorns is, in fact, the Hebrew word Rheems: the exact name of the animal figured for us by TAURUS. This gives a clue as to the nature and message of TAURUS.

We know that the day of the Lord is approaching, the day in which the Lord will visit judgment and retribution upon His enemies, those who have hated Him and defied Him.

We look again to a passage in Isaiah:

> "Come, my people, enter thou into thy chambers and shut the doors about thee: hide thyself as it were for a little moment, until the indignation be overpast. For, behold, the Lord cometh out of his place to punish the inhabitants of the earth for their iniquity: the earth shall also disclose her blood, and shall no more cover her slain."
>
> Isa. 26:20–21

Isaiah refers again to the fierce judgment that is to come when God lays aside His longsuffering, and patience for the good fruit of the earth:

> "The lord of hosts mustereth the host of the battle.
>
> They come from a far country, from the end of heaven, even the Lord, and the weapons of his indignation, to destroy the whole land. Howl ye; it shall come as a destruction from the Almighty."
>
> "Behold, the day of the Lord cometh, cruel both with wrath and fierce anger, to lay the land desolate: and he shall destroy the sinners thereof out of it."
>
> "For the stars of heaven and the constellations thereof shall not give their light: the sun shall be darkened in his going forth, and the moon shall not cause her light to shine.
>
> And I will punish the world for their iniquity; and I will cause the arrogancy of the proud to cease, and will lay low the haughtiness of the terrible. Therefore I will shake the heavens, and the earth shall be moved out of her place, in the wrath of the Lord of hosts, and in the day of his fierce anger.
>
> Everyone that is found shall be thrust through, and everyone that is joined unto them shall fall by the sword."
>
> Isa. 13:4b–6,9–11,15a

> "Through thee will we push down our enemies: through thy name will we tread them under that rise up against us."
>
> **Ps. 45:5**

These same thoughts of impending judgment are contained in the New Testament as well:

> "And Enoch also, the seventh from Adam, prophesied of these, saying, Behold, the Lord cometh with ten thousands of his saints, to execute judgment upon all, and to convince all that are ungodly among them of all their ungodly deeds which they have ungodly committed, and of all their hard speeches with ungodly sinners have spoken against him."
>
> **Jude 14–15**

Paul also warns of this Day that is to come:

> "And to you who are troubled rest with us when the Lord Jesus shall be revealed from heaven with his mighty angels, in flaming fire taking vengeance on them that know not God, and that obey not the gospel of our Lord Jesus Christ. Who shall be punished with everlasting destruction from the presence of the Lord, and from the glory of his power; When he shall come to be glorified in his saints and to be admired in all them that believe (because our testimony among you was believed) in that Day."
>
> **2 Thess. 1:7–10**

So glory, admiration and rejoicing are promised to the redeemed saints who are partaking in the day of judgment; but for those who have denied the Lord, hated Him, chosen to oppose Him, to ignore Him, and to ignore His warnings and appeals ... He is coming as the wild, fierce, unappeasable Rheem, the outraged Auroch, the thrusting, goring Unicorn, which shall destroy the land and cause the blood of the wicked to flow.

Do the Signs and stars also warn of this impending judgment and the Day of His wrath?

—NAMES FOR THE SIGN—

It is interesting to note that as TAURUS rises, SCORPIO sinks out of view. It is clear that when the Lord comes upon the scene in judgment, Satan will be destroyed and vanish from view.

TAURUS is named in Hebrew Shur, The Bull Coming from a root which carries the meaning of both Coming and Ruling. The Arabic and Syriac name is Al Thaur, and both have meanings the same as the Hebrew, The Bull Coming. The Greek name *Tauros* and the Latin *Taurus* both mean The Bull. However the various Coptic names add several new thoughts: Isis, The One Who Saves Mightily; Apis, The Head or Chief Who Comes; Horias, The Traveller Who Comes to Save; Statio Hori, The Station or Place of Horus—The One Who Comes to Save.

The name Isis as used here does not refer to the goddess who came later, but comes from the Hebrew verb "to save" with the addition of the Egyptian masculine pronoun 's' meaning This One Saves.

—NAMES OF THE STARS—

In all languages and cultures TAURUS was seen as the mighty rushing bull.

The brightest star in Taurus is Al Debaran, located in the lower eye, and carries the meaning of The Leader or The Governor. The second brightest star is El Nath (Arabic as in ARIES), in the tip of the upper horn, meaning The Wounded or the Slain. The next brightest identifiable star is Al Cyone in the Pleiades which means The Center.

There is a bright cluster of stars located in the upper shoulder of Taurus which bears the Arabic name, the Pleiades, in Hebrew named Chima meaning The Heap or The Accumulation. It consists of seven stars which according to mythology were the seven daughters of Atlas.[45] They were turned into doves and later into stars by Jove because of their virtue and affection for one another, and their sorrow over either the death of

---

45 The other six sisters in addition to Alcyone (Cyone), were Asterope, Merope, Electra, Maia, Celion, and Taigeta.

Part III - Kingdom and Judgment Established - TAURUS

their father or of one of their sisters. These stars have been associated by the ancients with Noah and the judgment poured out by God: Taurus apparently recognized as symbolic of judgment[46], and the doves of the Pleiades relating to the doves of Noah. So that from earliest time, this Sign has had an association with the flood (judgment poured out upon the evil, while the righteous are preserved).

The Hyades is another cluster of stars located in the left eye of TAURUS and this Hebrew name means The Congregated. This name symbolizes the tens of thousands of His saints, His chosen, His elect... the very apples of His eye.

Other stars which appear in TAURUS are Palilicum (Hebrew) meaning Belonging to the Judge; Al Thuraiya (Arabic), The Abundance; Wasat, Arabic for The Center or the Foundation; and the Latin named star Vergiliae, The Center, in Arabic known as Vertex[47], The Turned Upon or Rolled Around.

These latter star names, in particular, Al Cyone, Wasat, Vergiliae and Vertex introduce an interesting point. Some ancient astronomers thought that because these references had been made from antiquity to the Pleiades

---

[46] The astronomical symbol for TAURUS is (♉). This is explained by hieroglyphic authorities as a single boat on the surface of the earth. Thus relating TAURUS to the outpouring of God's judgment in the great flood of Noah's time. A fact of phenomenal impact in light of our interpretation of TAURUS as indicating the judgment yet to come.

[47] Nicholas Copernicus was born at Thorn, Prussia A.D. 1473. It was he who founded the Copernican system: placing the Sun as the center with all the planets revolving around it. Prior to 1543 all astronomers believed the earth to be the center of the universe, and that the stars and planets revolved around it.

Giordano Bruno was burned alive in Rome in A.D. 1600, by order of the Inquisition, for asserting that the earth was not standing still and was not the center of the universe.

Galileo Galilei (1564-1642) one of the greatest of the astronomers, was imprisoned in 1616 and again in 1633 for the same reason, the Pope ordering that all books should be destroyed that asserted the motion of the earth.

as the center, indicated that the Pleiades or Alcyone was the very center of the entire universe. Modern astronomers recognize it as an important asterim, or cluster of stars, and do note that many stars revolve around it, but discount the announcement in the 1800's that it was the center of the universe.

However this is particularly interesting since the asterim appears in the shoulder of TAURUS, which is a figure for the Messiah coming in the judgment of whom it was said:

> "For unto us a child is born, unto us a Son is given, and the government shall be upon his shoulder."
>
> **Isa. 9:6**

Jesus is spoken of in Colossians as:

> "... before all things, and by him all things consist."
>
> **Col. 1:17**

That is to say, that He is the force holding all things together, much like gravity.

God enquired of Job,

> "Knowest thou the ordinances of heaven? Canst thou set the dominion thereof in the earth?"
>
> **Job 38:33**

What are the ordinances of heaven that have an effect upon the earth?

The heavens, in accordance with God's plan and provision, cause the effects of gravity to affect the earth. God has caused the gravity of the earth to be in balance with that of other planets in the universe, so that we are neither crushed to the earth, nor float off into space to another planet with a stronger attraction. The effects of the heavens are felt in the tides, seasons, etc. Jesus's effect upon the earth is somewhat similar to gravity: He is what is holding this world together, just as gravity keeps us from flying off into space.

The Syriac name for the Pleiades is Succoth which means Booths and is also the name of the Feast of the Harvest, more commonly called the Feast of Tabernacles. This is particularly significant when we consider that the Feast of Tabernacles is the only Jewish feast day remaining to be prophetically fulfilled before the Lord's return!

DENDERAH

Denderah pictures a full bodied Bull in their zodiac. The Egyptians recognized this emblem by several names; Isis, Him Who Saves or Delivers, Apis, The Head, and Horias, The Traveller Who Comes to Save.

Illumination will next be gained from a mighty hunter, ORION.

ORION
(THE HUNTER)

The next constellation figure is one of the most famous of all those in the heavens; mentioned twice in Scripture and in much of the great secular literature; he is ORION, The Hunter. The picture presents him as a mighty man, a hunter poised as if about to strike his enemy or prey with the club in his uplifted strong right hand, aimed in the general direction of CETUS. With his left hand he holds victoriously aloft the severed head of a lion which he has defeated. His left foot is uplifted as if injured or as if about to crush an enemy. The river ERIDANUS has its source in that same foot. Girded around his waist is his famous belt from which hangs a sword, the hilt of which bears the head of a lamb. Much rich Scriptural symbolism is contained in this figure.

A Scripture which we considered previously may well also relate to such a figure:

> "Behold, I will send for many fishers, saith the Lord, and they shall fish them: and after will I send for many hunters,

and they shall hunt them from every hill and out of the holes of the rocks. For mine eyes are upon all their ways: they are not hid from my face, neither is their iniquity hid from mine eyes."

Jer. 16:16–17

This Scripture describes God sending hunters who will be involved in the pouring out of His judgment upon the world.

Orion is a hero of mythology who had supernatural powers, such as the ability to walk upon the waters of the sea without sinking, and he possessed all the heroic virtues. He was reported to have received a mortal wound in the foot from a scorpion, because he was the greatest of all the hunters. He was supposed to have accomplished many great works, such as making an underworld home for the gods of the fires. He was later made into a constellation in the heavens and placed opposite SCORPIO, so that he would rise as the scorpion set, indicating for all to see, his supremacy over his enemy. He was said to have been blinded while asleep by Atlas because of his love for the latter's daughter Merope. But after placing himself in a particular position so as to receive the full effects of the rising sun, he was restored and went forth with great haste and mighty anger to destroy his enemies.

In all these pagan perversions we can certainly see underlying traces of the true and pure story from which these myths sprung. They all relate to Jesus and His mighty acts! He it is who will mete out the severity and mercy of God.

FIG. 34   ORION   The Glorious One

—NAMES FOR THE SIGN—

The Hebrews call this figure Orion, with the meaning of One Coming Forth As Light. The Arabs had four names for him, Al Giauza, The Branch, Al Gebor, The Mighty, Al Mizam, The Prince, The Ruler, and Al Nagjed, The Prince, The Wounded. The ancient Akkadians named him Ur-Ana, The Light of Heaven.

—NAMES OF THE STARS—

The brightest star blazes forth from his right shoulder, Betelguez, The Coming of the Branch.

> "But who may abide the day of his coming? and who shall stand when he appeareth? for he is like a refiners' fire, and like fuller's soap."
>
> **Mal. 3:2**

The second brightest star is located in his foot, Rigol (Arabic), The Foot, or One Treading Underfoot. The third brightest is Belatrix, Hastily Coming located in the left shoulder. The next brightest stars are located in the belt, and bear Arabic names, Mintaka, meaning Dividing the Belt, Al Nitak, The Wounded, and Al Rai, The Bruising. There are many stars in this figure, some with names relating to his own nature or character and others to his actions.

The star in his left leg is named in Hebrew Saiph, meaning The Bruised, and again refers to the fact that the One who is to tread upon the head of the enemy is the same One who Himself is to be bruised as is foretold in Gen. 3:15 where this very word is used in that prophecy.

Other stars which apply apparently to the figure himself, are the two Chaldee names Hecke, Coming and Niphla, The Mighty (or The Mighty Coming). Two Hebrew-named stars carry a similar thought: Meissa, Coming Forth and Nux, The Strong (or The Strong Coming Forth). Another star with an Arabic name Thabit means Treading Upon. The Hebrew star Kesil (or Chesil) is mentioned in Job and Amos, where it is rendered Orion and means Bound Together, Constellations, or The Burly, Strong One, and apparently here refers to the nebulae in the sword.

Thus in these names we read of One who is "The Prince, The Ruler, The Light of Heaven" and "The Branch Who Is Coming Forth Swiftly, as Swiftly As Light," and who will, although Himself "Bruised and Wounded, Bruise and Tread Upon the Enemy." The One who is Coming Hastily will also be Mighty and Strong.

There is a star located at the bottom of the sword's scabard which is in reality a nebula, and can be seen with the aid of a telescope to contain an entire collection of nebulae. This is the One just described as The Light of Heaven whom Isaiah describes as a Great Light (9:2), whom John describes as The Great Light and who says of Himself, "I am the Light of the World" (Jn. 9:15).

The dual nature of Jesus is illustrated in the sword hung from ORION'S belt. He is seen in the head of the sword as the Lamb of God, the Lamb that was slain for us. The blade end of the sword implies His coming judgment with the sword. It has been said of Jesus that he will reach everyone: either with His great love, or for those who refuse that love, with a sword! The sword is designed for His great enemy whom He has beheaded, the "roaring lion," Satan. He has dealt him the fatal head wound as pictured in his uplifted left hand.

Also note that the tip of TAURUS's left horn touches the club of ORION in the picture as it does in many representations, indicating clearly that the club of ORION has the identical thrust as that of the horns of TAURUS, and that the two figures are synonymous. Both present the ministry of judgment to be poured forth by Jesus when the forebearance of God ceases.

DENDERAH

In the ancient zodiac of Denderah, ORION is pictured as a man coming forth and pointing to three bright stars, Bellatrix, Betelguez, and Rigol indicating his ownership of these stars. His name is given there as Ha-ga-T which means Ha, The Chief, Ga, Triumphs and T stands for the article The or This. Thus we can read, This Chief Triumphs. Also interesting is the fact that there are hieroglyphics located below the figure which spell Oar. Orion was spelled in ancient times Oarion. This name came from the Hebrew root word for light, used for example in Gen. 1:14, when God said "Let there be light." From this we can readily see the name of Orion meaning Coming Forth As Light.

The decan of ERIDANUS will amplify these truths.

ERIDANUS
(THE RIVER)

ERIDANUS is a river flowing forth from the uplifted foot of ORION, and flowing in a crooked, looping pattern beneath the paws of CETUS, the Sea-monster, and then out of sight downward off the chart toward the earth.

To what does this river pertain? I see two possibilities and perhaps both may be correct (more dual symbolism)—a positive message for the people of God and a negative one for His enemies. The positive message refers specifically and uniquely to the people of God. In this sense the River is the same as that poured forth by AQUARIUS from his urn. In this figure it comes from the uplifted foot, symbolizing the wounded heel, and the suffering of the Cross whereby the right was won to pour forth the Living Waters which continue to flow to the earth to bless the people of God.

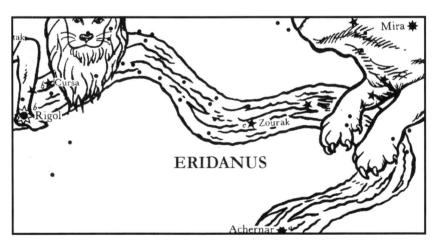

FIG. 35   ERIDANUS   The River

> "There is a river, the streams whereof shall make glad the city of God, the holy place of the tabernacles of the Most High."
>
> Ps. 46:4

> "I will open rivers in high places, and fountains in the midst of the valleys..."
>
> Isa. 41:18

> "And it shall come to pass, that every living thing that liveth, which moveth, whithersoever the rivers shall come, shall live, and there shall be a very great multitude of fish, because these waters shall come thither: for they shall live whither the river cometh."
>
> Ezek. 47:9

This river then illustrates the blessed river of living water and newness of life offered to the people of God in Jesus, and includes healing and fullness of life. The fact that CETUS' paws overlay the waters indicate his attempts to block the flow of blessings and even answered prayer for the fish-people (Dan. 10).

The other possible interpretation, which is negative in outlook and has its effect aimed at the enemies of God, is that this is the river of the judgment of God. That this river first touches the paws of CETUS is not surprising, nor that it then continues off the chart down toward the unnamed and unidentified enemies upon the earth who have chosen to link their fates with CETUS', those who have chosen to follow him rather than to accept the Author of Life eternal. To this thought Scripture bears ample testimony as does the theme of the adjoining Signs in this section of the heavens.

> "I beheld till... the Ancient of days did sit, whose garment was white as snow, and the hair of his head like the pure wool: his throne was like the fiery flame, and his wheels as burning fire. A fiery stream issued and came forth from before him ...

and judgment was set, and the books were opened. I beheld then because of the voice of the great words which the horn spoke; I beheld even until the beast was slain, and his body destroyed, and given to the burning flame."

Dan. 7:9–11

"The Lord reigneth; let the earth rejoice; ... righteousness and judgment are the habitation of his throne. A fire goeth before him, and burneth up his enemies round about... the earth saw and trembled."

Ps. 97:1–3

Our God shall come, and shall not keep silence: a fire shall devour before him, and it shall be very tempestous round about him. He shall call to the haven from above, and to the earth, that he may judge his people."

Psalm 50:3–4

These latter references seem more in keeping with the message and theme of the heavens and with the nature of the mighty judgment of God associated with both TAURUS and ORION.

Can the ancient names and stars help discern which type of river is intended here? Interestingly, the names lend themselves to both of our interpretations.

—NAMES FOR THE SIGN—

The ancient Hebrew name of ERIDANUS means River of the Judge or Ruler, and seems to follow the negative emphasis.[48] However, a different slant is to be seen at Denderah.

---

[48] A contrast is to be observed between the two rivers, ERIDANUS, reflecting judgment or curse, and the river of blessings pouring forth from the Urn of AQUARIUS. The latter was named by the Romans as Fluvius Aquarii, or The River of Aquarius.

Part III - *Kingdom and Judgment Established - ERIDANUS*

—NAMES OF THE STARS—

The brightest star Achernar (Hebrew) means The After Part of the River. The second brightest is named in Hebrew Cursa, Bent Down. Zourak, Flowing is the Arabic name for the third brightest. Several other stars named in Hebrew are in this river but are not identifiable as to exact position: Phaet, The Mouth of the River: Theemin, The Water, and Ozha, The Going Forth.

This river of judgment is combined with the figure of ORION in the following words of Scripture:

> "Behold, the name of the Lord cometh from afar, burning with his anger, and the burden whereof is heavy: his lips are full of indignation, and his tongue as a devouring fire. And his breath, as an overflowing stream shall reach to the midst of the neck... the breath of the Lord like a stream of brimstone..."
>
> **Isa. 30:27,28a,33b**

> "For, behold, the Lord will come with fire, and with his chariots like a whirlwind, to render his anger with fury, and his rebuke with flames of fire... For by fire and by his sword will the Lord plead with all flesh: and the slain of the Lord shall be many."
>
> **Isa. 66:15,16**

> "The mountains quake at him, and the hills melt, and the earth is burned at his presence, yea, the world and all that dwell therein. Who can stand before his indignation? and who can abide in the fierceness of his anger? his fury is poured out like fire, and the rocks are thrown down by him."
>
> **Nah. 1:5–6**

"But the day of the Lord will come as a thief in the night: in which the heavens shall pass away with a great noise, and the elements shall melt with fervent heat, the earth also and the works that are therein shall be burned up"

2 Pet. 3:10

"... and fire came down from God out of heaven, and devoured them. And the devil that deceived them was cast into the lake of fire and brimstone..."

Rev. 20:9–10

DENDERAH

The Egyptian Zodiac gives additional light upon this river. In their Zodiac the river is named Peh-Ta-T: We have learned that *T* means The or This; *Peh* means Mouth, River, and, *Aa* means Water: so we can read The Mouth of the River of Water. In their Planisphere the river commences at the urn of AQUARIUS and is seen continuing in ERIDANUS. Their figure would lend itself to the first possible interpretation. One does not negate the other, since both love and judgment were accomplished in the results of the bruising of the foot upon the Cross.

The thought of such immense destruction and fierce judgment is softened however by the gentle figure in the next Sign, AURIGA.

AURIGA
(THE SHEPHERD)

In the third decan of TAURUS is found the Gentle Shepherd, AURIGA, which is a perfect companion for the fierce and mighty figures of rushing TAURUS and ORION. They speak of the awesome judgment of God about to be poured out like a river of fire upon the unrighteous. But in AURIGA is seen the counterbalancing emphasis upon Jesus' love, and His coming in His role as the Gentle Shepherd, loving and concerned for the well-being of His beloved people.

PART III - *Kingdom and Judgment Established - AURIGA*

AURIGA is pictured as a shepherd holding an ewe in his left arm. Usually on the hand or wrist of that same arm are seen two little lambs. One is looking back, as does the ewe, at the fierce charge of TAURUS; the other is looking up into the face of the Shepherd. In his other hand AURIGA holds a pair of reins, which correspond to the BANDS seen in PISCES. This identifies him with ARIES as another representation of the holder of the reins of the Fish-people, or the people of God, represented here as sheep rather than fish.

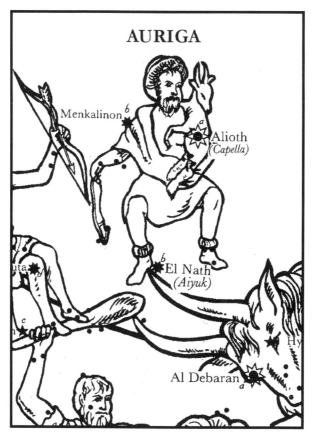

FIG. 36   AURIGA   The Shepherd

Aratus, the poet, in his description of AURIGA speaks of the Ewe and her lambs as well as their positions:

"She is both large and bright, but they—the kids— Shine somewhat feebly on Auriga's wrist."

Just such a gentle, compassionate Shepherd as the one pictured in the heavens is described in Scripture:

> "Behold the Lord will come with strong hand, and his arm shall rule for him: behold, his reward is with him, and his work before him. He shall feed his flock like a shepherd: he shall gather the lambs with his arm, and carry them in his bosom, and shall gently lead those that are with young."
>
> **Isa. 40:10–11**

> "The Lord is my Shepherd…"
>
> **Psalm 23:1**

Scripture tells us that the great Shepherd promised in the Old Testament is none other than Jesus, as Paul declares in the Letter to the Hebrews:

> "Now the God of Peace, that brought again from the dead our Lord Jesus, that Great Shepherd of the sheep…
>
> **Heb. 13:20**

Jesus also identifies Himself as the Shepherd:

"I am the good shepherd: the good shepherd giveth his life for the sheep." And again, "I am the good shepherd, and know my sheep, and am known of mine" (Jn. 10:14).

The Greeks who were able to come up with a story to fit every figure in the heavenly constellations were at a complete loss with regard to so gentle a figure as AURIGA. There was, however, a recognition by many of the ancients including the Greeks of a higher, deeper, grander wisdom contained in the figures so that they did not alter them but retained them in detail, hoping, no doubt, to later discover their true significance. Therefore, the constellation figures were maintained by man, not for the right reasons, but nonetheless they were preserved.

Also note the fact that the right heel of AURIGA is being pierced by the tip of the horn of TAURUS. This reminds of the truth that Jesus gave Himself for the sheep in self-sacrifice.

How say the Sign names and those of the stars?

—NAMES FOR THE SIGN—

AURIGA is the Hebrew word for Shepherd, the same word used in Isaiah 40:11 quoted just previously. To the Greeks AURIGA was known as Haeniochos meaning The Driver, or The Charioteer, which is the apparent source of the present tendency to call this figure as he still is in England today, The Wagoner. But this is an obviously inaccurate name, probably stemming from the Latin name Auriga which meant The Conductor of the Reins.

The English idea of a charioteer, no doubt came from the reins in his hand, although they did not recognize in them the BANDS of PISCES, and therefore attempted to explain his role as one who merely held the reins of horses. But it is clear from the Noetic roots in the name of AURIGA that its meaning was originally Shepherd as we have also seen him to be in Scripture. The stars' names attest to this same truth.

—NAMES OF THE STARS—

The brightest star is known by its Latin name Capella, The She-Goat, apparently from the Hebrew root Capra for atonement. The same star is known in Hebrew as Alioth, The Ewe or She-Goat. The figure of the goat (or sheep) is a prominent part of the constellation and is seen being held in the one arm of AURIGA and the reins in the other hand. It is as if the Good Shepherd has just removed the reins from her neck and set her free, in the glorious liberty of being "with" or "in Him."

Another Hebrew name appears in this constellation, Gedi, The Kids which are sometimes pictured as following behind AURIGA. This scene is perhaps what Jeremiah was describing when he wrote:

"And I will set up shepherds over them which shall feed

them: and they shall fear no more, nor be dismayed, neither shall they be lacking, saith the Lord."

Jer. 23:4

This state of peaceful rest for the people of God is further described by Ezekiel:

"Therefore will I save my flock, and they shall no more be a prey; and I will judge between cattle and cattle. And I will set up one shepherd over them, and he shall feed them, even my servant David; he shall feed them, and he shall be their shepherd.

And I the Lord will be their God ... And I will make with them a covenant of peace ... and they shall dwell safely in the wilderness, and sleep in the woods ... and they shall be safe in their land, and shall know that I am the Lord, when I have broken the bands of their yoke, and delivered them out of the hands of those who enslaved them."

Ezek. 34:22–25, 27

The second brightest star is to be seen in the bicep of his right arm and is named in Chaldean, Menkalinon meaning The Band or Chain of The Goats or Ewes. The lambs are freed but held safely in the arm of the Shepherd. Two other names in Arabic are of interest. The first is Maaz, The Flock of Goats, Kids. "Fear not little flock, for it is the Father's good pleasure to give you the kingdom." The other is El Nath (also appearing in ARIES and TAURUS), meaning The Wounded or The Slain, and speaks once again of the great sacrifice by which all this was purchased and made possible. Another star here bears an Arabic name which underscores the same truth, Aiyuk, meaning Wounded in The Foot.[49]

DENDERAH

---

[49] The root of this very word is used in describing the lameness of Mephibosheth in 2 Sam. 4:4.

PART III - Kingdom and Judgment Established - AURIGA

The Denderah story is similar and yet adds interesting additional truths. AURIGA is named Turn: The Sceptre, The Power. Turn, in fact, carries a scepter, the upper portion of which bears the head of a lamb, the lower portion is in the form of a cross. The animal's head signifies He Cometh. This also symbolizes the immortal life associated by the Egyptians with the sign of the cross from earliest history, and it indicates somehow that immortal life had something to do both with a Lamb and with the One to Come. The Egyptian hieroglyphic names also identify Turn as One Who Subdues or Tames.

The beautiful symbolism of this Sign as a whole reveals the terrible, awesome judgments of God to be poured out by TAURUS in his fierce rushing fury and ERIDANUS, The River of Fire, unleashed by ORION in accordance with that judgment. Yet, how like our loving Lord, to also give at the same time a revelation of Himself as the Gentle Shepherd. To His sheep He reveals Himself as the gentle, loving Shepherd, AURIGA, tenderly and compassionately nourishing the little lambs and comforting the Ewe so mercifully. This is none other than our Blessed Saviour whom we can but love and worship afresh as we see Him so lovingly portrayed for us.

Another two-fold revelation awaits us in GEMINI.

GEMINI

(THE TWINS)

The tenth Sign of the Zodiac, is GEMINI, THE TWINS, two youthful and jubilant figures seated side by side. The figure on the left is named Pollux or Hercules, and the figure on the right is named Castor or Apollo. The figure on the left is holding a club in a relaxed position. The figure on the right holds up an unstrung bow and arrow in his left hand while in the other, he holds a lyre or harp. The figure on the left is embracing the figure on the right and has his arm around the latter's waist.

The Latin names of these two figures are familiar from Scripture as the name of the ship upon which Paul sailed in Acts 28:11. The Greeks and Romans used to employ their names when swearing, a practice carried over today in the exclamations, "By Gemini," or the more modern "By Jimminy."

In mythology these were the sons of Jupiter, born in supernatural fashion, and renowned for their heroism. They were also reported to be seen in time of war leading armies of horsemen into battle. They were pictured in the temples of the Greeks as mounted on white horses and were considered to be great hunters. They were also reported to have cleared the seas of pirates and to have removed dangers to sailors from the seas and therefore, were considered to be the specific patrons of seafaring men. It was in this context, no doubt, that the ship in Acts bore their names. They were elevated to their position as a constellation by their father, Jupiter, who rewarded them for their devotion to one another. They were, in other accounts, considered somehow to be both kings, and divine saviours of mankind. In addition both were considered bestowers of special aid to mankind, serving as arbitrators and as warring judges, going forth at the head of avenging armies.

Part III - Kingdom and Judgment Established - GEMINI

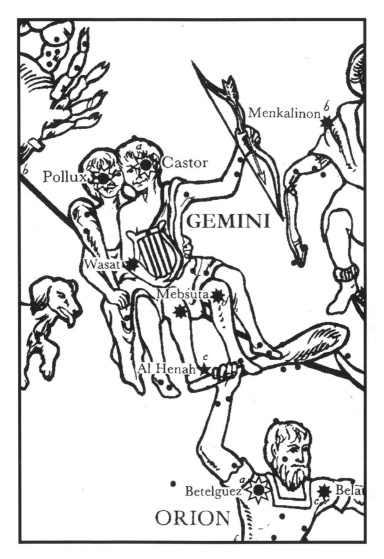

FIG. 37   GEMINI   The Twins

These two figures once again have the dual roles, and multifaceted natures of Jesus: Saviour-Suffering Servant; King-Priest; God-Man; King-Servant; Sacrificer-Sacrifice.

But more especially, I feel these figures present a glorious picture of the Bridegroom united with His beautiful, youthful bride. The figures indicate that the conflict is over and has been gloriously completed, as is seen in the previous Signs, and indicated here in the unstrung bow, and the club in relaxed position, as well as the presence of the harp upon which to sing the victory songs. It is clearly a time of rejoicing!

Foreshadowed here is the glorious future state of believers, the Church, as foretold in Scripture:

> "For thou shalt forget the shame of thy youth, and shall not remember the reproach of thy widowhood any more."

> "For thy Maker is thine husband; and the Lord of hosts is his name; and thy redeemer the Holy One of Israel; the God of the whole earth shall He be called... and hath called thee... as a wife of youth..."
>
> Isa. 54:4b–6

This is that which has occurred after the great catching up, which was considered in the Sign of ARIES; His church, His people, united with Him:

> "Then we which are alive and remain shall be caught up together with them in the clouds, to meet the Lord in the air: and so shall we ever be with the Lord."
>
> 1 Thess. 4:17

It should not surprise us that the two figures appear to be identical twins:

> "Beloved now are we the sons of God, and it doth not yet appear what we shall be: but we know that, when he shall appear, we shall be like him; for we shall see him as he is."
>
> 1 Jn. 3:2

This is the perfect fulfillment of Jesus' great priestly prayer portrayed graphically for us in the stars:

> "And now, O Father, glorify thou me with thine own self with the glory which I had with thee before the world was."

> "That they all may be one; as thou, Father art in me, and I in thee, that they also may be one in us; that the world may believe that thou has sent me. And the glory which thou gavest me I have given them; that they may be one, even as we are one."
>
> John 17:5, 21–22

> "Therefore I endure all things for the elect's sakes, that they may also obtain the salvation which is in Christ Jesus with eternal glory. It is a faithful saying: for if we be dead with Him, we shall also live with him: If we suffer, we shall also reign with him."
>
> 2 Tim. 2:10–12a

Pictured in the heavenly figure is the same prophesied in Scripture: a scene which could perhaps be a candid family snapshot taken at the Marriage Supper of the Lamb. This is a mystery clearly prophesied in Scripture but not yet realized: the Bride that will be one with Him in thought, word, and deed ... so identified with Him as to be almost indistinguishable from Him. "We shall be like him." "The image of Christ to be formed in you." "Christ in you," and like passages indicate that eventually He will have such complete sway over us and will work such a transformation in us that we will be exactly like Him—identically "twinned" to Him.

For the present we groan, as Paul says "within ourselves," realizing how far we are from that goal. We are still chained with a corruptible nature, but soon "this corruptible shall put on incorruptibility" and we shall in perfection "put on Christ."

Portrayed here are two youthful bodies, and yet they really, in a sense, represent one figure: Jesus linked with His Church, joint heirs and co-possessors with Him of all things. We possess His nature and shall be exactly like Him. He is uniquely the Son of God, yet we are also "sons of God." As a result of His birth as a man, and being reborn out of the grave, we have been "born again." We are the Bride formed out of His side, bone of His bone, flesh of His flesh. Just as Eve was the bride formed out of the side of the first Adam while he was asleep, so are we the Bride formed out of the side of Jesus, the second Adam, from which flowed the blood and the water while He slept the sleep of death for us, that we, like Eve, might come to life and be with him! He is the Bridegroom and we are the Bride. Yet both of us are referred to in Scripture as being the "man-child;" He first of all, and we in His image. We are to be to Jesus, as the Moon is to the Sun, reflectors of His Light. The glory is entirely His.

> "And there appeared a great wonder in heaven; a woman clothed with the sun, and the moon under her feet, and upon her head a crown of twelve stars;
>
> And she being with child cried, travailing in birth, and pained to be delivered.
>
> And she brought forth a man child, who was to rule all nations with a rod of iron: and her child was caught up unto God, and to his throne.
>
> And the dragon was wroth with the woman, and went to make war with the remnant of her seed, which keep the commandments of God, and have the testimony of Jesus Christ."
>
> **Rev. 12:1,2,5,17**

We do have the same Father in heaven, as Jesus so often stated. So it follows that we should be like our elder Brother, in whose image we were created.

So says the Scripture; how say the Signs and stars?

—NAMES FOR THE SIGN—

In viewing Scripture we have interpreted this Sign to be speaking of the commencing of the peaceful reign of Jesus Christ with His Beloved at His side, and as being the glory of "His Days."

> "In his days shall the righteous flourish; and the abundance of peace so long as the moon endureth. He shall have dominion also from sea to sea, and from the river unto the ends of the earth."
>
> **Ps. 72:7–8**

Part III - *Kingdom and Judgment Established - GEMINI*

GEMINI was originally known by its Hebrew name Thaumin, The United. The Hebrew, Arabic, and Syriac names carry a connotation of completion, the completion of a year, or the completion of a long betrothal, the consummation or completing of a thing long-awaited. In fact, the Hebrew name above is used in Exodus 26:24 in referring to the boards of the Tabernacle which are to be "twinned," that is, made exactly alike. The Syrians used the same name as the Hebrew with the same meaning while the Arabs named it Al Tauman, The Twins or The Pair, The Completely Joined. They also referred to this Sign as Clusus or Claustrum Hori meaning The Station or Place of the Coming One.

The Greek name is Didumoi, The Twins. The Latin name Gemini is also The Twins. However, in the Latin Vulgate the root word used in Gen. 25:24 to describe the births of the twins, Jacob and Esau, is the same word translated fellow in Zechariah in a prophecy referring to the Messiah: "The man that is my fellow." Its meaning is defined by Strong as "an associate, companion, a kindred man, comrade or another (of like kind)." Thus the kindred man to God, or "another fellow just like me" is coming.

Do the stars agree?

—NAMES OF THE STARS—

The brightest star in GEMINI is named in Greek and Latin, Castor, The Ruler or Judge, with the arrow signifying Coming In Haste. The second brightest star is Pollux meaning The Ruler or The Judge, bearing the club (or in some cases a branch) thus signifying that this one is also The Branch. He is sometimes called Hercules which we have already seen to mean The Strong One Coming To Labour or Suffer. In the left foot of Pollux is the third brightest star. Al Henah meaning The Hurt or Afflicted. The next brightest star is located in the knee of Castor and is named in Hebrew Mebsuta, which means Treading Underfoot. This name expresses the fulfillment of the prophecy of Romans 16:20, "The God of peace shall bruise Satan under your feet shortly."

Another star is Wasat (Arabic) meaning Established, As A Foundation, or Set, set up or appointed to rule.

There are also three stars whose names are known but which cannot be located with certainty: Propus — Hebrew for The Branch Spreading: and two with Arabic names Al Dira, The Seed or Branch and Al Giauza, The Palm Branch, or Stem (see Isaiah 11:1).

There is a unanimity in the names of the Sign and the component stars. This Sign tells of the perfect uniting or pairing, as in brotherhood or marriage, of two who will become comrades of God; they will together rule and judge. One of them is also seen to be the Seed and the Branch who has suffered, been afflicted in the foot, and laboured, but is now established upon His throne and flourishing and spreading as the palm tree. The other is to have a part in the final conflict, will bear arms, and will participate in the rejoicing afterwards, singing the other's praises, before joining with Him to judge and to rule.

DENDERAH

We have already noted that the ancient Egyptian name as handed down by the Copts is Pi-mahi or The United. The Denderah Zodiac figures GEMINI as a young man leading a woman by the hand. The young man has a tail signifying "This One Cometh." Thus we can see that the One Coming is to also be accompanied by, or to bring with Him, a young woman whom we take to be His newly acquired Bride whom He is leading to a place where she may share his glory with Him.

The following decans are hardly what we'd expect, but continue the story.

LEPUS
(THE HARE: THE ENEMY)

The first accompanying decan shows up on our chart as LEPUS, The Hare, The Rabbit, or The Enemy. He is springing away from SIRIUS and located right beneath the upraised foot of ORION who is about to stomp upon him.

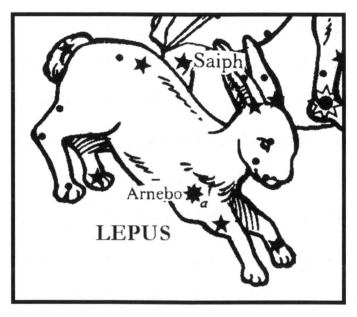

FIG. 38   LEPUS   The Enemy

Since ORION is about to trample LEPUS underfoot, we assume him to be a representation of the enemy, Satan. LEPUS is he that is spoken of in the last Scripture which we considered and who is to be "bruised under our feet shortly!"

Aratus says of LEPUS:

"Below Orion's feet, the Hare
  is chased eternally."

This pictures what will come to pass when, indeed, the Lord calls His church to His side, and seats her there for the Marriage Supper of the Lamb:

> "Let us be glad and rejoice, and give honor to him: for the marriage supper of the Lamb is come, and his wife hath made herself ready. And to her it was granted that she should be arrayed in fine linen, clean and white for the fine linen is the righteousness of saints.
>
> And he saith unto me, Write, Blessed are they which are called unto the marriage supper of the Lamb. And he saith unto me, These are the true sayings of God.
>
> And I fell at his feet to worship him. And he said unto me, see thou do it not! I am thy fellow servant, and of thy brethren that have the testimony of Jesus. Worship God; for the testimony of Jesus is the spirit of prophecy."
>
> "And I saw heaven opened, and behold a white horse; and he that sat upon him was called Faithful and True, and in righteousness he doth judge and make war.
>
> His eyes were as a flame of fire, and on his head were many crowns; and he had a name written, that no man knew, but he himself.
>
> And he was clothed with a vesture dipped in blood; and his name is called The Word of God.
>
> And the armies which were in heaven followed him upon white horses, clothed in fine linen white and clean.
>
> And out of his mouth goeth a sharp sword, that with it he should smite the nations: and he shall rule them with a rod of iron: and he treadeth the winepress of the fierceness and wrath of Almighty God.
>
> And he hath on his vesture and on his thigh a name written, KING OF KINGS, AND LORD OF LORDS."
>
> **Rev. 19:7–16**

This is what is visually presented here: the imminent destruction of the enemy and his forces, following closely upon the Lord taking His Bride unto Himself.

Do the Sign names and those of the stars fit into this scenario?

—NAMES FOR THE SIGN—

The Sign of LEPUS was called by the Hebrew's namc for its brightest star, Arnebo, The Enemy of Him That Cometh. The Arabians had a similar name Arnebeth, The Hare: The Enemy of Him That Cometh. The Latin name Lepus means The Hare Treading Underfoot. The same root word is used in Psalm 108:13 "Through God we shall do valiantly: for he it is that shall tread down our enemies."

—NAMES OF THE STARS—

The same consensus is reflected in the names of the individual stars within Lepus. There are three whose ancient names are available, in addition to the brightest star, Arnebo, already considered. The three, not identified as to position, are Nibal, The Mad, Rakis, The Bound (as with a chain), and Sugia, The Deceiver. All the star names agree in identifying this enemy and his nature. The three stars tell the nature, reaction and fate of this enemy. He is a "deceiver," as is plainly revealed in the Scriptures, is "mad," and will be "bound."

DENDERAH

Etched in the stone of the Denderah Zodiac we see the enemy of Him Who Cometh pictured as a Hoopee, an unclean Egyptian bird, standing over the serpent and both are under the upraised foot of Orion. This identifies even more clearly that this enemy is indeed Satan, The Old Serpent. The name given by the Egyptians for this figure was Bashti-Beki, which meant The Failing (Beki) of the Enemy Confounded (Bashti).

Another pursuer of LEPUS awaits us in the next decan.

CANIS MAJOR
(THE GREATER DOG: THE PRINCE)

The second decan presents another aspect of the One who is pursuing LEPUS, The Hare. He is figured in the charts as a dog sitting upright with a collar around his neck and his paws extended toward the Rabbit, as if temporarily restrained from pursuit. Dogs or wolves, as this was once thought to be, are both the natural enemies of rabbits, just as we have previously noted to be the case with hawks and eagles as natural enemies of serpents. This dog seems to be a sleek hunter, similar to a greyhound, bred for racing and catching just such prey as rabbits.

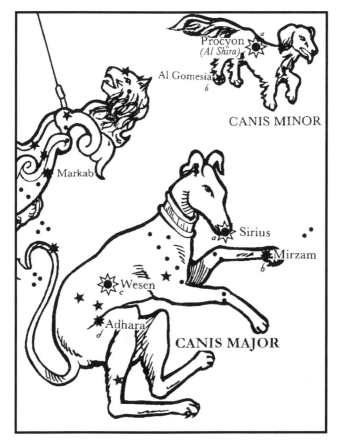

FIG. 39   CANIS MAJOR   The Prince

How does such an unlikely symbol relate to the unfolding theme?

—NAMES FOR THE SIGN—

CANIS MAJOR, The Greater Dog, has also been called The Wolf or The Dog in the past, but was known to the early Hebrews by the name given its brightest star, Sirius, The Prince. The names associated with this Sign make it readily apparent that this is certainly not merely an Egyptian dog which we are considering.

A prince is, of course, the son of a King. The other names also join in a chorus of princely terms. The Hebrew name by which the constellation came to be known is Abur, The Mighty. The Arabic name Al Habor has the identical meaning. The Egyptian name also concurs, Seir — The Prince, from which we get the words "Sire" or "Sir."

—NAMES OF THE STARS—

This Prince is none other than He spoken of in Isaiah 9:6:

> "Unto us a child is born, unto us a son is given: and the government shall be upon his shoulder: and his name shall be called Wonderful, Counselor, The Mighty God, The Everlasting Father, The Prince of Peace."

The brightest star, located in the nose, as mentioned above is Sirius (Heb.), The Prince. A form of this very word, *Sar* is used in the passage from Isaiah. Its root is very enlightening as it carries the sense To Make Oneself a Prince. That is just what Jesus did, in essence, through qualifying for His role, by His obedience, and His work upon the Cross.

Another Hebrew name for this brightest star is Ascher, Who Shall Come. Taking the two Hebrew names together, we have The Prince Who Shall Come. The Arabs called the same star Al Shira, Al Jemeniya, The Prince or Chief of the Right Hand.

> "Thine hand shall find out all thine enemies: thy right hand shall find out those that hate thee." Ps. 21:8

"... His right hand, and his holy arm, hath gotten him the victory."

Ps. 98:1

In many of the Messianic prophecies Jesus is spoken of as the right hand of God, the right arm, or the strong right arm, in addition to references to his being the Prince.

"... he (the enemy) shall also stand up against the Prince of princes...."

Dan. 8:25

"... from the going forth of the commandment... unto the Messiah the Prince shall be seven weeks and three score and two weeks..."

Dan. 9:25

The second brightest star located in the upper paw is Mirzam (Arab.), The Prince and had a second Arabian name Muliphen, The Leader or The Chief. The third brightest is Wesen (Arabic), located in the stomach, meaning The Bright, Shining, The Scarlet. The fourth brightest and last for which we have an ancient name is Adhara (Arabic); also Al Adra or Aludra, seen in the near thigh, and it means The Glorious. None of the names would have any relevance for a dog, but excite our hearts when we have the key to break the code, and see The Prince. This is the Mighty Prince who is also the commonly referred to "Prince of the Right Hand," and He is to be Glorious, Bright, and Shining when He comes to Lead.

The name Wesen is especially interesting because it is from the same Hebrew root word translated Scarlet used to describe the thread to be hung in the window by Rahab the harlot in the second Chapter of Joshua. That same scarlet thread speaks of the thread of blood throughout Scripture and points to the perfect blood to be shed by the very Prince, described prophetically here.

DENDERAH

Oddly enough, the Denderah version of CANIS MAJOR, holds the answer to one of the original mysteries which caused me to set out upon this quest in the first place, the mystery of Jesus being called a Nazarene.

The Egyptians present in Sirius a figure whom they called Apes, which name in Hieroglyphics and ancient Hebrew roots meant The Head Commanding, and Swiftly Coming Down in Victory. The Prince is figured by the hawk (Naz) the natural enemy of the serpent. The Greeks called this constellation the First or Great Dog, but originally saw it as The Wolf whose name was in Hebrew Zeeb (Wolf), but in Arabic meant This One Cometh. This indicates that This Prince is Coming to Reign. On his head the figure wears a mortar and pestle, which as mentioned earlier, indicates that he shall also be involved in bruising (the enemy).

Recall the dilemma that I had in the beginning, attempting to find the origin of the prophecy spoken of in Matthew 2:23, "And he came and dwelt in a city called Nazareth, that it might be fulfilled which was spoken by the prophets, He shall be called a Nazarene." There is no such prophecy recorded in Scripture; I was led in my search to the root word netser used for Branch by Isaiah in the Messianic prophecy recorded in Isa. 11:1. In this decan at Denderah we find mentioned in connection with The Coming Prince, the word Naz (Hawk, caused to come forth). Netser comes from a root "nazir" or "nat sar" meaning to keep or preserve as used in Isa. 26:3. "Thou wilt keep him in perfect peace, whose mind is stayed on thee." Seir we have seen means The Prince. If we combine the two Egyptian names Naz and Seir, we have the prophetic name of Naz-Seir or The Prince To Come Forth. So we see that the Netser (Branch) mentioned by Isaiah and the equally prophetic reference in the stars to The Prince To Come Forth (Naz-Seir) leads us again perhaps to the Naz-Seir-ene. Not one who merely lived in the little town of Nazareth, as no such prophecy is extant; but rather, this reference identifies The Prince to Come Forth as the One who was later to be born in Bethlehem.

Will the next decan, CANIS MINOR, also a dog, give a different view?

CANIS MINOR
(THE LESSER DOG: THE REDEEMER)

The third decan is seen as the second dog, CANIS MINOR, The Lesser Dog or Wolf, or as it was more anciently known, Procyon, The Redeemer. This animal is represented as a smaller dog who looks like a sheep dog, a symbol of Him who is the Redeemer and Protector of the sheep and is pictured as He is in Psalms:

> "O give thanks unto the Lord; for he is good: for his mercy endureth forever. To him that by wisdom made the heavens ... to him that made great lights ... the sun to rule by day ... the moon and stars to rule by night... and hath redeemed us from our enemies: for his mercy endureth forever."
>
> Ps. 136:1,5,7–9,24

And He is also the One whom Isaiah writes of:

> "And I will feed them that oppress thee with their own flesh; and they shall be drunken with their own blood, as with sweet wine; and all flesh shall know that I, the Lord am thy Saviour and thy Redeemer, the Mighty One of Jacob."
>
> Isa. 49:26

This sheep dog, then indeed represents the Redeemer and the Great Shepherd of the sheep. Just as we have been permitted to see dual figures of our Lord's nature and roles in GEMINI, now He gives two pictures of Himself as the Ruling Prince: one of Him coming victorious as in Sirius and the other coming as the loving, concerned, burden-bearing Shepherd and Redeemer.

He is pictured as being so identified with His sheep, His people, as to make it difficult to determine whether we are seeing a picture of the Redeemer or the Redeemed, for by the period of time illustrated here "We shall be so like him" as to literally be "one with Him."

PART III - Kingdom and Judgment Established - CANIS MINOR

FIG. 40   CANIS MINOR   The Redeemer

—NAMES FOR THE SIGN—

The earliest Hebrews knew CANIS MINOR by the name of its foremost star, Procyon, The Redeemer. Other names have not come down to us although apparently the Arabs knew the constellation by their name for the same star, given below.

—NAMES OF THE STARS—

The brightest star, located in the apparent heart of the figure, as already mentioned is named in Hebrew, Procyon, The Redeemer, certainly an unusual name for the lesser of two dogs in the heavens if any other interpretation were to be applied to the story than that which we are presenting.

The Arabians called this brightest star Al Shira, Al Shemeliya, The Prince or Chief of the Left Hand (corresponding to Castor). The Arabians named two other stars whose locations haven't come down to us, but their names have been preserved, Al Mirzam (as in CANIS MAJOR) The Prince or Ruler; and Al Gomeyra, Him Who Completes or Perfects.

> "The Lord will perfect that which concerneth me."
>
> **Ps. 138:8**

The second brightest star is located in the neck where the collar (or yoke) is attached, and bears the highly significant name Al Gomeisa which in Arabic means The Burdened, The Loaded, Bearing For Others. This is a perfect description of the ministry of Him who bore our burdens, and called to Himself all who were burdened and heavy laden and offered them rest, by taking their yoke and burdens upon Himself.

DENDERAH

The Denderah Zodiac presents in the third decan, a human figure with the head of a hawk and a tail added, thus signifying by the tail This One Comes, and by the hawk's head that the man coming is to be the natural enemy and destroyer of the serpent. The name given there bears this out, Sebak, apparently from the Hebrew word Shebah (to Make Captive) and meaning to the Egyptians Conquering or Victorious. Their complete name might be rendered "This One Comes Conquering, Victorious."

Thus the Egyptians also saw in the constellation of the LESSER DOG, the message of a Man coming to rule and to be victorious over his enemy.

A creature that would seem far more at home in a watery environment awaits in CANCER.

CANCER

(THE CRAB)

The next to the last major figure in the heavenly circuit is the extremely unlikely figure of a Crab. Notice that the Crab is facing LEO: and note that LEO and TAURUS are facing one another, forming bookends upon the final third of the heavenly story. The first one third of the heavenly story is set apart by two figures facing one another, VIRGO and SAGITTARIUS, and the center one-third is set apart by CAPRICORN and ARIES facing away from one another. These bookends constitute internal evidence to further corroborate our divisions of the story.

What is this Crab, and why does it appear in the heavenlies? A crab is a creature which lives in two environments, under the water and upon dry land. The body of Christ is also equipped for two environments, heaven and earth. There is another similarity. The crab possesses many legs, or members, which in hieroglyphics would indicate a multitude or multiplication. This is paralleled by the body of Christ which is composed of many members. John wrote of the multitudes of the redeemed, from every kindred, tribe and nation who will gather around the thrones of heaven.

The crab also has two appendages for grasping and holding on. Its claws enable it to hold on tenaciously. To hang on, or to hold on securely is a Christian trait, important for those of us who have been told that we must "hold fast that which is good" (1 Thess. 5:21), to "lay hold of the hope set before us" (Heb. 6:18), and more especially that we must "Fight the good fight of faith, lay hold on eternal life, whereunto thou art also called" (1 Tim. 6:12). So the Crab beautifully symbolizes the "Multitudes of the Redeemed who have lain hold upon eternal life."

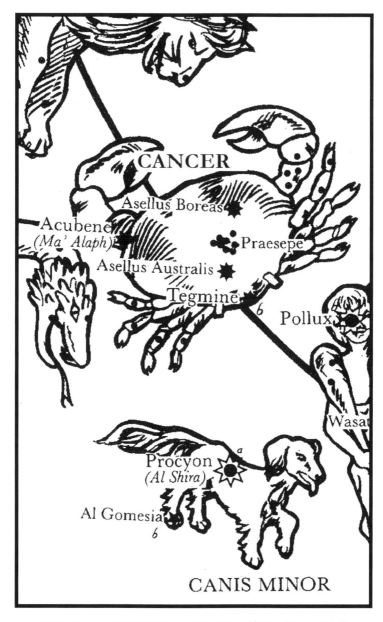

FIG. 41   CANCER   The Crab (The Sheepfold)

In this Sign we can see the fulfillment of God's promise to Abraham recorded in Genesis:

> "Look now toward heaven, and tell the stars if thou be able to number them ... so shall thy seed be."
>
> **Gen. 15:5**

> "I will multiply thy seed as the stars of the heaven, and as the sand which is upon the sea shore; and thy seed shall possess the gate of his enemies."
>
> **Gen. 22:17**

This latter passage, Paul explains in Galatians 3:16, speaks of the seed singular (i.e. Christ) of Abraham and those who are to be heirs according to the promise.

God "counted Abraham righteous" because he believed the promise made to him. However, Paul makes yet another startling statement concerning him in Galatians 3:18.

> "And the scripture, foreseeing that God would justify the heathen through faith, preached before the gospel unto Abraham, saying, In thee shall all nations be blessed."

God, I believe, on that heaven-lit night led Abraham out and had him look up at the starry heavens. He told him all or some of the very story which we have been reading here of the Seed, The Branch, The Coming King. Thus the Scripture can accurately state that God preached the gospel before unto Abraham. (The word translated "before" means prior or earlier, and also carries the meaning *above*.)

The Egyptians had a figure very different from the Crab in their Zodiac and yet there are some similarities. They used the Scarabaeus beetle, which they considered to be sacred. It is not possible to say with certainty which of the two symbols is the more ancient, although quite probably the beetle is of greater antiquity. However both have a beautiful message for us, if we can lay aside personal preferences and prejudices.

The Scarabaeus beetle, like the Crab goes through a variety of changes in its lifetime. It starts its life as a bug similar to other beetles living amidst the dirt and filth and decaying residue upon the surface or just under the surface of the earth. It lives in darkness and filth, yet within its being lies the spark of something greater or better than its present existence. When the beetle has fulfilled its appointed time a transformation begins. It, much like our caterpillar, develops a chrysalis in which it remains in suspended animation awaiting a resurrecting call from nature to begin a new life. Finally the foreordained moment arrives and the chrysalis is broken open to release a winged being totally unlike that which entered. This new being flies upward into the air of a more brilliant world of sunlight and glory than anything it has ever known before. With no thought of its former life, old things are passed away and a completely new life begins in a totally new dimension.

This correlates well with our "walk" as humans and as Christians. We, like the beetle, spend our days amidst the rot and decay of this planet encumbered with earthly problems and concerns until we finally complete our appointed rounds and enter into the sleep of death. The mummified state of the encased bug is not unlike the Lord's entombment or our own, yet for Him and for us there is something more, and we break forth from the grave. Death cannot hold us, for we belong to a different species now, and to a different world. Death has no power over us! We can fly freely toward heaven to enjoy a new lifetime that will last throughout eternity in a different climate and better environment than any we have ever known.

In light of the beetle's metamorphosis, it does not seem illogical that the Egyptians should choose it as their symbol of a perfect life; One who has progressed from darkness and filth into light and cleanliness, from death into resurrection life and from the miseries of earth to the glories of heaven. Whenever an Egyptian saw a Scarabaeus beetle, he was reminded of this process and the thought of a life after this life!

However, as beautiful as both symbols may seem, I am convinced that neither is the original form which occupied this position in the heavenly account. It was, I am sure, originally a figure which was associated in some way with a sheepfold or cattlefold. I base this, among other things, upon the names for the Sign.

—NAMES FOR THE SIGN—

CANCER was called by the ancient Hebrews, Sartan, or The One Who Holds, or Binds. The same meaning was understood in the Arabic name Al Sartan and the Syriac name Sartano. The Coptic name was Klaria, The Cattle Folds. This thought is also brought out in the name given to it by the Greeks, Karkinos, meaning The Crab: Holding, Encircling The Possession. The Latin name apparently includes an Arabic root Cer, Encircling, so that even our familiar name Cancer means The Crab Encircling.

—NAMES OF THE STARS—

The ancient names of the stars give additional light and guidance as to which is the true message of the original. The same Hebrew and Arabic name for the brightest star in the shoulder of the lower claw Acubene, means The Sheltering, or Hiding Place. Another name for this star was Ma'alaph, meaning Assembled Thousands.

The next brightest individual star is Teqmine (Hebrew) at the rear of the body meaning Holding, which was probably also the star the Greeks called Nepa, Grasping. Another star is called in Arabic Al Himarein, The Kids or The Lambs. Two other significant stars are marked upon the charts above and below Praesepe as Assellus Boreas, The Northern She-Ass and Assellus Australis, The Southern She-Ass. Praesepe(Hebrew) is a nebula and one of the brightest clusters of stars in the heavens, visible normally to the naked eye. It contains a great multitude of stars and is known to modern astronomers by the name The Beehive, a place which holds bees. However, Praesepe's ancient name, The Multitude, The Offspring, is more enlightening.

These names concerning sheep in their folds all seem relevant, save the two She-Asses. How do they fit Scripture? A blessing was given to Issachar, and the tribe which followed him bore upon their standards the symbol of two-asses.

"The sceptre shall not depart from Judah, nor a lawgiver from between his feet, until Shiloh come; and unto him shall the gathering of the people be.

"Binding his foal unto the vine, and his ass's colt unto the choice vine; he shall wash his garments in wine, and his clothes in the blood of grapes;

"Issachar is a strong ass crouching down between two burdens" (pens, according to Rotherham, sheepfolds, according to the R.S.V.); "And he saw that rest was good, and the land that it was pleasant; and bowed his shoulder to bear, and became a servant unto tribute (task, work, R.S.V.)."

Gen. 49:10,11,14,15

Issachar foreshadows the One who has two folds or two flocks, one who indeed bowed his shoulder to bear for them their burdens and sorrows: One who took their yoke upon Himself in the form of a man that He might bring them home to a haven having accomplished a great work or task for them. These two references to the meek and lowly ass may well be clues directing us to the One who Himself became meek and lowly and entered into Jerusalem as a King "riding upon an ass and upon a colt the foal of an ass" as predicted by Zechariah 9:9.

DENDERAH

The Egyptians, recorded by Ulugh Beigh, called this Sign in Coptic Klaria, The Cattle Folds, and they also referred to it as Statio Typhonis, The Station or Place of Him Who Smites and Is Smitten! The stars declare the place won for His people by the One who was Himself smitten while smiting His enemy. The Scarabaeus beetle, symbol of resurrection life, occupies the place of CANCER in Denderah as it also does at Egypt's Esneh temple and in a less ancient Hindu Zodiac of 400 B.C.

There is a clear reference in all the Sign's names and all the stars' names to a sheepfold, a holding place or resting place for the flock. This is brought out in yet another name applied to this Sign, the Arabic word *Khan* which means The Traveller's Resting Place, and *Ker* or *Cer* as noted means Encircled or Embraced. Thus *Khan-Cer* or Cancer, as the Romans used it, means The Traveler's Resting Place For The Encircled or The Embraced.

Here is a heavenly picture of a prophecy in Scripture: that the pilgrims and sojourners upon this planet who were searching for, and trusting in, "a heavenly city whose Maker and Builder was God," have found that place and are pictured here as enjoying that heavenly rest, embraced by their Blessed Lord. This figure was foreshadowed in the previous Sign when we saw the figure for the Church, Castor, being embraced by Pollux the representation of Jesus Christ. Scripture describes this scene of the sheep of God being embraced by the Good Shepherd in Isaiah 40:11.

> "He shall feed his flock like a shepherd; he shall gather the lambs with his arm, and carry them in his bosom, and shall lead those that are with young."

Clearly this Sign holds a message of the flock of Jesus Christ gathered unto Himself as His Body in the heavenly sheepfold. They are held securely by Him, safe from all enemies in a place of rest and peace. All enemies are far off, the body sheltered from all conflict or combat. It is a time of blessed peace as intimated in GEMINI by the unstrung bow; here by the sheep at rest in the fold.

We shall see these thoughts amplified and made even more clear for us in the following decans.

URSA MINOR
(THE LESSER SHEEPFOLD)

The first decan of CANCER is URSA MINOR. The Lesser Bear, or as it is commonly known in the Americas, The Little Dipper, and its larger companion are probably two of the most familiar constellations in the heavens. On the older star charts it was normally pictured as the smaller of two bears, very unusual bears, unlike any others in existence, for they have very long tails. What could this bear and its larger companion connote? The presence of a bear is especially puzzling since bears are not native to any of the countries which produced the Zodiacs.

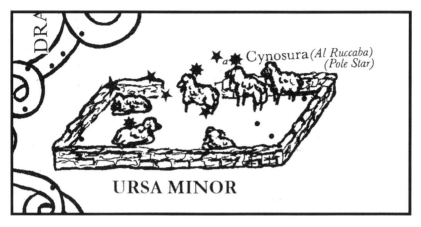

FIG. 42   URSA MINOR   The Lesser Sheepfold

On our chart the Lesser Bear is the LESSER SHEEPFOLD located near the center of the heavens with the sheep and fold under the feet of enthroned King CEPHEUS. This configuration is indubitably the earliest and most ancient, and most original symbol for this constellation, as is confirmed in the names associated with the Sign and its stars. The most ancient names applied to this figure and its larger companion do have to do with the greater and lesser sheepfolds, or holding places for sheep or a flock.

> "Hear the word of the Lord, O ye nations, and declare it in the isles afar off, and say, He that scattered Israel will gather him, and keep him, as a shepherd doth his flock.
>
> For the Lord hath redeemed Jacob, and ransomed him from the hand of him that was stronger than he. Therefore, they shall come and sing... and shall not sorrow any more at all."
>
> **Jer. 31:10–12**

> "Thou leddest thy people like a flock by the hand of Moses and Aaron."
>
> **Ps. 77:20**

> "For thus saith the Lord God: Behold, I, even I, will both search my sheep, and seek them out.
>
> I will feed them in a good pasture, and upon the high mountains of Israel shall their fold be: there shall they lie in a good fold...
>
> I will feed my flock, and I will cause them to lie down, saith the Lord God.
>
> And they shall no more be a prey to the heathen, neither shall the beast of the land devour them; but they shall dwell safely, and none shall make them afraid."
>
> **Ezek. 34:11,14,15,28**

He says that He shall provide for, and cause this flock of His to lie down in safety and rest. Jesus also speaks of a "little flock" which can readily be correlated to this figure.

> "But rather seek ye the kingdom of God; and all these things shall be added unto you. Fear not little flock; for it is your Father's good pleasure to give you the kingdom."
>
> **Lk. 12:31–32**

Jesus also went on in the famous passage concerning His role as the Good Shepherd to say:

> "And other sheep I have which are not of this fold; them also must I bring, and they shall hear my voice; and there shall be one fold and one shepherd."
>
> **John 10:16**

So He clearly states in the Scripture that there are two sheepfolds, that He is to be the One Shepherd over both and shall ultimately combine the two. These are the sheep for which He said He would lay down His life.

Do the ancient names of the Sign and its stars bear this out?

—NAMES FOR THE SIGN—

URSA MINOR was anciently called by the Hebrews for its second brightest star Kochab, in the upper right section of the fold, which meant waiting Him Who Cometh. There are a number of other ancient star names present in this constellation none of which have any relevance to bears. Aratus apparently used the name Cynosure to refer to the entire constellation. This is from the name of the brightest star in the constellation, Cynosura meaning The Center, or The Center of The Constellations.

This is of phenomenal import! These stars were named thousands of years ago, when this star which is now the Pole Star, around which all others seem to rotate, was not then the Pole Star. When these Zodiacs were drawn, the Pole Star was located in the constellation of DRACO (the Dragon, symbolic of Satan). The Dragon Star, or Alpha Draconis, was then the Pole Star. There has been a change in the powers in the spiritual realm; the kingdom of our Lord and Saviour, Jesus Christ, is being established; and power has been wrested away from Satan; the keys of Hell, as well as Heaven, now belong to Jesus, as Revelation describes. There has also been a change in the positions of the heavenly bodies. Due to the slow progression of the heavens, the center of the heavens has now moved into the constellation of Jesus' Lesser Flock. Now the Pole Star is located in a Sign emblematic of the kingdom of our Lord. Just as control has passed to Jesus in the spiritual realm, so has the pictured physical control of the heavenlies passed over into His kingdom; the center of the heavens has been removed out of a constellation symbolizing Satan into this one symbolic of Jesus' kingdom.

This Pole Star has also been known by name to the Arabs as Al-Ruccaba, The Pole Star; The Turned Upon, or The Gate of The Enemy. How could these primitive people have known that eventually the Pole Star would change to become this star upon which the entire heaven now seems to turn? Obviously, they in their natural wisdom could not have known. Thus, the only possible explanation is that the story in the heavens was indeed written by none other than the Divine Author.

Part III - Kingdom and Judgment Established - URSA MAJOR

—NAMES OF THE STARS—

The two brightest stars, Cynosura, and Kochab, we have mentioned. All the other stars bear Arabic names: Al Pherkadain, The Calves; Al Gedi, The Kid; and Al Kaid, The Assembled. The one exception has a Latin name Areas or Arctos meaning the Travelling Company.

All the names agree that this is a company of sheep, or people, who are awaiting Him who comes, and will be His assembly. The next decan will build upon and add to this imagery.

DENDERAH

The ancient Dederah Zodiac contains no bear either. It rather shows a picture of a wolf or jackal standing upon a ploughshare which comes tearing through, or bruising, the ground. It is named Api-Feni or The Head of the Serpent. The One who is to bruise the head of the serpent is described again. The plough in this figure probably led to this constellation being called the Plough, as it is today on the continent.

The larger companion of our SHEEPFOLD awaits in URSA MAJOR.

URSA MAJOR
(THE GREATER SHEEPFOLD)

URSA MAJOR is usually seen today as either a larger bear[50], similar to the one described in URSA MINOR, or especially in America, as The Big Dipper. This name was given to the figure since its seven major stars form the figure of a dipper similar to those carried on the covered wagons during the settlement of the American West, to dip water from the water barrels. However, the original form was that of a Sheepfold.

---

50 According to Aratus, Jupiter secretly transferred both bears to heaven from a cave in Crete. (Crete has no bears, but both herds and flocks are plentiful there).

The sheep leaving the enclosure, form the handle of "the dipper;" significantly, they head toward the sickle in the hand of BOOTES. The sickle is the implement for harvesting grain or souls.

—NAMES FOR THE SIGN—

The Big Dipper, probably the best known of all constellations, was originally called by the Hebrews Ash and means The Assembled. Job mentions Arcturus with his sons incorporating the three bright stars in the handle as sheep following the shepherd figure, Bootes. The Arabs call this constellation Al Naish or Annaish, The Ordered or Assembled Together, (as in a Sheepfold).

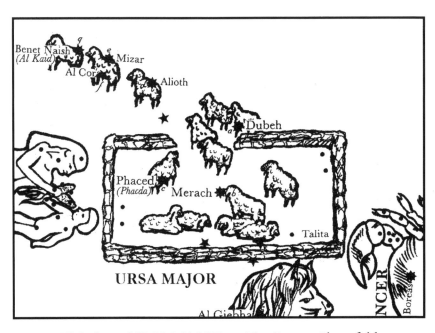

FIG. 43   URSA MAJOR   The Greater Sheepfold

—NAMES OF THE STARS—

The stars tell the same tale. The brightest star is Dubheh (Arabian) for a Herd of Animals. The second brightest star bears a Hebrew name Merach, meaning The Flock; the same in Arabic means The Purchased. The third brightest star is Phaced, or Phacda (Arabic) meaning Visited, Guarded, Numbered. (His people are like the stars of the heavens and the hairs upon their heads are both named and numbered).

The next brightest star is Alioth (Hebrew) represented by the sheep at the upper left corner of the sheepfold, meaning as it did in AURIGA, The She Goat, The Ewe (a type of the Church). The next brightest is the next sheep closer to BOOTES, and carries the name, Mizar meaning Separate or Small. In the same sheep is Al Cor (Arabic), The Lamb. The star closest to the Shepherd is next in order of brightness, Benet Naish (Arabic), The Daughters of The Assembly. This is also called Al Kaid (Arabic), The Assembled. The small star in the lower right corner of the sheepfold bears the name Talita or Talitha, The Little Lamb.[51]

The remaining unidentifiable stars all seem to echo the same message: El Acola (Arabic), The Sheepfold; Megrez (Hebrew), Separated, as The Fold, Cut Off in The Fold; Cab'd al Asad (Arabic), The Wealth of the Multitude; El Kaphrah (Arabic), The Protected, The Covered (this same name meant in Hebrew, The Redeemed, The Ransomed); Dubheh Lachar (Arabic), The Latter Flock. The Greeks gave names to four stars: Helike, meaning A Company of Travellers; Amaza, Coming and Going; Arctos, Travelling Company, and finally Calisto, The Sheepfold, Set or Appointed. The Latin name Ursa meant either The Bear or The Strong.

It is clear now that these two figures represent the two flocks of which Jesus spoke, the two segments of His body, which together contained all His sheep. But these sheep are not lost, nor in danger. They are safely in the folds, at rest, enjoying safety, the protection of the Shepherd, and are accompanied by the Lamb. They have been assembled, numbered, and are being guarded. They represent a great multitude.

---

51 This very word was used by Jesus in Mark 5:41 as he raised Jairus' daughter from the dead, saying to her, "Talitha, cumi."

DENDERAH

The Egyptians at Denderah presented URSA MAJOR as Fent-Har, The Enemy of the Serpent from *Fent*, Serpent and *Har*, Who Terrifies, thus The One Who Terrifies the Serpent. It is pictured as a female swine, natural enemy of the serpent, coming holding a ploughshare, the implement for bruising.

Therefore, Denderah illustrates the same theme; the final decan holds additional confirmation. But what could a ship have to do with such a message? We shall see in ARGO.

ARGO
(THE SHIP)

The third and final decan of Cancer presents the figure of a ship, ARGO. Its sails are furled and the rowing oars are forward as if the ship is about to be backed into its dock. The ship is adorned with two figures, the head of a Lion atop the stern of the ship looking forward toward the bow and toward LEO, the Lion in the next Sign. The second figure is the head of a man at the water line who appears to be bearing the entire ship on his back.

Of this great heavenly ship, Aratus the poet sang centuries ago.

"Stem-formost hauled; no mark of onward-speeding ship. Sternward she comes, as vessels do When sailors turn the helm On entering the harbour: all the oars backwater And gliding backward, to an anchor comes."

This is a picture of that glorious, heavenly homecoming of all the company of fellow strugglers, of all the pilgrims and saints who have completed their appointed rounds upon the earth and have won the right to a glorious homecoming.

FIG. 44   ARGO   The Ship

In myth and legend this was the ship of the argonauts who, along with Jason sought the golden fleece. The golden fleece was a treasure which desperately needed to be regained, having been lost to mankind, stolen by a clever, devious enemy. It symbolizes or was a perversion of the loss by mankind through Adam in the Garden, of that greatest of treasures—a close walking, talking relationship with God which was his right or gift because of innocence or his sinless state. It might be said of the argonauts that they were in reality seeking to regain what had been lost to them through sin: righteousness and a right relationship with God, the means by which they could reenter Paradise.

ARGO graphically represents the joyous, victorious completion of that journey and mission as the travellers return home, to enter that harbour of safety where no storm can touch them. The ship and its company of passengers are safely at rest in their homeport, with all the dangers of their journey behind them, all trials completed and the victory won. This company in the Ark, ARGO, with the True Jason at its helm, has reached its home port. Its destination is the Heavenly Zion which is similar to what was spoken by Isaiah:

> "Therefore the redeemed of the Lord shall return, and come with singing unto Zion; and everlasting joy shall be upon their head; they shall obtain gladness and joy, and sorrow and mourning shall flee away."
>
> **Isaiah 51:11**

All of the sixtieth chapter of Isaiah describes this glorious time, but especially the following verses appear relevant to the heavenly ship:

> "Lift up thine eyes round about, and see: all they gather themselves together, they come unto thee: thy sons shall come from far, and thy daughters shall be nursed at thy side. Then thou shalt see, and flow together, and thine heart shall fear, and be enlarged; because the abundance of the sea shall be converted unto thee, the forces of the gentiles shall come unto thee."
>
> **Isaiah 60: 4–5**

> "Who are these that fly as a cloud, and as the doves to their windows? Surely the isles shall wait for me, and the ships of Tarshish first, to bring thy sons from afar, their silver and their gold with them, unto the name of the Lord thy God, and to the Holy One of Israel, because he hath glorified thee, ... and they shall call thee, the city of the Lord, the Zion of the Holy One of Israel."
>
> **Isaiah 60: 8–9,14**

Part III - Kingdom and Judgment Established - ARGO

"The sun shall be no more thy light by day; neither for brightness shall the moon give light unto thee: but the Lord shall be unto thee an everlasting light, and thy God thy glory. Thy sun shall no more go down; neither shall thy moon withdraw itself; for the Lord shall be thine everlasting light, and the days of thy mourning shall be ended."

Isaiah 60:19–20

—NAMES FOR THE SIGN—

The most ancient Hebrew name for this figure was ARGO which meant The Company of Travellers. The same name and meaning were assigned to the constellation by the Greeks and the Romans.

Throughout the centuries some have seen in this heavenly ship a picture of Noah's Ark. Peter wrote that the Ark of Noah was a type, a figure for Jesus Himself, as well as the later catching away of God's people. That catching away would be God's vehicle for carrying His own away from His wrath, the final judgment. However, the eight persons aboard that vessel could hardly qualify as a multitude and therefore that interpretation must give place to the one we have taken here.

—NAMES OF THE STARS—

The stars chime the same chorus. The brightest star is Canopus (or Canobus), The Possession of Him Who Cometh. The star Markab is to be seen in the forepart of the hull and means in Hebrew Returning From Afar. The other stars in this constellation are not identified as to position, but bear significant Hebrew names, Sephina, The Multitude, Tureis, The Possession, and Asmidiska, The Released Who Travel. The final two stars bear Arabic names Soheil, The Desired, and Subilon, The Branch.

The names of the stars and the Sign make it clear that this ship represents a company of travellers, a multitude, the possession of Him who comes. The released multitude which travels is the possession of, or belongs to the Branch, the Desired One, whom we have found referred to in all the Signs since His first appearance in VIRGO. The Branch, with His redeemed multitudes out of every tribe, and tongue, and nation has returned to the home port—heaven—with His flock, that they might be with Him forever where He Himself is.

DENDERAH

At Denderah ARGO's place is occupied by a Sign entitled Shes-En-Fent meaning (*Shes* – The Son or Offspring; *En* – Rejoicing over; *Fent* – The Serpent), The One Who Comes Rejoicing Over the Serpent. The figure shown is that of a huge steer or bull (named *Ba*—Who Comes) with the ***crux ansata*** (the cross with the loop), the emblem of life, around its throat. This figure is reminiscent of TAURUS and the sacrifice which made Satan's defeat possible.

Additional insight may be obtained from another Zodiac, the one Kirchner presents in his Egyptian planisphere. Kirchner presents ARGO not as one but two large galley ships with ram's heads upon them. Two ships parallel the two sheepfolds in CANCER, URSA MAJOR and MINOR; and also the dual roles of the Lamb of God, as seen in ARIES. The last piece to the puzzle will be found in the glorious and majestic figure of LEO.

LEO
(THE LION)

The twelfth and final Sign of the Zodiac which will complete the story is LEO — The Lion. LEO is represented as a full grown, fine specimen of a beast not seated nor reclining, as so many of our figures have been seen, but rather springing up, about to pounce upon his prey.

The same figure is prefigured in the book of Revelation, the Lion of Judah rousing Himself. In the fifth chapter of Revelation there is description of One seated upon the throne of heaven with a book in his right hand, sealed with seven seals. That this greatly desired document was sealed, and none was found worthy to open the seals caused the Apostle John great grief. He wept greatly, because all of man's inheritance was unavailable to mankind, until he was comforted by one of the elders who said to him,

> "Weep not; behold, the Lion of the tribe of Judah, the Root of David, hath prevailed to open the book and to loose the seven seals thereon."
>
> Rev. 5:5

This greatly desired document was apparently figurative of the great treasure, the title-deed stolen through subtlety and deceit from mankind, through Adam, until a hero should come who had the power, wisdom and might to recover it. This title-deed contained the full restoration to mankind of his lost relationship with the Father, the absolution of the disinheritance which had taken place in the Garden at the fall, and the loosing of all the blessings of God upon His long-lost children. God the Father longed to restore to mankind the blessed state which He had envisioned for them, and in fact had given them at the beginning. However, the full restoration necessitated the coming of One worthy to loosen the seals. The seven seals indicate the complete separation and the estrangement of this document from mankind.

FIG. 45 LEO The Lion

But praise be to God, One has been found worthy. The Lion of the tribe of Judah is worthy!!!

> "And they sang a new song, saying, Thou art worthy to take the book, and to open the seals thereof: for thou wast slain, and has redeemed us to God by thy blood out of every kindred, and tongue, and people, and nation: and has made us unto our God kings and priests; and we shall reign on the earth."
>
> Rev. 5:9–10

In the Revelation account John writes that after the seals were broken open, the various judgments of God began to be poured out upon the earth, upon His enemies.

John had earlier been instructed to write what he beheld, and he wrote of the joy which he observed in heaven upon the opening of the seals and of the scroll. He was so instructed, I believe, in order that we in these last dark days might also have the hope of the glorious conclusion, in knowing that the Lion of the Tribe of Judah has prevailed, that the story will end in victory for the forces of right. The Army of the Lamb does win in the end, as the Elders saw and rejoiced. The same message can be read in this Sign in the heavens.

The earliest people saw in this Lion, this king of beasts, One whose coming was to be associated with violence and wrath being poured out upon the Lion's enemies and with a great flaming forth at them. When a lion's roar thunders through the jungle all his enemies shudder. So shall it be when the Lion of Judah rouses Himself, opens the seals, and pours forth His wrath upon His enemies.

This Coming One has been seen by His people as the Lamb, the Gentle Shepherd, and so He is; but that this gentle, meek, silent, and uncomplaining Lamb is capable of great wrath, the Scriptures also plainly state:

> "And the heavens departed as a scroll when it is rolled together; and every mountain and island were moved out of

their places.

"And the kings of the earth, and the great men, and the rich men, and the chief captains, and the mighty men, and every bondman, and every free man, hid themselves in the dens and in the rocks of the mountains;

"And said to the mountains and rocks, Fall on us, and hide us from … the wrath of the Lamb.

"For the great day of his wrath is come; and who shall be able to stand?"

Rev. 6:14–17

Scripture is also replete with references to the wrath and the fury of the Lion[52] when it is roused, as the coming of the wrath of God:

"Therefore, I will be unto them as a lion; as a leopard by the way will I observe them.

"I will meet them as a bear that is bereaved of her whelps, and I will rend the caul of their heart, and there will I devour them like a lion: the wild beast shall tear them."

Hos. 13:7–8

"And he said, the Lord will roar from Zion….

"Will a lion roar in the forest when he hath no prey?

"Surely the Lord God will do nothing, but he revealeth his secret unto his servants, the prophets.

"The lion hath roared; who shall not fear? the Lord God hath spoken who can but prophesy?"

Amos 1:2a, 3:4,7–8

---

52 Jesus, the Lion of Judah (Rev. 5:5 & Gen. 49:8–9), David a type (Ps. 18:6–17).

"The Lord shall go forth as a mighty man, he shall stir up jealousy like a man of war: he shall cry, yea, roar: he shall prevail against his enemies."

Isa. 42:13

"Now consider this, ye that forget God, lest I tear you in pieces, and there be none to deliver."

Ps. 50:22

"Therefore, wait ye upon me, saith the Lord, until the day that I rise up to the prey: for my determination is to gather the nations ... that I may pour upon them mine indignation, even all my fierce anger: for all the earth shall be devoured with the fire of my jealousy."

Zeph. 3:8

Thus the Scripture describes God coming forth in His awesome wrath. How does the Sign in the heavens echo this message?

—NAMES FOR THE SIGN—

LEO was known to the ancient Hebrews as Arieh, The Lion Rending or Tearing. To the Arabs he was Al Asad, The Lion Who Rends or Who Makes Waste. The Syrian name Aryo had the same meaning, The Lion Who Rends. The Coptic name for this figure was Pi-Mentekeon, The Plucking Asunder. The Greek word for lion, Leon as well as the Latin word Leo both were used as names for the Sign and the former word was used in writing the Scriptures[53]. The Latin name, when used in Hebrew, carries the same thought it does when used by the Arabs and Syrians, that of Leaping Forth as a Flame, or Coming Vehemently. It is used in that sense in Ex. 3:2 when referring to God speaking out of the burning bush.

—NAMES OF THE STARS—

The names of the stars continue the same thoughts. The brightest

---

53 (Sept. Gen. 49:9, N.T. Rev. 5:5)

star in Leo is Regel or Regulus (Hebrew) in the foreshoulder, meaning The Treading Under Foot. The next brightest star, located in the tail, is Denebola (Hebrew), The Judge or Lord Who Cometh Quickly. The third brightest is Al Giebha (Arab), The Exaltation, located at the top of the back in the mane. Two other Hebrew-named stars are Zosma, located at the highest part of the hindquarters, meaning The Shining Forth and Sarcam, The Joining.[54]

Three additional Arabic-named stars complete our list: Minchir al Asad, The Lion's Punishing, Tearing or Piercing; Denab Alaced, The Judge Who Cometh, Who Seizes; and finally Al Dafera, The Enemy Put Down. The latter phrase certainly indicates defeat for the enemy, but apparently implies even more, as this is a phrase still used today in referring to the putting to death of a horse.

The names in this Sign of LEO, echo the message read in Revelation: that One is coming forth with vehemence and great wrath, a mighty Lion who will rend and tear his enemies asunder. He shall also trample them under foot; His coming is that of a judge who will come quickly to punish, tear and seize the enemy, who will be completely put down. At the same time the coming will be a great shining forth, and an exaltation of the One coming!

By now we expect the three unlikely accompanying decans to have a parallel message.

---

54 This name, The Joining, points us back to the solution to the riddle of the Sphinx, and where to start our story: Sphinx means To Bind Closely Together, or to be joined.

HYDRA
(THE SERPENT)

The first decan of LEO begins the description of the consummation of the victory which He shall win. HYDRA is seen as a long winding serpent encompassing the entire right third of the heavenly circle. The long undulating body of this serpent has just one coil near the neck, but the body does have two other identifying features: near the center is a bird pecking at it, and a large two-handled cup placed upon it. LEO, in the act of pouncing, seems to be leaping upon the head of this serpent, HYDRA.

Initially, in mythology, Hydra was the female serpent, "The Mother of All Evil." Later the name and gender were changed to Hydrus but retained its evil character, and its meaning was rendered as "the Father of Lies." The ancient Persians called this constellation of a starry serpent, The Serpent of Eve! This is indeed Satan, although at the twilight of his career. No longer is the serpent grasping for power, throne, or crown, as we have previously seen him, but is rather fleeing for his very life from the wrath of the Lion.

> "And there was war in heaven: Michael and his angels fought against the dragon; and the dragon fought and his angels, And prevailed not; neither was their place found any more in heaven.
>
> "And the great dragon was cast out, that old serpent, called the Devil and Satan, which deceiveth the whole world: he was cast out into the earth, and his angels were cast out with him."
>
> **Rev. 12:7–9**

Thus LEO with his feet upon HYDRA's head, pictures the fulfillment of the prophecy that the Lion of Judah would come to trample underfoot, to rend, and to put all his enemies beneath his victorious feet.

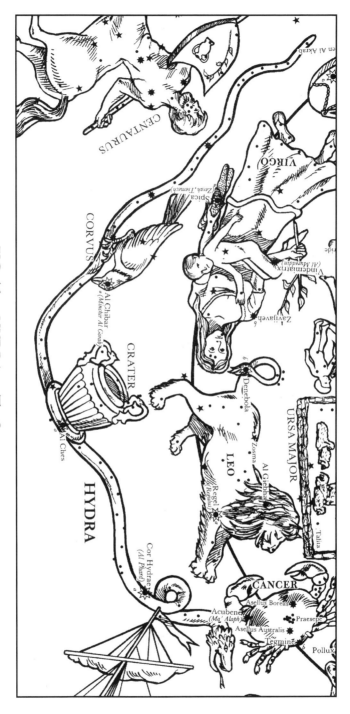

FIG. 46 HYDRA   The Serpent

—NAMES FOR THE SIGN—

The Sign names focus upon the serpent as the great enemy of God with clarity. The ancient Hebrew name for this sign, Hydra, means he is The Abhorred.

—NAMES OF THE STARS—

The brightest star in this constellation is located just behind the coil in the neck, and is called by modern astronomers by its Latin name, Cor Hydrae, The Heart of The Serpent, but its ancient Arabic name is of far more significance, Al Phard, meaning The Separated, or The Excluded, The Put Out of the Way. These are particularly fitting names: Satan is indeed the separated one, excluded from all the blessings of God, excluded from heaven at the beginning and to be eternally separated from God, at least until his final destruction. He is especially the one put out of the way, out of the way of the people of God, out of God's way, and out of the Way, as the people of God have been called the people of "The Way."

Two additional stars named by the Arabs are of interest: Al Drian, also means The Abhorred: Minchir al Sugia, meaning The Piercing, Punishing, or Tearing to Shreds of the Deceiver.

All the stars and names of the Sign agree that this is indeed the symbol of the end of the dominion of the serpent. The serpent's kingdom has been vanquished and brought down. The enemy, the serpent himself, has been excluded from fellowship with other forms of life and has become seen as he truly is, the Abhorred of God.

DENDERAH

This very thought is repeated in the names and figures of the ancient Denderah Zodiac. There HYDRA is presented as a serpent also under the Lion's foot. The hieroglyphic name *Knem* is beneath the figures of the Lion and serpent: Knem means He Who Triumphs or Conquers. From this word Knem are derived both the words "king" and "khan", the latter meaning fixed or established. Thus in Denderah, too, the point is plainly made that the coming Lion-King has defeated the serpent which is being trampled under foot.

What does the CUP indicate?

CRATER
(THE CUP)

The second decan, CRATER, The Cup, is composed of 13 stars; thirteen being the symbolic number for apostasy in the Scriptures. The cup, CRATER, is on the chart as a cup, or ancient mixing bowl for wine, with two handles. It has been placed upon the back of the serpent and is so closely fixed upon, or identified with, the serpent that the same stars are considered to be in both constellations.

The handles are formed by serpents spewing forth something from their mouths in our drawing, which is copied from a secular scientific publication, Jamieson's Celestial Atlas. Jesus used similar phraseology:

> " So then because thou art lukewarm, and neither cold nor hot, I will spue thee out of my mouth."
> **Rev. 3:16**

CRATER is that cup with which we have come to be familiar in Scripture, the cup of God's wrath!

> "For in the hand of the Lord there is a cup, and the wine is red; it is full of mixture; and he poureth out of the same: but the dregs thereof, all the wicked of the earth shall wring them out, and drink them."
> **Ps. 75:8**

> "Upon the wicked he shall rain snares[55], fire and brimstone, and an horrible tempest: this shall be the portion of their cup."
> **Ps. 11:6**

One must choose either to accept the cup of Salvation and fellowship with the Lord (symbolized by Communion), or else drink the cup of trembling and of His wrath. The cup of Salvation or the cup of wrath ... the choice is clear, one cup or the other shall be drunken from. For believers

---

55 quick burning coals

the choice is embodied in our blessed cup of Communion and the priority of fellowship with our God: in partaking of it we reaffirm the importance of His Body and Blood in our lives.

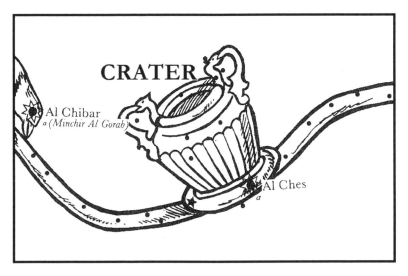

FIG. 47 CRATER The Cup

John, the Revelator, with whose writing we commenced our Scriptural consideration of LEO, also saw and described such a cup of God's wrath:

> "If any man worship the beast and his image, and receive his mark in his forehead, or in his hand, The same shall drink of the wine of the wrath of God, which is poured out without mixture into the cup of his indignation; and he shall be tormented with fire and brimstone in the presence of the holy angels, and in the presence of the Lamb."
>
> **Rev. 14:9b–10**

"And one of the four beasts gave unto the seven angels golden vials full of the wrath of God, who liveth forever and ever."

"And I heard a great voice out of the temple saying to the

seven angels, Go your ways, and pour out the vials (bowls) of the wrath of God upon the earth."

Rev. 15:7,16:1

"And the seventh angel poured out his vial into the air; and there came a great voice out of the temple of heaven, from the throne, saying, It is done."

"And the great city was divided into three parts, and the cities of all nations fell: the great Babylon came in remembrance before God, to give unto her the cup of the wine of the fierceness of his wrath"

Rev. 16:17,19

"And the devil that deceived them was cast into the lake of fire and brimstone, where the beast and the false prophet are, and shall be tormented day and night forever and ever."

Rev. 20:10

This Scripture describes the total destruction and elimination of the great enemy of God.

—NAMES FOR THE SIGN—

Both the Hebrews and the Arabians knew this Sign anciently as Al Ches, The Cup. This name was also the name of the brightest star in the constellation located on the right side. This star, along with the second brightest that has no name of which we are aware, form the base of the cup.

DENDERAH

The Egyptians of Denderah pictured CRATER as a female figure wearing a plume atop her head, holding a vase or cup in each hand. There are hieroglyphic characters beneath, which apparently mean Sent Forth or Poured Forth (as water from her vase). This plumed figure well may represent the angel seen by John in the passage just quoted, pouring forth the bowls of God's wrath upon an apostate world. The two cups could even indicate the double portion prescribed for Babylon:

> "Come out of her, my people, that ye be not partakers of her sins, and that ye receive not of her plagues. For her sins have reached unto heaven, and God hath remembered her iniquities. Reward her even as she rewarded you, and double unto her double according to her works: in the cup which she hath filled to her double."
>
> Rev. 18:4b–6

The message of CRATER is clear and consistent throughout. The time of the pouring forth of God's wrath has come, and its awesome contents must be allowed to fall upon the enemies and haters of God. This righteous judgment must come forth from the Throne of God that they might be totally destroyed and removed from the scene, eliminated, that the next phase of God's plan might be initiated.

The third decan, CORVUS, will accentuate and amplify the destruction of the great enemy, Satan, as the personification of his system or kingdom and as the representative of all his followers, who shall also be destroyed.

CORVUS
(THE RAVEN)

The final decan of the heavenly account portrays the fulfillment of the prophecy that the birds of the heavens would be summoned to feast upon the dead corpses of the enemies of God. We see CORVUS, The Raven, pictured slightly to the rear of the Cup pecking or feasting upon the flesh of the writhing body of the serpent.

> "And I saw an angel standing in the sun; and he cried with a loud voice, saying to all the fowls that fly in the midst of

heaven, Come and gather yourselves together unto the supper of the great God;

That ye may eat the flesh of kings, and the flesh of captains, and the flesh of mighty men, and the flesh of horses, and of them that sit on them, and the flesh of all men, both free and bond, both small and great."

Rev. 19:17–18

The final destruction of Satan and his armies is described graphically in this star picture as merely a corpse to be eaten by the birds of the air—a bit of despicable refuse upon the roadside, fit only for consumption by the carrion birds designed for such a task.

—NAMES FOR THE SIGN—

The Hebrews knew this Sign as Chima, The Accursed. The Arabians called the figure Al Gorab, The Raven.

—NAMES OF THE STARS—

The brightest star in this constellation is located in the eye of the raven, Al Chibar which means in Arabic The Joining Together. The same star was called Al Chiba in Hebrew meaning The Curse Inflicted, or The Accursed. Another star bore the Arabic name Minchir al Gorab and meant The Raven's Piercing or Tearing to Pieces.

Thus the stars' names and the picture unite again in relating the message: the Raven with its claws in the flesh and its beak piercing the body of the serpent points to Satan's death and destruction at the hands of the victorious King of Kings and Lord of Lords. It says to us, the battle is over, the conflict finished: what was uttered in the throne room in the presence of John is pictured here. The story is complete.

PART III - *Kingdom and Judgment Established* - *CORVUS*

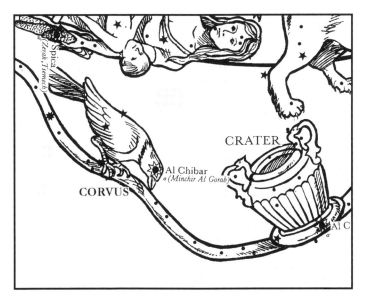

FIG. 48   CORVUS   The Raven

The body of the defeated enemy has been given over to the birds of the air as a thing totally undesired, undeserving of notice, honor or respect. It does not even merit burial, but rather is left as a bit of carrion for the bugs and birds—no one else has any interest in it. Even the skitterish carnivorous birds aren't afraid of him any longer. The bird isn't attacking, its wings are at its sides, calmly eating. This is almost exactly the scene proclaimed by Samuel of the situation at the defeat of Goliath by David (and the Lord).

> "This day will the Lord deliver thee into mine hand; and I will smite thee, and take thine head from thee; and I will give the carcases of the host of the Philistines unto the fowls of the air, and to the wild beasts of the earth; that all the earth may know that there is a God in Israel."
>
> **1 Sam. 17:46**

That is exactly what has happened in this scene. The head has already been taken figuratively by PERSEUS, HERCULES, and by ORION, and here the body is being consumed.

DENDERAH

The ancient Egyptians pictured CORVUS as a bird perched upon the body of the serpent behind the figure of a Lion. They named the figure aptly The Great Enemy and gave it the hieroglyphic name Her-Na. (*Her* we saw in Cancer meant Him Who Terrifies, and *Na* means to Fail or to Break). Thus this hieroglyphic name is The Great Enemy (Who Used To Terrify Us) Failing or Being Broken.

The great theme of the heavenly story is once again that which was outlined in Genesis 3:15. The ultimate conclusion of the great conflict between the seed of the woman and the seed of the serpent, is displayed in the heavens by the total devastation of the great enemy and the giving of his body to the birds and the beasts to feast upon. This one who so presumptuously attempted to set himself up against the God of heaven is disposed of without a shred of honor or respect!

Our God Reigns!!!!

THE TWELVE LABOURS

Literature, history and mythology all make reference to "the twelve labours of Hercules." These we have already seen to be perversions of truths about the Messiah. According to the legends, these twelve heroic deeds were performed by Hercules to improve the lot of mankind.

It is evident that God in His wisdom chose twelve emblematic figures in the heavens to represent twelve particular truths concerning the Messiah-Saviour. These Signs were designed to convey twelve major truths which God wanted the people of earth to know regarding His Messiah-Son whom He would send. The names of the Signs summarize the message, in the sacred language[56] by which they were known to our earliest ancestors.

It is as if the Lord had said to earliest man "When you behold the stars called...

THE VIRGIN

Remember the SEED of the woman is appointed to come, to be despised, to be pierced, but also to be The DESIRED, The KING, and the SHEPHERD-GUARDIAN of His people.

THE SCALES

Remember One who comes to pay a price in THE SCALES WEIGHING, that He might purchase His redeemed people. He will make that payment and finish His work upon THE CROSS, and will offer Himself up TO BE SLAIN, thereby winning A KINGLY CROWN.

---

56 Manetho, Egyptian historian during the reign of Ptolemy I and II, about 300 B.C., wrote of records preserved in the "sacred language" from before the flood. "When Manetho says that Hyk is 'king' in the sacred tongue, he identifies the sacred with the ancient Hebrew language." (Mazzaroth)

THE SCORPION

Remember Him engaging in THE CONFLICT with the ACCURSED enemy. While HOLDING THE SERPENT, He receives a bruise in His own heel, but do not forget that THE BRANCH KNEELING shall bring about THE WOUNDING and PUNISHING of the enemy.

THE ARCHER

Remember THE GRACIOUS ONE GOING FORTH as the Sent of God, who shall triumph in the end, SPRINGING UP AS THE FISHING EAGLE; although He must first be sacrificed as a Lamb upon THE ALTAR before defeating THE DRAGON and being exalted over all.

THE GOAT-FISH

Remember the Great Atonement Slain for us, CUT OFF but not for Himself, DESOLATE, WOUNDED, and falling, to rise again, and to raise and save His people from wrath by THE POURING OUT OF WATER.

THE WATER-POURER

Remember Him WHO GOES to heaven AND RETURNS to pour from THE WATER BUCKET the blessing of rivers of Living Water into the awaiting MOUTH OF THE FISH, representing His people. This is THE BRANCH, WHO RETURNS FROM AFAR, WHO RETURNS AS IN A CIRCLE and Who shall joyfully, and gloriously pour forth blessings.

THE FISHES

Remember Him who owns and upholds THE FISHES, the multitudes of His redeemed people, UNITED to Himself and to one another in THE BAND of love. He comes quickly, rejoicing, to reign as THE BRANCH, THE KING who shall rule in righteousness, when His CHAINED AND

AFFLICTED church shall be set free from bondage and from the power of the enemy.

THE LAMB

Remember THE LAMB SENT FORTH so that all might look upon Him that was bruised and pierced, that His people, His Bride might be raised up to His throne to be THE ENTHRONED with Him, being delivered from THE BOUND enemy by their Redeemer, THE BREAKER of their bonds.

THE BULL

Remember Him Who comes as THE BULL, THE APPOINTED JUDGE OR RULER, The Branch COMING FORTH AS LIGHT making available THE RIVER of Life, and as THE SHEPHERD of His flock.

THE TWINS

Remember He is THE UNITED, both as the Son of God with the Son of Man, and as One with His people; also that THE ENEMY OF HIM WHO COMES shall be put under the feet of Him who is to be both THE PRINCE and THE REDEEMER.

THE SHEEPFOLD

Remember THE ONE WHO HOLDS in a place of safety prepared for those faithfully AWAITING HIM WHO COMETH, the great company of the Lord's people, His possession in all ages and countries, the sheep of His fold, THE ASSEMBLED, THE COMPANY OF TRAVELLERS who will be caught up to be with Him forever.

THE LION

Remember Him as the Victorious LION of Judah triumphing over the ABHORRED enemy, who is seen firmly placed beneath His feet and receiving THE CUP of His wrath, which is THE CURSE INFLICTED and fulfilled.

This astounding message was written thousands of years ago in the stars by the hand of One who loved us so much that He wanted us to be sure to know the Truth when He came.

TITLE

The title of this book comes from Psalm 19:

> "The *heavens declare* the glory of God; and the firmament shewth his handiwork. Day unto day uttereth speech, and night unto night sheweth knowledge. There is no speech nor language, where their voice is not heard. Their line is gone out through all the earth, and their words to the end of the world. In them hath he set a tabernacle for the sun, Which is as a bridegroom coming out of his chamber, and rejoiceth as a strong man to run a race. His going forth is from the end of the heaven, and his circuit unto the ends of it: and there is nothing hid from the heat thereof."
>
> **Ps. 19:1–6**

The first half of this Psalm, quoted above tells that man should know and understand the existence of God because of his creative works. The latter half speaks of man knowing Him by means of His laws, His statutes, and His Word. The Holy Spirit gives a commentary upon this passage in the New Testament. In Romans we read:

> "So then faith cometh by hearing, and hearing by the word of God. But I say, Have they not heard? Yes verily, their sound went into all the earth, and their words unto the ends of the world."
>
> **Rom. 10:17–18**

This passage underscores and explains another passage in the first chapter of Romans, where it states that man is without excuse for not knowing and honoring God properly, for, it says "God hath shewed it (that which needs to be known of Him) to them."

May we be caused to see and to seek Him to whom the stars and Signs testify.

CONCLUSION

"And all the host of heaven shall be dissolved, and the heavens shall be rolled together as a scroll: and all their host shall fall down, as a leaf falleth off from the vine, and as a falling fig from the fig tree."

Isa. 34:4

"And the heaven departed as a scroll when it is rolled together..."

Rev. 6:14

The story is complete! The heavenly scroll upon which it has been recorded can now be rolled up as it will, one day soon for ever, when the earth shall be judged ... but while time remains, THERE IS STILL AN OPPORTUNITY TO RESPOND TO WHAT HAS BEEN LEARNED. This isn't the end... it can be the beginning!

If you feel that what we have found in the heavenly message is something more than mere coincidence, and

(1) that there has been an Intelligence behind the design, the numbering, and the naming of the stars and the Signs,

(2) that there has been a purpose in the careful preservation of these truths—even though by unbelievers and men of science who did not realize the significance of the message which they were preserving,

(3) that there is a message contained by design which calls attention prophetically to the Coming One, and

(4) if you have come to recognize that Coming One as JESUS CHRIST, the same One presented by God The Father in the Scriptures as the MESSIAH, the DOOR of the sheep, the OPENER of THE WAY into heaven ...

Then I encourage you to take a step further in the search for Truth and to carefully read the next section.

As a rational man, I must conclude that if only a few stars had possessed names which had been significant and referred to the Gospel account recorded in Scripture, it could have been coincidence. However, when hundreds have, and have fit so perfectly, so exactly with the other account, I must conclude that the Author of both is the same and Divine, and that I owe it to myself to get to know more about him.

SALVATION...
A RELATIONSHIP IS OFFERED

How You May Be Saved

Are you saved? This question may be one for which you have a clear-cut affirmative answer, or it may leave you unsure of where you stand, or to what it really refers. The question is simply asking you... Do you know Jesus Christ as your personal Lord and Saviour? Have you invited Him into your heart (Revelation 3:20), received forgiveness for all your sins, and been born again into life eternal? Do you know, for example, if you had been killed this morning in an auto accident, that right now you would be in the presence of Jesus? If you aren't sure, read on.

The question of salvation is an all-encompassing one, because when one understands what is being offered, when one is "saved" or "born again," it affects every aspect of your being: body, soul and spirit, not just for now but for all eternity.

There are several things that God wants us to know concerning ourselves, concerning His Nature, His provision and the relationship which He desires us to have with Him.

God Wants You To Know—That a Problem Exists

1. **All are sinners and no one can save himself.**
   "For all have sinned, and come short of the glory of God" (Romans 3:23).
   "There is none righteous: no, not one" (Romans 3:10).
2. **We are all under the sentence of death.**
   "For the wages of sin is death" (Romans 6:23).
   "Wherefore, as by one man sin entered into the world, and death by sin: and so death passed upon all men, for that all have sinned" (Romans 5:12).

God Wants You To Know—That a Solution Exists

3. Jesus has already provided a means of salvation.

"God commendeth his love toward us, in that, while we were yet sinners, Christ died for us" (Romans 5:8).

"God so loved the world, that he gave his only begotten Son, that whosoever believeth in him should not perish, but have everlasting life. For God sent not his Son into the world to condemn the world; but that the world through him might be saved" (John 3:16–17).

"For Christ also hath once suffered for sins, the just for the unjust, that he might bring us to God" (1 Peter 3:18).

God Wants You To Know—That You Must Do Something

4. **You must repent of your sins.** Repent means to confess them to Him and turn your back upon them.

"If we confess our sins, he is faithful and just to forgive us our sins, and to cleanse us from all unrighteousness" (1 John 1:9).

God Wants You to Know—Who Jesus Is

5. Jesus is God's Son.

"... I saw the Spirit descending from heaven like a dove, and it abode upon him ... And I saw and bare record that this is the Son of God" (John 1:32,34).

6. Jesus is God (He is divine: God in the flesh).

"For many deceivers are entered into the world, who confess not that Jesus Christ is come in the flesh. This is a deceiver and an antichrist" (2 John 7).

Salvation - A Relationship Is Offered

God Wants You To Know—
That Jesus Has Offered Salvation and All That it Entails

7. You have a decision to make.

"He that believeth on the Son hath everlasting life; and he that believeth not the Son shall not see life ..." (John 3:36).

"How shall we escape, if we neglect so great salvation? (Hebrews 2:3).

"Behold, I stand at the door, and knock: if any man hear my voice, and open the door, I will come in to him, and will sup with him, and he with me" (Revelation 3:20).

"But the gift of God is eternal life through Jesus Christ our Lord" (Romans 6:23b).

Eternal life can begin for you this very moment if you will make the decision to receive Jesus Christ.

How do we do it?
How do we accept Jesus' offer of salvation?

Paul tells us in Romans 10:9–11,13:

> "That if thou shalt confess with thy mouth the Lord Jesus, and shalt believe in thine heart that God hath raised him from the dead, thou shalt be saved. For with the heart man believeth unto righteousness; and with the mouth confession is made unto salvation. For the scripture saith, whosoever believeth on him shall not be ashamed. For whosoever shall call upon the name of the Lord shall be saved!"

There it is! Whosoever shall call upon His name. If you believe, you can now call upon His name and be saved! If you'd like to do that now, please pray with me:

"Lord, Jesus Christ, I confess to You now that I am a sinner, and that I cannot save myself—I need You. I cannot cleanse myself from my sins. I confess them to You and I am sorry for them all. I ask You now to forgive me for all my sins and to wash me and cleanse me of them with Your blood which You shed for me.

By a decision of my will, I now open the door of my heart to You and I invite You to come into my heart, to rule in my heart, as my Saviour, as my Lord, as my King, and as my God. I thank You now for coming into my heart and for the assurance of heaven when this life is over.

Amen."

If this book has been a blessing to you, and especially if you have decided to dedicate your life to the Divine Author of the message which The Heavens Declare ... please write us and let us rejoice with you.

What Is The Real Value Of These Truths

Certainly we do not need the gospel recorded in the stars to complete the revelation of Jesus Christ, nor to obtain Salvation, for these are made abundantly available to us through the Scripture. However, they are important for at least the following reasons:

1.) God has given them. He in His wisdom has provided them as Signs for mankind. Therefore, it ill-behooves us to ignore them.

2.) They corroborate the account recorded in Scripture (not that we as believers need corroboration, but unbelievers and sceptics may thus be reached).

3.) They serve to build faith and to strengthen love and appreciation of the power of God, who is able to tell things in advance of their happening in great detail which He has also said He would:

"And now I have told you before it comes to pass, that, when it is come to pass, ye might believe." **Jn. 14:29**

God has chosen to abundantly confirm and prove His own word to us by prophetically predicting in advance things to come. He has even given as a test of a prophet's authenticity, that the thing prophesied must come to pass (Deut. 18:20–22).

4.) It is a blessing to know that God so loves and cares for us that He has left yet another message for us. His desire to communicate further demonstrates His love and concern toward us. The discovery of this message is somewhat similar to finding a letter from a deceased loved one. Even though it tells nothing new, it serves as a reminder of the departed's love.

5.) These accounts can also provide another means of reaching the lost, and unlocking the jail doors of those held prisoner by Satan in the clutches of the occult bondage of astrology.

These truths serve to restore to us ground that has been yielded to Satan and his forces. Christians should not fear the figures in the heavens for all the starry host testify to the God of the Bible. "The Heavens Declare the glory of God."

This information if used properly and lovingly will provide an effective tool for witnessing to those ensnared by astrology. Shortly after teaching this material for the first time early in 1974, a woman who had attended several of the sessions introduced me to her daughter. She told me in an aside that the young woman was "deeply into astrology" and unwilling to receive anything that had to do with the Lord.

I complimented the daughter on the beauty of the solid gold Aquarius pendant which she was wearing and asked if she'd be interested in hearing about the True Aquarius? She responded in the affirmative and I led her to our prayer room. After a brief discussion of the truths contained in the original zodiac figure which led into an explanation of Salvation, she accepted Jesus as her personal Lord and Saviour. Several people who have heard this teaching have returned to tell of being able to witness to members of their families because they knew these truths. There is tremendous power for witnessing resident within these truths!

What About Astrology?

Many have embraced the teachings of astrology and relied upon its premise of revealing the future. However, many have also come to see the fallacy of its claims. St. Augustine was such a one. He wrote that he gave up astrology upon learning that a wealthy landowner and a slave on the landowner's estate were born at exactly the same time.

Augustine's reasoning is similar to the fallacy represented in the case of identical twins who should, according to astrological logic, have identical tendencies, life styles, and lives, but most often do not.

The Bible is even stronger, not basing its refutation of astrology simply upon the inaccuracy of it, but rather upon God's prohibition against it, as a rejection of Him and His will.

> "And when they say unto you, seek unto them that have familiar spirits, and unto wizards that peep, and that mutter: should not a people seek unto their God?
>
> Isa. 8:19

The Bible recognizes that some do foolishly believe in astrology, but warns both the faithful and the foolish not to be deceived:

"... Learn not the way of the heathen, and not be dismayed at the signs of heaven; for the heathen are dismayed at them."

Jer. 10:2

"Great trouble shall... come upon thee ... for the abundance of thy sorceries, and for the great abundance of thine enchantments. For thou hast trusted in thy wickedness:

"Thou hast said, None seeth me. Thy wisdom and thy knowledge, it hath perverted thee... Stand now with thine enchantments, and with the multitude of thy sorceries ... Let now thy astrologers, the stargazers, the monthly prognosticators" (horoscopes = monthly prognostications) "stand up and save thee ... they shall be as stubble ... none shall save thee."

Isa. 47:9–15

"When thou art come into the land which the Lord thy God giveth thee, thou shalt not learn to do after the abominations of those nations. There shalt not be found among you anyone ... that useth divination (fortune-telling) or an observer of times (casters of horoscopes)... for all that do these things are an abomination unto the Lord."

Deut. 18:9–10

A further example of the true source of the power behind fortune-telling and of God's stand against it is to be found in the book of Acts, where we read that Paul cast out a spirit from a young girl possessed with a spirit of divination. The spirit was called divination (or fortune-telling) which is when someone can supernaturally discern the future but not by the power of God. Otherwise, a man of God would not, nor could not, cast out such a spirit.[57]

---

57 Acts 16:16-18. For additional truth about casting out spirits, see *Pigs in the Parlor*. And for information on Familiar Spirirs, see *Confronting Familiar Spirits*. Both are by Frank Hammond.

God in His word is equally explicit in forbidding the worship of the figures or the stars of the heavens (called Sabatinism), in passages such as the following:

> "But ye have borne the tabernacle of your Moloch and Chiun; your images, the star of your god, which ye have made unto yourselves. Therefore will I cause you to go into captivity..."
>
> **Amos 5:26–27b**

Astrology is also illogical because of the astronomical principle of the *precession of the equinoxes*[58]. Simply stated, this refers to the effect caused by the gradual change in the direction of the earth's axis of rotation, which causes the planetary bodies to move in relation to the earth about 50.2" per year and therefore to take approximately 25,800 years to return to the same point of observation.

This truth strikes a death blow to the very heart of astrology, for today when the sun is supposed to be in Aries as at the vernal equinox, it is really in Pisces. So, if you were told that you were a Gemini, then you are instead a Taurus, for the movement amounts to about thirty days or a full Sign.

It is not difficult to see why the scientific community has so little regard for this pseudoscience, and it is clear from all we've seen why Christianity stands opposed to it.

> "All things work together for good to them that love God, to them who are the called according to his purposes."
>
> **Rom. 8:28**

The truth of this Scripture can be applied here. God could use even the distorted purposes of those practicing the ancient art of astrology — with which He forbade His people to be involved — to preserve truths about Himself which He had chosen to reveal in the star names. The source

---

58 This truth of the "precession of the equinoxes" was well known to the early Babylonian astronomers, which gives a further indication of how well developed their grasp of the science was.

is unimpeachable from the standpoint of bias; those espousing astrology are opposed to the claims of Salvation and the promises of Jesus Christ, preferring to rely upon fatalistic guidance from the stars rather than the answer to prayer.

A person who believes that his or her life has been programmed unalterably into the stars from the moment of birth (or point of conception depending upon which brand of astrological interpretation you prefer) would find little merit (or hope) in prayer, having been taught that "the die is cast" and that his or her kismet, karma, or fate is fixed.

Christianity, on the other hand, presents the offer of a living relationship with Him who can change your destiny! May the Divine author of the heavenly story cause you to seek Him evermore.

Map of the Heavens

Spanning the following two pages is a complete map of the heavens. This includes the 12 major constellations and their associated Decans.

We have placed a slight repeat on the right hand page of the diagram so that no pictorial information is lost in the fold of the book. This way, each constellation and decan can be seen in their entirety.

The Heavens Declare

252

The Heavens Declare

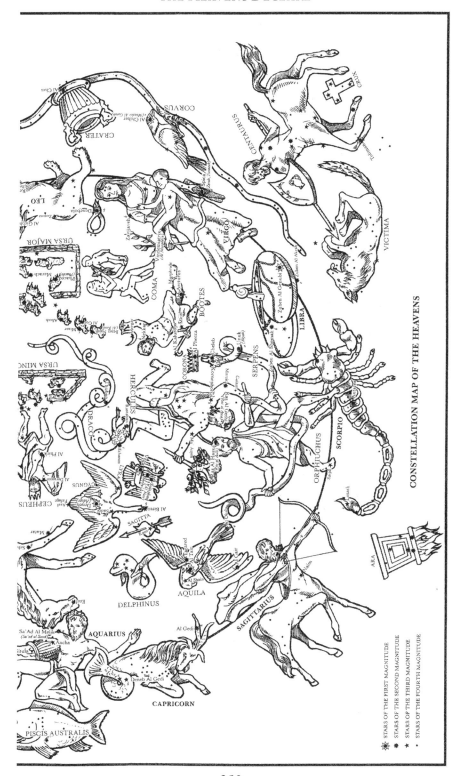

CONSTELLATION MAP OF THE HEAVENS

BIBLIOGRAPHY

Adam, Ben	*Astrology: The Ancient Conspiracy* (Originally *The Origin of Heathendom*)	USA, 1963 England, 1937
Baird, J. A.	*The Power of the Gospel*	USA, 1982
Baker/Zim	*Stars, Rediscovering*	USA, 1951
Bayne, Samuel G.	*Pith of Astronomy*	NY & London, 1896
Bjornstad/Johnson	*Stars, Signs & Salvation in the Age of Aquarius*	USA, 1971
Broome, J. H.	*Astral Origin of the Emblems*	London, 1881
Broome, J. H.	*On the Signs of the Zodiac*	London, 1861
Brown, R.	*Phainomena*	London, 1885
Browne, R.	*A System of Theology*	London, 1728
Budge, E. W.	*Babylonian Life & History*	London, 1884
Bulfinch, T.	*Bulfinch's Mythology*	USA, 1979 (1855)
Bullinger, E. W.	*The Witness of the Stars*	London, 1893
Bullinger, E. W.	*Names & Order of the Books of the Bible*	London, 1895
Bunsen, J. B.	*Egypt's Place in Universal History*	London, 1848
Clayton, P. A.	*The Rediscovery of Ancient Egypt*	Grt. Britain, 1982
Dent, C.	*The Testimony of the Stars*	London, 1879
Dent, C.	*Letters* (of F. Rolleston)	London, 1867
Dilitzsch, F.	*Babel & The Bible*	London, 1903
Drummond, Sir W.	*Origines*	London, 1824
Drummond, Sir W.	*Two Discourses*	London, 1809
Dupuis, C. F.	*Was Christ a Person or the Sun?*	London, 1857
Edwards, A. B.	*A Thousand Miles Up the Nile*	London, 1982 (1877)
Faber, G. J.	*Origin of Pagan Idolatry Vol. I.*	Grt. Britain, 1816
Flamsteed, J.	*Catalog of Stars*	London, 1798
Flamsteed, J.	*An Account of the Rev. John Flamsteed*	London, 1835

Bibliography

Frazer, J. G.	*The Golden Bough*	USA, 1890-1981
Gall, J.	*An Easy Guide to the Constellations*	London, 1870
Hawkins, G. S.	*Stonehenge Decoded*	Glasgow, 1965
Horsley, Bishop	*Nine Sermons*	London, 1815
Jamieson, A.	*A Celestial Atlas*	London, 1822
Jones, Owen	*Views on the Nile*	London, 1843
Kang/Nelson	*The Discovery of Genesis*	St. Louis, 1979
Lamb	*The Phenomena & Dionesia* (translation of Aratus)	London, 1848
Lewis, Sir G. C.	*An Historical Survey of the Astronomy of the Ancients*	London, 1862
Mansoor, M.	*Biblical Hebrew*	USA, 1977
Martin, M. E.	*The Friendly Stars*	USA, 1907 & 1964
Maunder, E. W.	*Astronomy of the Bible*	London, 1908
Miller, H.	*Testimony of the Rocks*	London, 1857
Osburn, W.	*Ancient Egypt*	London, 1846
Osburn, W.	*Religions of the World*	London, 1857
Pember, G.	*Earth's Earliest Ages*	London, 1876
Richardson, D.	*Eternity in Their Hearts*	USA, 1981
Roberts, P.	*Christianity Vindicated in Series of Letters*	London, 1800
Rolleston, F.	*Mazzaroth: Or, The Constellations*	*London, 1862-1875*
Seiss, J.	*Gospel in the Stars*	Phila., 1855-1885
Smyth, W. H.	*Cycle of Celestial Objects*	London, 1881
Smyth, W. H.	*Popular Astronomy, Vol. I, II.*	London, 1855
Steidl, P.	*The Earth, The Stars, and The Bible*	USA, 1979
Watts, Isaac	*Knowledge of the Heavens & The Earth*	London, 1760
Webb, E. J.	*Names of the Stars*	London, 1952
Williams, I.	*Genesis—Selections*	London, 1861

Index of Star & Sign Names

Name	Definition	Location
Aar	A Stream	P. Aust.
Abur	The Mighty	Can Mj.
Achernar	The After Part of the River	Eridan
Acubene	The Sheltering, or Hiding Place	Cancer
Adarah	The Pure Virgin	Virgo
Adhara	The Glorious	Can Mj.
Adhil	The Afflicted	Androm
Adige	Flying	Cygnus
Adom	The Cutting Off	Crux
Adrenosa	The Virgin Who Carries	Coma
Afeichus	The Serpent Held	Orphiu.
Aiyuk	Wounded In The Foot	Auriga
Akrab	The Conflict	Scorpio
Al Adra	The Glorious	Can Mj.
Al Akrab	Wounding Him Who Cometh	Scorpio
Al Asad	The Lion Who Rends, or Who Makes Waste	Leo
Al Azal	The Branch or Shoot	Virgo
Al Beze	The Despised	Centau.
Al Bireo	Flying Quickly	Cygnus
Al Cair	The Piercing	Aquila
Al Ches	The Cup	Crater
Al Chiba	The Curse Inflicted, The Accursed	Corvus
Al Chibar	The Joining Together	Corvus
Al Cor	The Lamb	Urs.Maj.
Al Cyone	The Center	Taurus
Al Dabih	The Sacrifice Slain	Capric.
Al Dafera	The Enemy Put Down	Leo
Al Debar an	The Leader, or The Governor	Taurus
Al Derab (Al Deraf)	Coming In A Circle	Cepheus
Al Deramin	Coming Quickly As In A Circle	Cepheus
Al Dib	The Reptile	Draco
Al Dira	The Seed, or Branch	Gemini
Al Drian	The Abhorred	Hydra

Al Dshabeh	The Slaying of The Sacrifice	Capric.
Al Gebor	The Mighty	Orion
Al Gedi	The Kid	Urs.Min.
Al Gedi	The Kid, or Goat	Capric.
Al Genib	Who Carries Away	Perseus
Al Genib	Who Carries	Pegasus
Al Ghoul	The Evil Spirit	Perseus
Al Giauza	The Palm Branch, or Stem	Gemini
Al Giauza	The Branch	Orion
Al Giebha	The Exaltation	Leo
Al Giscale	The Strong One	Hercul.
Al Gomeisa	The Burdened, The Loaded, Bearing For Others	Can.Mi.
Al Gomeyra	Him Who Completes Or Perfects	Can.Mi.
Al Gorab	The Raven	Corvus
Al Gubi	Heaped Up, High	Libra
Al Habor	The Mighty	Can.Mj.
Al Hamal	The Sheep Gentle, and Merciful	Aries
Al Henah	The Hurt, or Afflicted	Gemini
Al Himarein	The Kids, or Lambs	Cancer
Al Haut	The Fish	Pisces
Al Iclil	An Ornament, or Jewel	Corona
Al Kaid	The Assembled	Urs.Maj.
Al Kaid	The Assembled	Urs.Min.
Al Katurops	The Shepherd's Crook	Bootes
Al Kaus	The Arrow	Sagitta
Al Maach (Al Amak)	The Struck Down	Androm.
Al Mara	The Afflicted	Androm.
Al Mirzam	The Prince, The Ruler	Orion
Al Mirzam	The Prince, or Ruler	Can.Mi.
Al Mosealah	Delivered To The Grave, Sheol, Hades, or Hell	Androm.
Al Mugamra	The Completing, or The Finishing	Ara
Al Mureddin	Who Shall Come Down, Who Shall Have Dominion	Virgo
Al Nagjed	The Prince, The Wounded	Orion
Al Naim	The Gracious One	Sagitt.

Al Naim, Al Sadira	The Gracious One Who Strives	Sagitt.
Al Naish (Annaish)	The Ordered, or Assembled Together	Urs.Maj.
Al Nesr	The Eagle	Lyra
Al Nitak	The Wounded	Orion
Al Okab	Wounded in the Heel	Aquila
Al Oneh	The Subdued, The Weakened	Perseus
Al Phard	The Separated, The Excluded, The Put Out of the Way	Hydra
Al Phecca	The Shining	Corona
Al Pherkadain	The Calves	Urs.Min.
Al Phiratz	The Broken Down	Androm.
Al Phirk	The Redeemer	Cepheus
Al Rai	The Bruising	Orion
Al Rai (or Errai)	He Who Bruises Or Breaks, The Shepherd	Cepheus
Al Risha	The Band, or Bridle	Band
Al Ruccaba	The Pole Star, The Gate of the Enemy, The Turned Upon	Urs.Min.
Al Samaca	The Upheld	Pisces
Al Sartan	The One Who Holds, or Binds	Cancer
Al Shain	The Bright, or The Scarlet Colored	Aquila
Al Shaula	The Dart	Sagitt.
Al Sheratan	The Bruised, The Wounded	Aries
Al Shira, Al Jemeniya	The Prince, or Chief of The Right Hand	Can.Mj.
Al Shira, Al Shemeliya	The Prince, or Chief of the Left Hand	Can.Mi.
Al Tair	The Wounding	Aquila
Al Tauman	The Twins, The Pair, The Completely Joined	Gemini
Al Thaur	The Bull Coming	Taurus
Al Thuraiya	The Abundance	Taurus
Al Waid	Him Who Is About To Be Destroyed	Draco
Al Warida	The One Who Comes Forth	Sagitt.

Index of Star & Sign Names

Al Zubena	The Purchase, Redemption, or Gain	Libra
Algol (Al Ghoul)	Coming and Going, Rolling Around (i.e. The Head)	Perseus
Alioth	The Ewe, or She Goat	Auriga
Alioth	The She Goat, The Ewe	Urs.Maj.
Almah	The Virgin	Virgo
Aludra	The Glorious	Can.Mj.
Alyah	The Accursed	Serpe
Amaza	Coming, and Going	Urs.Maj.
Amroo	The Lamb	Aries
An-nas-sur-ra	High In Rising: i.e In Heavenly Position	Urs.Min.
Ancha	The Vessel of Pouring Out, The Urn	Aquari.
Andromeda	The Chained Woman, Set Free From Death	Androm.
Antares	The Wounding	Scorpio
Apes	The Head Commanding, Swiftly Coming Down In Victory	Can.Mj.
Api-Aatl	The Strong Chief, Chief of the Strong	Corona
Api-Bau	The Chief, or Head, Who Cometh	Orphiu.
Api-Fent	The Head Of The Serpent	Urs.Min.
Apis	The Head or Chief Who Cometh	Taurus
Apollo (Castor)	The Ruler, or Judge Coming In Haste	Gemini
Aquarius	The Rising Up of, or The Pouring Forth of Water	Aquari.
Ara	The Altar	Ara
Aram	Utter Destruction, Curse	Ara
Areas, Arctos	The Travelling Company	Urs.Min.
Arctophylax	The Guardian of The Arctos, The Greater Flock	Bootes
Arctos	A Travelling Company	Urs.Maj.
Arcturus	He Cometh	Bootes
Arc turns	The Assembled	Urs.Maj.
Argo	The Company Of Travellers	Argo

Arided	He Shall Come Down	Cygnus
Arieh	The Lion Rending, or Tearing	Leo
Aries	The Lamb, Coming Forth	Aries
Arnebeth	The Hare	Lepus
Arnebo	The Enemy Of Him That Cometh	Lepus
Aryo	The Lion Who Rends	Leo
Aschere	Who Shall Come	Can.Mj.
Asedah	To Be Slain	Victima
Asedaton	To Be Slain	Victima
Asellus Australis	The Southern She-Ass	Cancer
Asellus Boreas	The Northern She-Ass	Cancer
Ash	The Assembled	Urs.Maj.
Asmeath	A Sin-Offering	Centaur.
Asmidiska	The Released Who Travel	Argo
Aspolia	The Place Of The Desired Branch	Virgo
Ataroth	A (King's) Crown	Corona
Atatah	A Kingly (Royal) Crown	Corona
Athik	Who Breaks	Perseus
Auriga	The Shepherd	Auriga
Auriga	The Conductor of The Reins	Auriga
Azel	Who Goes and Returns Quickly	Cygnus
Baraziggar	The Altar, or The Sacrifice of Righteousness	Aries
Bashti-Beki	Confounded, Failing: The Failing of the Enemy Confounded	Lepus
Baten Kaitos	From the Belly of the Whale	Cetus
Bau	The One Who Cometh	Hercul.
Bau	The Coming One	Bootes
Bau	He Who Cometh	Ara
Bellatrix	One Hastily Coming	Orion
Benet Naish	The Daughters of the Assembly	Urs.Maj.
Bershaush	The Breaker	Perseus
Betelguez	The Coming of the Branch	Orion
Bethulah	The Virgin	Virgo
Bethulto	The Virgin	Virgo
Bezeh	The Despised	Centaur.
Biham	A Flock of Kids or Lambs	Pegasus

Bootes	He Cometh, The Coming One	Bootes
Cab'd al Asad	The Wealth of the Multitude	Urs.Maj.
Caiam	The Treading Underfoot	Hercul.
Calisto	The Sheepfold, Set or Appointed	Urs.Maj.
Cancer	The Crab Encircling	Cancer
Canopus (or Canobus)	The Possession of Him Who Cometh	Argo
Capella	The She Goat	Auriga
Caph	The Branch	Cassio.
Capricorn	The Goat	Capric.
Carnebus	The Wounding	Orphiu.
Castor	The Ruler, or Judge: Coming In Haste	Gemini
Cephus	The Branch, The King	Cepheus
Cephus	The Branch	Cepheus
Cetus	The Sea Monster	Cetus
Cheicus (or Caucus)	To Come as in a Circle	Cepheus
Cheleb Afei,	Aesculapius, Orphiuchus; The Serpent Holder	Orphiu.
Cheleb, Chelbalrai	The Serpent Enfolding	Serpen.
Chiba	The Accursed	Corvus
Chima	The Pleiades, The Heap, or The Accumulation	Taurus
Chiron	The Executer	Sagitt.
Chiron (or Cheiron)	The Pierced, or Who Pierces	Centaur.
Claustrum Hori	The Station or Place of the Coming One	Gemini
Clusus	The Station or Place of the Coming One	Gemini
Coma	The Desired, The Longed For	Coma
Cor Hydrae	The Heart of the Serpent	Hydra
Cor Scorpii	The Heart of the Scorpion	Scorpio
Corona	(Corona Borealis) The Crown, The Northern Crown	Corona
Corona Borealis	The Northern Crown	Corona
Croton	The Purchaser	Sagitt.
Cursa	Bent Down	Eridan.

Cygnos	The Swan Circling	Cygnus
Cygnus	Who Comes and Goes, or Circles	Cygnus
Cynosura	The Center, The Center of the Constellations	Urs.Min.
Dagim	The Fishes	Pisces
Dalaph	Pouring Out Of Water	Delphin.
Dalaph	Coming Quickly	Delphin.
Dat Al Cursa	The Set (Queen) Enthroned	Cassio.
Deli	The Water Urn	Aquari.
Delphinus	The Dolphin	Delphin.
Deltoton	The Triangle, or High (Arab = Lifted Up)	Aries
Delu	The Water Urn	Aquari.
Deneb	The Lord, or Judge Cometh	Aquila
Deneb	The Lord, or Judge Cometh	Cygnus
Deneb Al Gedi	The Lord, Judge, or Sacrifice Cometh	Capric.
Deneb Aleced	The Judge Who Cometh, Who Seizes	Leo
Deneb Kaitos	The Judge of Cetus Cometh (mod. Arab. Tail of the Whale)	Cetus
Dene bo la	The Judge, or Lord Who Cometh Quickly	Leo
Desma	The Bound	Androm.
Didumoi	The Twins	Gemini
Diphda	The Overthrown	Cetus
Drakon	Trodden Down	Draco
Dubheh	Herd Of Animals	Urs.Maj.
Dubheh Lachar	The Latter Flock	Urs.Maj.
El Areola	The Sheepfold	Urs.Maj.
El Asieh	The Bowed Down	Draco
El Athik	The Fraudful	Draco
El Kaphrah	The Protected, The Covered	Urs.Maj.
El Kaphrah	The Redeemed, The Ransomed	Urs.Maj.
El Nath	The Wounded, The Slain	Auriga
El Nath	The Wounded, or The Slain	Taurus
El Natik (El Nath)	The Wounded or The Slain	Aries

Enif	The Branch	Pegasus
Eridanus	The River of the Judge or Ruler	Eridan.
Ethanin (or Etanino)	The Long Serpent or Dragon	Draco
Fafage	The Glorious Shining Forth	Cygnus
Fent-Har	The One Who Terrifies the Serpent	Urs.Maj.
Fent-Kar	The Serpent Ruled	Lyra
Fent-Kar	Fent—Serpent; Kar—Enemy	Sagitta
Fom Al Haut	(Fomalhaut) The Mouth of The Fish	P. Aust.
Gedi	The Kids	Auriga
Gedi	The Kid, or Cut Off, Hewn Down; A Sacrifice Slain	Capric.
Gemini	The Twins	Gemini
Gemma	The Pearl	Corona
Giansar	The Punished Enemy	Draco
Graffias	Swept Away	Libra
Grumian	The Subtle	Draco
Guiam, or Caiam	Punishing	Hercul.
Ha-Ga-T	This Chief Triumphs	Orion
Haeniochos	The Driver, or The Charioteer	Auriga
Harpocrates	Justice, or Victim of Justice	Victim
Hazanethon	The Branch	Coma
Heke	Coming	Orion
Helike	A Company of Travellers	Urs.Maj.
Her-Fent	The Serpent Accursed	Draco
Her-Na	Him Who Terrifies The Great Enemy Broken	Corvus
Herakles	The Mighty Man	Hercul.
Hercules	The Mighty Man	Hercul.
Hercules (Pollux)	This One Comes To Suffer	Gemini
Homan	The Water	Pegasus
Horias	The Traveller Who Comes to Save	Taurus
Horus	The Coming One	Victim
Hupei Tirion	The Station of The Pouring Out; or Place of His Coming Down	Aquari.
Hupenius	The Station of Bearing, (or Place of Birth)	Capric.

Hyades	The Congregated	Taurus
Hydra	The Abhorred	Hydra
Hydrokoeus	The Pourer Forth of Water	Aquari.
Hyk	The King	Cepheus
Icythus	The Fish	Pisces
Isidis	Attack of The Enemy	Scorpio
Isis	One Who Saves Mightily	Taurus
Kaphar	To Cover (Atonement)	Libra
Kar Knem	Who Fights; The Bruised, Trodden Upon	Perseus
Karkinos	The Crab; Holding, Encircling The Possession	Cancer
Kaus (or Al Kaus)	The Arrow	Sagita
Kesil (or Chesil)	Orion: Bound Together, Constellations, The Burly One	Orion
Kesith	The Bending of The Bow	Sagitt.
Khan	Traveller's Resting Place, or Inn	Cancer
Khau	The Longed For; A Multitude, Fish, or Hoped For	Delphin.
Khu-or-Bakh	The Enemy Ruled, Bowed Down	Scorpio
Knem	He Conquers	Sagitt.
Knem	He Who Triumphs or Conquers	Hydra
Knem + Kannu	The Subdued, The Bruised + Victory	Cetus
Knemu	The Appointed Dieth, Is Bruised	Centaur.
Komephorous	The Branch Kneeling	Hercul.
Krios	The Lamb	Aries
Klaria	The Cattle Folds	Cancer
Kochab	Waiting Him Who Cometh	Urs.Min.
Lepus	The Hare, Treading Underfoot	Lepus
Lesath	The Perverse	Scorpio
Libra	The Scales	Libra
Lupus	The Wolf	Victima
Lycos	The Wolf	Victima
Ma'alaph	Assembled Thousands	Cancer
Ma'asad	The Slaying, The Destroying	Capric.
Ma'asym	The Sin-Offering	Hercul.

Maaz	The Flock of Goats, Kids	Auriga
Mara	Utter Destruction, Curse	Ara
Markab	Returning From Afar	Argo
Markab	Returning From Afar	Pegasus
Marsic	The Wounding	Hercul.
Matar	To Cause To Overflow (Mod. Arab. Lucky Star of the Rain)	Pegasus
Mebsuta	Treading Underfoot	Gemini
Medusa	The Trodden Underfoot	Perseus
Megeros	Contending	Orphiu.
Megrez	Separated, as in The Fold; Cut Off in the Fold	Urs.Maj.
Meissa	Coming Forth	Orion
Menkalinon	The Band, or Chain of The Goats or Ewes	Auriga
Menkar	The Bound, or Chained Enemy	Cetus
Merach	The Flock	Urs.Maj.
Merach	The Purchased	Urs.Maj.
Merga	Who Bruises	Bootes
Mesartim	The Bound, or The Binding	Aries
Minchir al Asad	The Lion's Punishing, Tearing, or Piercing	Leo
Minchir al Gorab	The Raven's Piercing, or Tearing To Pieces	Corvus
Minchir al Sugia	The Piercing, Punishing, or Tearing To Shreds of Deceiver	Hydra
Mintaka	Dividing The Belt	Orion
Mira	The Rebel	Cetus
Mirac (Mizar)	The Coming Forth as an Arrow	Bootes
Mirach	The Weak	Androm.
Leo	The Lion	Leo
Leon	The Lion	Leo
Mirfak	Who Helps	Perseus
Misam al Thuraiya	(Nebula)	Androm.
Mizar	The Bound	Androm.
Mizar (or Izar)	The Preserver, or Guardian	Bootes
Mirzam	The Prince	Can.Mj.

Mizar	Separate, or Small	Urs.Maj.
Mozanaim	The Scales Weighing	Libra
Muliphen	The Leader, or The Chief	Can.Mj.
Murphride	Who Separates	Bootes
Naim	The Gracious (or Delighted In)	Sagitt.
Nekkar	The Pierced	Bootes
Nepa	Grasping	Cancer
Nibal	The Mad	Lepus
Niphla	The Mighty, or The Mighty Coming	Orion
Nun-Ki	The Prince of The Earth	Sagitt.
Nuno	The Fish Lengthened Out (As In Posterity)	Pisces
Nushata	The Going or Sending Forth	Sagitt.
Nux	The Strong, or The Strong Coming Forth	Orion
Oar (Oarion)	(Ancient Name For Orion) Coming Forth As Light	Orion
Okda	The United	Pisces
Orion	One Coming Forth As Light	Orion
Orphiuchus	The Serpent Held	Orphiu.
Ozha	The Going Forth	Eridan.
Palilicium	Belonging To The Judge	Taurus
Parthenos	Maid Of Virgin Pureness	Virgo
Pegasus	Coming Quickly, Joyfully	Pegasus
Peh-Ta-T	The Mouth of The River Of Water	Eridan.
Per-Ku-Hor	This One Cometh To Rule	Cepheus
Perets	The Breaker	Perseus
Persea	The Stretched Out	Androm.
Perseus	The Breaker	Perseus
Phaced (Phacda)	Visited, Guarded, Numbered	Urs.Maj.
Phaet	The Mouth (of The River)	Eridan.
Pholas	The Mediator	Centaur.
Pi-Cot Orion	The Fish, Congregation, or Company Of Him That Cometh	Pisces
Pi-Maere	The Gracious Going Forth (or The Beauty of His Coming Forth)	Sagitt.

Index of Star & Sign Names

Pi-Mahi	The United	Gemini
Pi-Mentekeon	The Plucking Asunder	Leo
Pisces	The Fish, Multiplying	Pisces
Piscis Hori	The Fish Of Him Who Comes	Pisces
Pleiades	The Center	Taurus
Pollux	The Ruler, or Judge	Gemini
Porrima	The Virgin	Virgo
Praesepe	The Multitude, The Offspring (mod. — The Beehive)	Cancer
Procyon	The Redeemer	Can.Mi.
Prometheus	The Deliverer, or Branch, Who Cometh	Virgo
Propus	The Branch Spreading	Gemini
Proximo	The Nearest	Centaur.
Pulcherima	The Most Beautiful	Bootes
Rakis	The Bound (Arab. As With A Chain)	Lepus
Ras Al Thalita	The Head of The Triangle	Aries
Ras-al-Awa	The Head of The Desired One	Orphiu.
Ras-al-Awa	The Head of The Desired	Hercul.
Ras-al-Gethi	The Head of Him Who Bruises	Hercul.
Ras-al-Hagus	The Head of Him Who Holds	Orphiu.
Rastaban	The Head of The Subtle, or The Head of The Serpent	Draco
Regel (Regulus)	The Treading Underfoot	Leo
Regnum Ammonis	Reign of Ammon; The Dominion or Government Established	Aries
Regulus	Treading Underfoot	Cepheus
Rex Centaurus	The King—The Centaur	Centaur.
Rigol	The Foot, or One Treading Underfoot	Orion
Rosh Satan	The Head of The Adversary, or The Head of Satan	Perseus
Rota neb	Swiftly Running (as Water In A Trough)	Delphin.
Rotaneu	Swiftly Running (as Water In A Trough)	Delphin.

Ruchba	The Enthroned, The Seated	Cassio.
Ruchba er Rami	The Riding of The Bowman	Sagitt.
Sa'ad al Melik	The Record of The Pouring Out	Aquari.
Sa'ad al Naschira	The Record of The Cutting Off	Capric.
Saad al Suud	He Who Goeth and Returneth; The Pourer Out of The Stream	Aquari.
Sadr	Who Returns, as in a Circle	Cygnus
Sagittarius	The Archer Who Sends Forth The Arrow	Sagitt.
Saiph	The Bruised	Orion
Saiph	Bruise	Orphiu.
Salisha	The Exalted, The Chief	Aries
Sarcam	The Joining	Leo
Sartan	The One Who Holds, or Binds	Cancer
Sartano	The One Who Holds, or Binds	Cancer
Scalooin	Swift (as Flowing of Water)	Delphin.
Scham (or Sham)	Destroying	Sagitta
Scheat	Who Goeth and Returneth	Aquari.
Scheat	He Who Goeth and Returneth	Pegasus
Sebak	This One Comes Conquering, Victorious	Can.Mi.
Seir	The Prince	Can.Mj.
Sephina	The Multitude	Argo
Sera	Victory	Crux
Serpentarius	The Holder of The Serpent	Orphiu.
Set	Set Up, or Appointed as a Ruler	Gemini
Set	Set Up as a King or Queen	Androm.
Set	The Queen, The Daughter	Cassio.
Shedar	The Freed	Cassio.
Shelyuk	The Fishing Eagle	Lyra
Shes-En-Fent	The One Who Comes Rejoicing Over The Serpent	Argo
Shes-nu	The Desired Son	Coma
Shur	The Bull Coming (Ruling)	Taurus
Sirius	The Prince	Can.Mj.
Sirra	The Chained	Androm.
Situla	A Small Urn For Drawing Water	Aquari.

Smat	One Who Subdues, Rules, or Governs	Bootes
Soheil	The Desired	Argo
Spica	An Ear of Corn, The Seed of Corn	Virgo
Statio Hori	The Station or Place of Horns, The One Who Comes To Save	Taurus
Statio Typhonis	The Station, or Place of Him Who Smites and is Smitten	Cancer
Su-At	The Bird of The Nile (He) Coming	Aquila
Subilah	Who Carries	Virgo
Subilah	Who Bears	Coma
Subilon	The Branch	Argo
Subilon	The Spike (or Ear) of Corn	Virgo
Succoth	The Pleiades, Booths; Feast of Tabernacles	Taurus
Sugio	The Deceiver	Lepus
Sulaphat	Springing Up	Lyra
Sunbul	An Ear Of Corn	Virgo
Sura	The Lamb	Corona
Sura	The Lamb (accdg to Ulugh Beigh)	Victima
Taleh	The Lamb Sent Forth	Aries
Talita (or Talitha)	The Little Lamb	Urs.Maj.
Tametouris Ammon	The Reign of Ammon; The Dominion or Government Established	Aries
Tarared	The Wounded	Aquila
Tauros	The Bull	Taurus
Taurus	The Bull	Taurus
Terebellum	Sent Forth Swiftly	Sagitt.
Tes-Ark	This (One) Cometh From Afar	Cygnus
Tesmech	The Branch	Virgo
Thabit	Treading Upon	Orion
Thaumin	The United	Gemini
Thaumin	The United	Gemini
Tegmine	Holding	Cancer
Theemin	The Water	Eridan.
Thera	The Beast	Victima
Thuban	The Subtle	Draco

Thusiasterion	The Altar	Ara
Toliman	The Heretofore and The Hereafter	Centaur.
Toxotes	The Archer	Sagitt.
Triophas	Treading Underfoot	Orphiu.
Turn	The Sceptre, The Power	Auriga
Tureis	The Possession	Argo
U-Or	He Who Cometh (lit. He To Come, He To Come)	Band
Unuk	Encompassing	Serpen.
Ur-Ana	The Light Of Heaven	Orion
Urkab er Rami	The Bowman (or The Rider)	Sagitt.
Ursa	The Bear, or The Strong	Urs.Maj.
Ursa Major	The Great Bear, The Big Dipper, The Greater Sheepfold	Urs.Maj.
Ursa Minor	The Lesser Bear, Little Dipper, The Lesser Sheepfold	Urs.Min.
Vega	He Shall Be Exalted	Lyra
Vergiliae	The Center	Taurus
Vertex	The Turned Upon, or Rolled Around	Taurus
Victima	The Victim	Victima
Vindemiatrix	The Son, or The Branch Who Cometh	Virgo
Virgo	The Virgin	Virgo
Wasat	Established, as a Foundation	Gemini
Wasat	The Center, or The Foundation	Taurus
Wesen	The Bright, The Shining, The Scarlet	Can.Mj.
Yofee	The Enthroned, The Beautiful	Cassio.
Zavijaveh	Gloriously Beautiful	Virgo
Zeeb	Wolf: (Arab = This One Coming Quickly)	Can.Mj.
Zerah	Corn, or Seed	Virgo
Zosma	The Shining Forth	Leo
Zourak	Flowing	Eridan.
Zuben Akrabi	The (Redemption) Price of the Conflict	Libra

Zuben al Akrab	The (Redemption) Price of the Conflict	Libra
Zuben al Genubi	The Price Which Is Deficient	Libra
Zuben al Shemali	The Price Which Covers	Libra
Zugos	A Yoke, Cross-Bar, or Balance Beam	Libra

The Blood Covenant

ISBN 0892280298

THE BLOOD COVENANT
by H. C. Trumbull

The original, recognized, authoritative resource for old-world covenants, by Henry Clay Trumbull.

The Blood Covenant is one of the least understood, and yet most relevant covenants for our understanding of God's dealings with man, throughout the Bible. This covenant of life & death spans the entire sacrificial system of the Old Testament, and is the basis for the Act of Communion in the Church today.

Impact Christian Books
www.impactchristianbooks.com
1-800-451-2708

Other Titles by H. C. Trumbull

The Salt Covenant
by H. C. Trumbull

The original source book for information about covenanting in salt and its significance. Draws from the scriptural uses of covenants of salt and blood in the Bible. Why is Salt a substitute for Blood in making covenants? Why did Lot's wife become a pillar of Salt? Why does Jesus refer to his followers as 'Salt of the Earth'? Why did God give the kingdom to David and his sons forever by a Covenant of Salt?

Find out, in a book by the author of the best selling *Blood Covenant*.

ISBN 0892280794

The Threshold Covenant
by H. C. Trumbull

How did Moses and the Israelites know what God meant when he said, "It is the Lord's Passover?" Why was blood required on the thresholds of the Hebrew homes in Egypt? What role does the threshold play in the marriage covenant? Why is a bride carried over the threshold?

This fascinating sequel to the *Blood Covenant* will give deeper understanding to the role of threshold covenants in Scripture, including a surprising revelation concerning the Passover Covenant.

ISBN 0892280751

Keys to Unlock Bible Prophecy

ISBN 0892280980

The 3rd Tower of Babel

by Stephen Banks

The most exalted image of Jesus Christ, the symbol of His Second Coming, has been overlooked during centuries of biblical research.

Now, from the pages of Zechariah, Isaiah, and Daniel, this remarkable symbol of the Messiah is revealed.

Through this symbol of Jesus Christ you will find the key to unlock a 5000 year mystery involving the Ark of the Covenant, the coming New World Order, and the Second Coming of Jesus Christ.

Do Your Relationships Produce
Bondage or Joy?

Does someone manipulate you?
What are the symptoms of an ungodly relationship?
Are you tormented with thoughts of a former lover or friend?
Are you free to be all that God intended you to be?

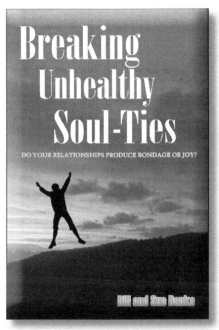

0892281391

"Here at last is a thorough and theologically sound treatment of a little understood subject" - from the *Foreword* by Frank Hammond

Breaking Unhealthy Soul-Ties (PAPERBACK OR E-BOOK)
by Bill & Sue Banks

Unhealthy soul-ties involve the control of one individual over another, and can be one of the most difficult blocks to spiritual freedom. Some relationships are healthy and bring blessings into our lives; other types of relationships can bring demonic bondage to our souls. This book assists the reader in diagnosing both healthy and unhealthy relationships, and offers positive steps to personal freedom.

Miraculous Testimonies of Spiritual Warfare!

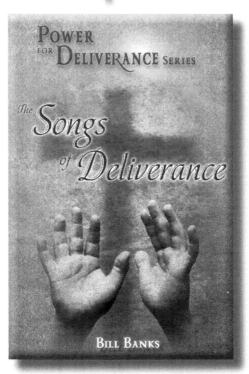

089228031X

POWER FOR DELIVERANCE - THE SONGS OF DELIVERANCE
BY BILL BANKS

This **book,** or **e-book**, shows that there is help for oppressed, tormented, and compulsive people, and that the solution is as old as the ministry of Jesus Christ. From over 30 years of counseling and ministering deliverance, in the United States and abroad, Bill Banks highlights the common root causes of emotional and mental torment, and walks the reader through steps to be set free. Read numerous case studies of people who have been delivered from their torments and fears, including testimonies of over 60 spirits...

Drugs	**Anger**	**Cancer**	**Pornography**	**Perversion**
Fears	**Harlotry**	**Hatred**	**Witchcraft**	**Rebellion**
Cocaine	**Rejection**	**Temper**	**Occult Spirits**	**Childlessness**
Terror	**Torment**	**Suicide**	**Disobedience**	**Unforgiveness**
Smoking	**Murder**	**Bitterness**	**Homosexuality**	**Foolishness**
Sleeping Disorder		**Abuse of Women**	**& more!**	

Bill Banks on Healing

Alive Again
By Bill Banks

0892280484

(PAPERBACK OR E-BOOK)

One of the greatest healing testimonies in print. A healing from cancer lasting over 30 years! And a powerful explanation of the baptism of the Holy Spirit, including prayers to receive this special touch from the Lord.

With six different terminal conditions, and numerous malignant tumors, read how one man sought the healing accounts in Scripture for strength and encouragement. Follow his story as he fights to live during 6 months of chemotherapy, radiation, and dialysis, and then is told he has only 48 hours to live! When the doctors gave up - God didn't. Find answers to the questions: Is It God's Will To Heal? And, Does God Want To Heal You?

Also available as an *Audio Book* on
Compact Disc!

Listen to an excerpt now at:
www.impactchristianbooks.com/alive

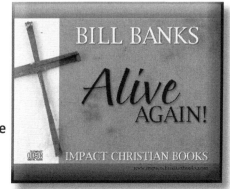

A Skeptic Discovers ANGELS Are Real!

0892280484

A Skeptic Discovers Angels are Real!
by Bill Banks

Skeptical of angelic accounts? So was this author, such accounts to him were too much to believe. Then he began to meet people, heads of ministries and missionaries, who had life-changing encounters with angels! This book contains a total of 11 miraculous encounters with angels, and concludes with a vision and revelation about heaven.

A mysterious hitch-hiker, a woman at the Garden Tomb in Jerusalem, and a bus driver, all disappear into thin air. A missionary's car in France runs on empty for hours, while it is protected by a mysterious van. A motorcyclist picks up a passenger, and his broken, gangrenous leg is instantly healed. And more!

Impact Christian Books
www.impactchristianbooks.com
1-800-451-2708

Impact Christian Books

THESE BOOKS ARE AVAILABLE THROUGH YOUR LOCAL BOOKSTORE,
OR YOU MAY ORDER DIRECTLY FROM
IMPACT CHRISTIAN BOOKS

Website: www.impactchristianbooks.com

Phone Order Line: **1-800-451-2708**
(314)-822-3309

Address: **Impact Christian Books**
332 Leffingwell Ave. Suite #101
Kirkwood, MO 63122
USA

- You may also request a free Catalog -

Made in the USA
San Bernardino, CA
09 February 2015